Exploring the Flea Markets of France

Exploring the Flea Markets of France

A COMPANION GUIDE FOR VISITORS AND COLLECTORS

Sandy Price

THREE RIVERS PRESS/New York

Published by Three Rivers Press, 201 East 50th Street, New York, New York 10022. Member of the Crown Publishing Group.

Random House, Inc. New York, Toronto, London, Sydney, Auckland
www.randomhouse.com

Three Rivers Press is a registered trademark of Random House, Inc.

Printed in the United States of America

Design by Cindy LaBreacht

Library of Congress Cataloging-in-Publication Data
Price, Sandy
Exploring the Flea Markets of France: A Companion Guide for Visitors and Collectors / Sandy Price
Includes bibliographical references and index
1. Flea Markets—France—Handbooks, manuals, etc. I. Title.
HF5482.15.P74   1999   99-12531
381'.192'0944—dc21

ISBN 0-609-80411-1

10 9 8 7 6 5 4 3 2 1

First Edition

To Jim

Acknowledgments

I am deeply indebted to the following people for their assistance and encouragement to me during this long process—Liz Pinto, Daphne Intrator, Catharine Yolles, Naomi Duguid, Jeffrey Alford, Ethan Poskanzer, Judy Nisenholt, Joni Boyer, June Stapleton, Andrew Oliver, and, most of all, my long-suffering spouse, Jim, and my children. Also, much gratitude is owed to Liv Blumer, my agent; Jessica Schulte, my editor; and Bob Blake, who prepared the maps for this book.

Contents

Exploring the Flea Markets of France

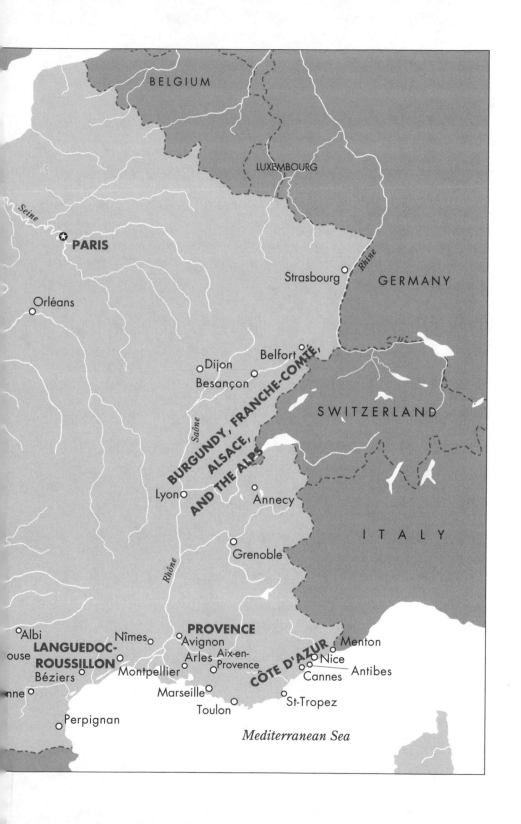

Introduction

I t could be anywhere in France—Provence or the Côte d'Azur, the Loire or
the Alps. The *place* is full of people—strolling, talking, laughing—and the
array of color is overwhelming. You can feel your breath quickening as you
arrive. Alongside the square may be a church, some public buildings, boutiques, or a little garden; it is sometimes difficult to tell because of all the
activity about you.

You eagerly join the milling crowd. For the next hour or two, all sense of
time is lost. You move from overflowing stall to overflowing stall, completely
captivated and absorbed.

The crowds thicken as the day progresses and now you must pay close
attention as you thread your way along so you don't miss a thing. You hear
people around you chatting and laughing, and bargaining with vendors.
While serious, the negotiations are good-humored, both parties playing their
roles to perfection.

As your eyes become adjusted to all the activity, you spot something you
covet, perhaps hidden in a pile of things on the ground or prominently displayed on a stall table. You stand gazing at it for a while, pondering whether
you really want it, whether you can afford it, what you'd be prepared to pay
for it, and how you are going to get it home. Then, abandoning yourself to its
charms, you take the plunge and bargaining begins until victory is yours.
Clasping your new purchase in your hands, suddenly very wide-awake and
energized, you move on to the next stall. Your pulse quickens. Just down the
way, you've spotted something else really great.

You have joined the French in one of their favorite pastimes—scouring
the flea markets—an activity that they call *la chine*. What they are looking

at and buying, in markets all over France, is sometimes referred to as *brocante*. *Brocante* is the term used for old, used objects—both decorative and practical—of no apparently great age or value. The closest word in English is *collectibles*. It's not antiques and it's not junk, although any given item might be considered one or the other. *Brocante* is the nebulous space in between; that the boundaries are not clear makes it all the more enjoyable.

Thanks in part to recent books, visitors are now generally well aware of the wonderful food markets of France, so much a feature of daily life. Many do not know, however, about the more than two hundred flea or *brocante* markets held regularly in villages, towns, and cities in every region of France. Like the food markets, they are part of the way of life in this country—a place where people get together, to browse and to buy.

On flea market day—often weekly, but sometimes monthly—vendors begin arriving before dawn, in cars or vans loaded with their wares. Streets may be closed off to other traffic as the setting up begins. Makeshift tables are erected, or sometimes the things for sale are set out on the ground, in cartons or on blankets. Collectibles of all kinds are arranged and displayed, under large parasols protecting them from rain, or vendors from the sun. It can take hours to unpack and set up, and what does not get sold will have to be carefully rewrapped and reloaded at the end of the day. You hear the vendors talking quietly together as they work, the steam from their coffees rising in the morning air.

And then the market begins, sometimes early in the morning, with dealers and truly obsessed collectors arriving first to inspect the goods as they are unloaded. Some markets are held only in the morning, with vendors packing up and leaving by noon or soon after, while others continue until late afternoon. The noise rises as the day progresses, and the banter escalates into lively chatter. By midmorning, some vendors have pulled out baguette sandwiches to get them through until lunch—they may have breakfasted as early as 4 A.M. On cold days, some pour themselves an early glass of Ricard or wine, to ward off the chill.

A feeling of festivity is in the air. Occasionally there is live music—a violinist or perhaps a street organ-grinder. There may be a woman pushing a coffee-and-snack cart down the rows, announcing the selections on offer as she goes. Trucks parked nearby sell sausages and *frites* or kabobs and Turkish coffee.

Who can explain the fascination we have for even the most simple objects of everyday life in decades past—little wooden coffee mills, copper pots, corkscrews, wire egg baskets, mustard yellow garden pots, or café tables and chairs in tarnished colors? Maybe it is a desire to escape the mass production and vulgarity of our own era and experience. By surrounding ourselves with a few beautiful things from what we imagine to be a saner, more elegant, and gentler age, we hope to transcend, even just a little, our own frenetic world. The café au lait bowls, the old straw baskets, and the 19th-century steamer trunk sitting in the corner of our apartment give a pleasure we can hardly define; they make our environment seem calmer, more real, and more in tune with the past.

It is not only the things sold at the flea markets that provide a sense of stability and timelessness. The markets themselves play a similar role by their regularity and certainty. Bear in mind that flea markets have been going on in France for over a century, as is the case with the Puces de St-Ouen in the north end of Paris. Whatever else is going on in the world, you know that, on this or that day, at such and such time and place, there will be a flea market, just as there has been, in many cases, for years.

While the markets represent stability and certainty, at the same time there is a wonderful unpredictability about what you will find there. It is that thrill of anticipation and excitement—not just the ambience and comparatively reasonable prices—that keeps people coming back and makes the markets so much more appealing than antique shops and *brocante* stores.

If you are a tourist, you will be just as attracted to the flea markets as are collectors. Many are located in appealing settings, and usually in the quaintest and most historical part of town. Sometimes, searching out a market will take you deep into the countryside, unveiling little villages you would not otherwise see. Both the character of the markets, and the things you will find there, reveal the extraordinary regional diversity of France. Even the more down-to-earth markets, while not glamorous or visually splendid, uncover a side to life often hidden from visitors—the wide spectrum of social classes and the multiethnic nature of modern France.

Openness and accessibility are the hallmarks of the markets. Whether or not you speak French, and even if you are just there to browse and relax, you can share in the experience. There are no lineups, no schedules, and rarely any admission fees. Strolling along in the fresh air while you look through the market stalls—and then perhaps sitting down to take in the scene at a nearby café—is a truly congenial way to spend some time in France.

How to Use This Book

You may have been to France before and may already be familiar with the markets and the collectibles to be found here. You may be a first-time visitor, bitten by the collecting bug at home or elsewhere in your travels, who thinks it would be fun to check out the scene in France. Or you may be someone looking for more real experiences when you visit other countries, something beyond museums and galleries.

Whatever your situation, this book is a companion guide to your travels in France, steering you to the kinds of flea markets that will suit your tastes and desires, and accompanying you as you go.

The book is divided into essentially two parts—the first gives you general information about visiting the markets and about the things that are collected in France. The second is a region-by-region, in-depth exploration of the flea markets. Below is an outline of the next ten chapters, and an explanation of their structure, to help you use them.

PRACTICAL ADVICE ON VISITING THE FLEA MARKETS

This chapter gives you the general information you need for visiting the markets—how to get there, when to go, how to double-check market schedules, what to bring, how to protect against theft, how to communicate, how to know what to buy, how to tell if something is fake, how to bargain, what facilities you'll find nearby, how to transport your purchases back home, what customs regulations apply, and what else to read on French collectibles and the flea markets.

5

WHAT TO LOOK FOR IN THE MARKETS

This chapter lists and describes some 30 items, of all kinds, that are collected in France and found at the flea markets. They are discussed alphabetically for easy reference. You will get ideas both about what you should look out for in the markets and what you might want to collect.

REGION-BY-REGION DESCRIPTIONS

The next eight chapters are a region-by-region guide to the flea markets of France (starting in the Côte d'Azur, in the southeast, and moving in a counterclockwise direction, ending up in Burgundy, Franche-Comté, Alsace, and the Alps). The regions selected are those of the greatest interest to visitors. For easy reference, all of the regional chapters use the same format (with a slight variation in the case of Paris), as follows:

LIST OF THE MARKETS: At the beginning of each chapter a list is provided of regular markets in that region, organized by days of the week for handy reference as you travel. It tells you where the market is located, how many vendors generally to expect, and the hours. The markets profiled in the chapter are marked with an asterisk. A dollar symbol indicates those markets charging an entrance fee. A map of the region also pinpoints the markets that are profiled, in bold. Many other market towns are also marked, as are some tourist centers, to help you plan.

REGIONAL OVERVIEW: This section gives you general information about the region, under the following headings:

Getting Oriented: About the Region
Market Rhythms: When They're Held/When to Go
Market Flavors: How They Look/How They Feel
The Collectibles: What You'll Find/What to Look For
Buying: Price Levels/Bargaining Opportunities
Getting Around: How to Travel/Where to Go

MARKET CLOSE-UPS: This section profiles individual flea market towns, and their markets, within the region. In selecting those featured, diversity—in terms of market size, level, schedules, and geographic location—has been a primary goal.

Each market profile follows the same format—a quick-reference summary, followed by a description of both the place and the market.

The summary begins by listing the number of vendors generally found at the market. It then rates the market; three categories are rated, using a rough rating system of from one to four fleurs-de-lis (with ❧ the least and ❧❧❧❧, of course, the most)—Price/Quality Range, Scenic Value, and Amenities Nearby. Each is explained below:

PRICE/QUALITY RANGE: This category indicates the range or level of the market; that is, from a low-end, low-priced market to a high-quality, high-priced market. (While quality and price do not always go together, they do generally coincide and are combined as one category here.)

SCENIC VALUE: This category rates the aesthetic appeal of the market (in terms of both its natural and human-made surroundings).

AMENITIES NEARBY: This category indicates the level of amenities (cafés, restaurants, food markets, washrooms) in the vicinity of the market.

The collectibles generally found at the market are listed under the heading "Featured Items," followed by the "When, Where, How" section, which tells you when the market is held (day and times) and where it is located; where appropriate, directions are given from the train station to the market. In cases where it is applicable, the names of other nearby markets that are described in the text (not simply referred to) are listed, under "Other Markets Discussed." Finally, the phone number of the town's tourist office is provided.

The remainder of each market-town profile is descriptive, broken into three sections—the first tells you a little about the town in which the market is held; the second, titled "The Market," describes the market itself in detail (its ambience, the collectibles found, prices, and bargaining); and the third, "Other Things to Do," lists appealing cafés and restaurants, museums of particular interest to collectors, and other nearby markets.

Paris is treated differently because it is a city rather than a region. Instead of giving an overview of the place, a history of the flea markets of Paris is provided. Otherwise, the same format is used as for the regional chapters, until the section "Market Close-Ups." Here, since there is no new town or city to talk about, the discussion moves immediately to the market itself. Also, in addition to an "Other Things to Do" heading under each market, there is an "Other Things to Do in Paris" section at the end of the chapter, suggesting a few other cafés and restaurants to try out in the center of the city. Unique also to this chapter is a list of charity shops in Paris for bargain hunters to check out.

NOTE TO READERS

This book discusses the markets in terms of regions of France, to better assist you in your travels. While generally corresponding to the delineations of these regions in other guidebooks, they are, likewise, somewhat subjective. As in other guidebooks, the boundaries selected do not necessarily correspond to current political or administrative regions, historical regions, or even social and cultural divisions, but rather are defined with all of these factors in mind (or sometimes one, as opposed to another). Also, in a couple of cases I have added a new, somewhat idiosyncratic, consideration, that of visiting the flea markets.

The extensive list of markets at the beginning of each of the regional chapters is included to give you as much information about the flea markets in France as possible. Of course, while the information provided in the lists has been checked, I cannot personally verify that it is accurate in every case; things change without warning, and it's always best to call ahead to check that the information provided is still accurate.

Since market times listed in this book can only be approximate (since flea market vendors are not entirely predictable, nor are estimates by organizers always correct), try to leave yourself plently of leeway to be sure to make it to the markets you want to see. Also, in this vein, the number of vendors listed is only an estimate, and will vary from season to season and even week to week. The "Featured Items" section of each individual market profile lists the things I have seen in the market, and that I expect you will see as well; however, given the fluidity and unpredictability of the wares that appear in the markets, from visit to visit, there can be no guarantee that you will find the same things I did.

While phone numbers listed in this book are as current as possible, as are museum times, they are always subject to change. With regard to phone numbers, if you are calling from outside France, drop the first number, the 0.

All distances in this book are in kilometers, rather than miles, as France uses the metric system. However, temperatures are given in Fahrenheit as well as Celsius. Prices, of course, are in francs, in part because the value in dollars (American and Canadian) will vary with changes in the exchange rates. Euro prices are not given, since the Euro will not be used for general purchases until 2002, although prices may be posted in both francs and Euros long before then. (There are about 6.6 francs to the Euro.) Town and city populations are based on the town or city proper, not including the surrounding area.

While I have attempted in this book to provide the most accurate and up-to-date information possible regarding the flea markets, museums, cafés and restaurants, buses and rail travel, purchasing, shipping and mailing, customs, and so on, please be aware that this information is subject to change. Neither I nor the publisher can accept responsibility for omissions or errors contained in this book or for your experiences while traveling.

Three terms appear throughout this book and are not repeatedly defined or explained—*brocante, la chine,* and *le chineur. Brocante* is a slightly nebulous term that means collectible or used goods, whether decorative or utilitarian, of no enormous value or antiquity. *La chine* is the term the French use for the activity of scouring markets and looking for treasures, while a *chineur* is, essentially, a keen collector.

Visiting the flea markets of France is, above all, tremendous fun. If you like to collect, you will love doing it here; not only will you find some really interesting and beautiful things to bring home, you may also get a few great bargains.

Collecting aside, the markets are also just a great place for those who crave being part of a real scene when they travel—being among local people, doing what they're doing, and seeing how they live. The flea markets let you do just that.

Practical Advice on Visiting the Flea Markets

One of the great features of the flea markets of France is their accessibilty—both literally, in terms of getting there, and figuratively, in the sense of providing an easy and hassle-free experience. Compared to other activities that tourists engage in—which sometimes feel more like work than entertainment—visiting the markets is refreshingly simple; you set your own pace and you decide how you want to proceed.

This chapter gives you some tips to help make the experience as enjoyable as possible—on how to get there, when to go, how to double-check schedules, what to bring, how to protect against theft, how to communicate, how to decide what to buy, how to tell if something is fake, how to bargain, what facilities you'll find nearby, how to transport your purchases home, what customs regulations apply, and what else is available to read on the markets and French collectibles.

HOW TO GET THERE

In deciding which mode of transport to use in France—car or train—you will no doubt take into account a number of considerations, apart from the flea markets. The most basic one is the general objective of your trip—that is, do you want to tour the French countryside, visiting lots of little towns and villages, or is it your aim to see the big towns and cities, scouring galleries and museums? In the first case, having a car is highly convenient and advantageous; in the second, train travel is well suited to your plans.

To the extent that visiting the flea markets figures in your decision-making, their typical location becomes relevant. Many of the markets are held in towns and cities that are easily accessible by train (on the French national train service, the SNCF), and often via the high-speed trains, called the TGV. Train service is extensive in this country, reaching surprisingly small communities (sometimes via SNCF-operated connecting bus service); it is also punctual and reliable, except during the occasional strike.

Most markets accessible by train are within a short 10-to-15-minute walk from the station (and are also often located in the same part of town as other sites you'll want to visit). If you are heading to the market from your hotel—and you are staying in the center—you can almost invariably get there, in this case as well, on foot or by public transit. (This is also the easiest way to get around, in big cities at least, since finding a parking spot in the center of French cities is notoriously difficult and can also be quite expensive.)

Some markets are located outside town. This is most likely to be the case with junk markets or especially large ones, which crowded city centers cannot easily accommodate. Even when public transport is available to get to these markets, service may be confusing and sporadic (especially on a Sunday morning when they are sometimes held). Other markets, located in small villages, may not be readily accessible by either train or bus; in such a case, you may have to take a taxi from a nearby town, if you do not have a car. (For transportation tips specific to the region you will be visiting, consult the relevant chapter, under the heading "Getting Around: How to Travel/Where to Go.")

The bottom line is this: while you don't need a car to visit most of the flea markets, having one is sometimes desirable. Also, a car is convenient for visiting a large number of markets in a short time (such as two, or even three, in one day, for example), since it will invariably be easier and faster than traveling by train. Finally, if you plan to buy a lot of collectibles, particularly bulky ones, a car is the way to go.

Cost considerations may, however, be an important factor. Renting a car in France is often not cheap (particularly with automatic transmission)—although, of course, more economic when shared among a few people—and gas is expensive (up to three times what you pay in North America, for example). Moreover, the autoroutes, while fast and convenient, have tolls, which rapidly add up. Finally, many hotels (at least in the cities) charge a pretty hefty fee for overnight parking.

Train travel, on the other hand, is quite reasonable if you buy a rail pass before you leave for France. Passes often give you unlimited travel for the number of days you select (up to a set maximum), to be completed within a fixed time. (Conditions vary based on the different passes offered.) Such passes are very convenient; you select the days you want as you go, activating your pass for that day simply by filling in the date. Reservations are not necessary, except on the TGV (which will cost you a small supplement); on other trains, you simply jump on and travel as far as you want, in any direction, for the entire day. A first-class pass is a good idea; it's not that much more expensive than a second-class one, and the seating is much more spacious and comfortable.

I recently spent a couple of weeks traveling on a rail pass to flea markets all over northern France, using Paris as my base and usually returning there each night. It was great; no train was ever more than a minute or two late, and I avoided the stress of driving in France (which, for North Americans, is significant, since the French drive much faster than we do. While the speed limit on the autoroutes is usually 130 kilometers per hour, many drive at speeds far in excess of that).

Whether you go by train or car, plan your route ahead of time. If you don't have a detailed city or town map, you can almost always pick one up at the tourist office when you arrive; you can sometimes even get one for the next stop on your itinerary, if it is in the vicinity. Ask the staff to mark out the route to the market, especially if it is located outside the center of town; you are not likely to find signs posted along the road to guide you to the site. If you are hoping to take public transit, you can also get information from the tourist office about bus routes and schedules.

WHEN TO GO

What season of the year is preferable for visiting the markets? What time of day is best to arrive? While the answer to both questions varies according to the region and your objectives, there are some general tips.

As for the time of year to come, two, sometimes conflicting, factors are the weather and crowds. From late spring to early fall, the weather is usually at its best (although it can be hot during this period, particularly in the south). This is also generally the height of the tourist season; the markets are at their liveliest then, but prices will tend to be somewhat higher and the crowds can be annoying. The winter, in most parts of France (except the Côte d'Azur and, to a lesser extent, Provence and Languedoc-Roussillon), can be a bit grim—wet and raw (despite what anyone tells you to the contrary)—and should, in most regions, be avoided, unless bargain hunting is your primary interest. All in all, the mid to late spring and early to mid fall are the best times to come —it's not too hot; the markets, while not crowded, are still lively; and prices are less influenced by the tourists.

Weather factors other than heat and cold can also affect your market experience. At some markets, vendors carry on despite rain, although in somewhat reduced numbers, while rain will really drive sellers away at other markets. (It's hard to say what the attitude is likely to be in any individual case, except that vendors tend to be more hardy when the market is monthly, rather than weekly.) In any event, since rain really does put a damper on things, think twice before venturing to the flea market on a rainy day.

Wind can also be a factor, particularly in Provence, where the infamous mistral blows periodically down the Rhône valley (apparently, most often in winter). Depending on its force, on cold days this wind may affect the number of vendors turning up at markets in its path. However, while bothersome, the mistral is almost never strong enough to really put a damper on a market, and as compensation, the views of the surrounding countryside on such days are incredibly clear.

The best time of day to come to the flea markets depends both on the season and your objectives. General tourists, primarily interested in the markets as a part of their discovery of the region, should usually plan to arrive in the late morning (except in the heat of summer, when coming somewhat earlier— or late in the afternoon, in the case of all-day markets—is best). In the late morning the markets are in full swing and at their liveliest. Also, in winter, this part of the day can be quite mild, in marked contrast to earlier on, when you may well encounter frost and fog. Even in the south, those few morning hours can make a great difference; by 11 to 11:30 A.M. in Nice, for example, it will often be warm enough in January to sit outside in the cafés and restaurants.

Once noon hits, vendors often take a long break for lunch (especially in the south), and while this is a somewhat entertaining sight, it is not optimal for either general sight-seeing or purchasing.

For those who go to the markets mostly to buy, it is, of course, best to arrive early. At some of the big morning-only markets, really keen collectors and bargain hunters arrive before dawn or soon thereafter. At these markets, you will see people—often dealers—scouring the stands in the dark with flashlights, even peering into boxes as they are being unloaded from cars and vans.

The most important tip regarding market times is this: whatever the official hours (and even those can vary, depending on whom you talk to), some vendors may pack up and leave much earlier, either because they've had a bad day or because that is their practice. To ensure that you catch a market at its peak, arrive well before its scheduled end. However, if you do end up arriving late in the day, near the market's scheduled end, one potential advantage is that you may get a great bargain on something that a vendor does not want to have to pack up again and take home. (This is the case particularly with bulky and fragile items.)

CHECKING MARKET SCHEDULES

Many flea markets (particularly in the large centers) have been held in the same spot, on the same day, for many years and do not vary. Indeed, regularity and predictability are among the markets' great attractions. However, a few will always be subject to a change in location or time, or to cancellation. Also, when markets fall on holidays or coincide with special events, they may not proceed as usual, and you may want to check beforehand.

To confirm that a market will actually take place on the day you are planning to come, call the local tourist office. (The phone number is provided for the market towns featured; check the "Market Close-Ups" section of each of the regional chapters.) While not invariably reliable on the flea markets, tourist offices often have someone on staff who can assist you in English, and their hours of operation are fairly extensive. If the staff has no knowledge about a particular market or is not certain about its schedule during your stay, ask that someone call the city hall (the *mairie*) on your behalf. The *mairies* administer a fair percentage of the markets and will usually have accurate information about the ones within their mandate.

WHAT TO BRING

A fundamental rule of flea marketing is to bring along only those things that you really need, since everything else will soon feel like a real encumbrance. Do not, for example, cart along a coat, an umbrella, or a big bag unless it is absolutely necessary. I often go without a purse, with just some cash in my pocket or in a travel pouch strung around my neck. This is not only safer against theft, it is also liberating, leaving your hands free to rummage through the goods. You don't really need a purse, anyway; almost all vendors deal only in cash. If you feel the need to have some identification with you, do as one of my friends does and just bring along a photocopy of the relevant pages of your passport.

Also, if, like me, your interests lie in bizarre objects of little apparent value (that is, real treasures whose true value is not yet evident to others), then bring a lot of coins with you, instead of large bills. (In France, coins now go up to 20 francs.) Not only is it convenient to have small change on hand, it avoids the embarrassment you'll feel if, having bargained someone down to 20 francs for some old pitcher or wire basket, you then try to pay with a 200-franc bill. Do not, however, attempt to unload any of the *centimes* you have collected in your travels—such a stratagem will be flatly refused. (Vendors are so keen to avoid any coin less than a franc that, sometimes, if you don't have the exact amount, they will simply take what you do have and forget the rest.)

Another general objective in your attire is to look like everyone else at the market. You are likely to get better deals if you don't stand out, even if it is clear as soon as you begin talking that you are not French. Wear casual clothes; more comfortable for browsing, they will also help dispel any notion that you are a rich tourist, a goal that is clearly in your best interest. Avoid bringing a camera, unless taking pictures at the markets is a big objective for you; a camera definitely pegs you as a tourist and also tends to send the message (whether or not it's valid) that you are well-heeled, to boot.

While traveling light is your biggest aim, do bring along a lightweight cloth or nylon bag for your purchases, or even a couple of strong plastic bags; vendors often use the flimsy bags supplied in the supermarkets. Vendors usually have paper or other wrapping material on hand, but to be safe, you might consider bringing along an old newspaper to further protect your purchases.

Basically, the rules on what to bring are dress light, dress down, carry cash and a couple of bags, and you'll have a great time.

PROTECTING YOURSELF AGAINST THEFT

Unfortunately, a special caution must be issued about protecting yourself against theft. Although violent crime remains low, petty theft is sadly a problem in France (as in a lot of places). Since tourists are usually less savvy than the locals and tend to carry more cash and other valuables on their person, they are obvious targets. Also, flea markets (like many other spots frequented by tourists) are busy places, where people are distracted and, thus, more vulnerable to pickpockets and theft.

If you are traveling by car, don't leave anything of any value in it; this includes the trunk, even if it's one of those trunks where nothing can be seen from the outside. No one in France is at all surprised when you tell them that your car has been broken into, which indicates the extent of this problem. (We managed to have all of our suitcases, and everything else, stolen from our trunk while parked for two hours at midday in the center of Aix-en-Provence.) In France, license plates include the number of the administrative department in which the car is registered, and rental cars tend to be registered in the same department. Thus, your car's license plate is a pretty fair signal that it's a rental, making you a prime target for would-be thieves. So, don't take any chances; always unload your bags at the hotel before going to the flea market or anywhere else.

HOW TO COMMUNICATE

After many years of observing (with both great interest and amusement) the relationship between the French and the English-speaking world, I have concluded that those little tensions that sometimes arise (which are almost always minor) often stem from a complete misinterpretation of the behavior of the other party.

You will occasionally hear English-speaking people claim that the French are rude and arrogant. While one may encounter such people here (as every-where else), my experience has really been to the contrary. It is, however, true that the French are often formal, polite, and correct—a style that is some-times misconstrued as haughty and cold.

Similarly, the French are sometimes guilty of misreading the English-speaking world, particularly those from North America. I have watched French friends misinterpret a familiar or casual manner—which, in North America, would be read as a sign of friendliness and congeniality—as brash, disrespectful, and impolite.

The potential for cross-cultural miscommunication should be borne in mind when you are visiting the flea markets. The safest strategy is to adopt a polite and correct manner in your dealings with people, even if doing so feels slightly unnatural and wooden. Always observe the little formalities so well entrenched in social discourse in France; for example, here people address each other as *monsieur* or *madame,* and the failure to do so is generally con-sidered rude. Also, even the smallest transaction (such as buying bread or a newspaper) begins with the greeting *bonjour* (followed by *monsieur* or *madame*) and almost invariably ends with *merci, bonne journée.* (In stores, people, upon entering, will often address this greeting to everyone there, including other customers.)

Do the same in the markets. Begin each conversation with a greeting—*bonjour, monsieur,* or *madame*—and commence any inquiry with *s'il vous plaît.* Always use *vous* (the formal word for "you"), rather than *tu* (the famil-iar term), even though *tu* is now used as a matter of course by some of the younger, more casual crowd. (While the French may sometimes permit them-selves a wider and more freewheeling range of behavior in their dealings with each other, it is safer not to assume that this flexibility also extends to you.)

It is not a crime to be unable to speak French, and you should not feel embarrassed if you do not. However, it is appropriate and polite to show some recognition of your situation; the failure of so many visitors to do so, whether out of embarrassment or arrogance, may be a reason for any resentment you encounter. If you speak only the most basic French, begin conversations by explaining that fact (even if it is painfully obvious), and then ask the people you are addressing if they speak any English. Whether they do or don't, you will have shown the respect that is due and are then free to try to convey your meaning in English, if necessary. People you encounter will be much more receptive and helpful if you follow this approach.

You will not usually have too much difficulty getting by in the flea markets if you do not speak French. Vendors, particularly in urban areas and tourist centers, often speak at least a few words of English, even if it is limited to conveying prices. Learning some rudimentary phrases—and numbers—

before you travel, so that you can make a purchase at the flea markets, is of course a good idea. If this is beyond you, and you run into difficulties, simply point out what you are interested in and use a piece of paper to write down prices. I have seen people bargaining with vendors in this way, and while not ideal, it does work.

Below are some basic phrases that may help you to get by in the markets:

S'il vous plaît, monsieur (madame)...
Excuse me, sir (madam)...

Je m'excuse, mais je ne parle pas très bien le français.
I'm sorry, but I don't speak French very well.

Parlez-vous anglais?
Do you speak English?

Pourriez-vous m'expliquer d'où ça vient?
                    ...à quoi ca sert?
                    ...comment ça fonctionne?
Could you tell me where that comes from?
            ...what it's for?
            ...how it works?

Ça vaut combien?
How much is this?

La pièce ou pour l'ensemble?
Each one or for all of them?

C'est joli, mais c'est un peu trop cher pour moi.
It's nice, but it's a bit too expensive for me.

Est-ce votre dernier prix?
Is that your lowest price?

Pourriez-vous me faire un prix?
Could you give me a lower price?

Est-ce que vous accepteriez ___ francs?
Would you take ___ francs?

Merci, je vais y réfléchir.
Thanks, I'm going to think about it.

Je regrette, mais je n'ai pas de monnaie.
I'm sorry, but I don't have the exact change.

Pourriez-vous l'emballer avec du papier?
Could you wrap it in some paper?

Auriez-vous un sac?
Would you have a little bag?

Merci, bonne journée.
Thank you, good day.

HOW TO KNOW WHAT TO BUY

One of the most basic, and yet hard to answer, questions is what to buy or what to collect at the flea markets. The next chapter introduces you to a number of collectibles that you might not otherwise appreciate when you first encounter them.

However, your primary guide should be your own reactions and tastes. If something appeals to you, although you're not sure why (or even what it is), pay attention to that feeling. I began collecting many things in this way; for some reason (color, texture, shape, function, or simply emotional appeal), an object grabbed me and I started to become a collector of it, only later learning that other people felt the same way. Since most of the things you are likely to fall for in this way are not expensive, you can permit yourself a few such indulgences. Of course, you should try to back up your initial impressions with some actual knowledge, and for this simply ask the vendors for help; they are generally quite knowledgeable and usually willing to share information with you.

Sadly, one must exercise restraint on one's exuberance at the markets. While many things (as I know) can be packed in with your luggage, some just cannot; you should therefore take into account before you begin bargaining that you might incur some expense shipping the items home. On the other hand, bear in mind that you will probably not often get to France, so that sometimes a bit of a leap of faith is warranted. Try to imagine how you'll feel about that object when you look at it in your living room ten years from now.

HOW TO TELL IF SOMETHING IS FAKE

Unfortunately, as reported in French *brocante* magazines, fake items (for example, a copy of a collectible) do turn up in the flea markets (as elsewhere) from time to time. It is difficult to protect yourself against this problem. If the item is of a modest value, the consequences of it being a fake are not great, in one sense, but it is still very annoying.

While experts can provide advice on how to spot fakes among specific collectibles, little guidance can be given about how to identify fakes generally. The best way to protect yourself is to acquire as much knowledge as you can beforehand about the collectible in question—how it generally looks, what color it usually is, what decoration it normally has, what its markings (if it has any) generally look like (for example, in the case of Quimper ware), how it feels to hold, what the typical signs of age are, what kinds of fakes (if any) have been spotted, etc. You can try to do some of this by reading everything you can find on the item you want to collect before you come to France. Also, once you arrive, try to familiarize yourself, as much as possible, with what that collectible looks like in the flesh, by going to museums and by frequenting flea markets and antique fairs.

Other than that, a little common sense is of some worth. If the item looks far too pristine for the age it is supposed to have (for example, it has no signs of wear and no nicks or defects of any kind), then you may well wonder about its authenticity. If it is different from other examples of its genre, or much less expensive than most such items, questions may also arise. Make inquiries of the vendor, then assess the credibility of the answers. If you have concerns but are willing to take a chance, take those doubts into account in deciding what price you are willing to pay. (Also, if you are a novice, remember that not everything sold in the flea markets is old.) My general rule of thumb (which is certainly not invincible) is that the more beaten up a thing looks, the more likely it is to be the genuine article.

THE FINE ART OF BARGAINING

Some people are not interested in quibbling over the price of things at flea markets. However, for many, a substantial part of the enjoyment comes from feeling that they not only bought something great, but that they managed to get it at a good price. Generally, in the French flea markets, the price quoted (no tax is added) is at least 10 to 15 percent more than the vendor is actually willing to accept. Bargaining is almost always expected—not considered bad form.

In some cases, negotiating is conducted like a theatrical performance. I have encountered some vendors who are clearly masters of the art (that is, both proficient in psychological games-playing and prepared to exercise their skills to the hilt), although most are just straightforward merchants or ordinary folks who simply want to get a fair price for their wares. Whatever the situation, below are a few useful tips to ensure that the negotiating is as beneficial to you—the sometimes hapless purchaser—as possible.

First, ask yourself before you begin bargaining whether you really know anything about the value of the thing you are interested in buying. If you don't, there's nothing wrong with that, but bear it in mind in any offer you make. Also, don't completely trust the vendor's claims as to the object's age, origins, or value; even though well-meaning, they may not be right. Check the item for any defects before you start negotiating. This can be problematic because, at a certain point, this advice begins to conflict with another basic rule, which is not to show that you are really keen to buy. Above all else, do not give the impression that, no matter what the price, you would be prepared to pay it, even if that happens to be true. Such a sentiment is betrayed by picking the thing up several times, talking excitedly to your friend about it, or telling the vendor how nice or unusual you find it.

A good strategy, if you've got the patience, is to point to a few other things and ask about them first, before zeroing in on the object you really want (I have to confess that I am not always able to follow this advice). Some crafty *chineurs* also advocate throwing the cherished item in with a few other things, requesting a price for the lot, and then confining the inquiry to the one thing that they do want. The thinking here is that a lower price will be quoted for the desired object that way. Another strategy is to bargain the price down on the thing you covet to close to what you are willing to pay, and to then try to throw in something else that you also like. Some vendors are more prepared to add another item than to further reduce the price.

If the object you covet has any defects at all, point them out, but do it in a low-key way, conveying the impression that you are somewhat (but not overly) concerned about them. (Although they might not actually bother you, even slight imperfections do reduce the value of things.) Don't push it too far, however; vendors are usually well aware of flaws and will quickly counter that they have been taken into account in the price.

Some people feign ignorance about the things they covet; for example, adopting a kind of bewildered or dubious look when told the age or provenance of an item, even though they are well aware of what it is. I have seen this taken to extremes, with prospective purchasers blithely professing that merely an object's charming color or shape has attracted their interest. Such a stratagem is not only unconvincing, it is also unlikely to succeed; it may prove, as well, to be counterproductive, by annoying the vendor.

This is not to say that dramatic gestures by buyers never have their place; they do, especially in markets where such tactics are employed by vendors. Particularly in the south, I have seen buyers head-shaking dubiously and mock-hesitating, even starting to walk away in midnegotiation, only to be called back by vendors anxious to sell. (The much talked about north-south behavioral divide is, no doubt, an overgeneralization; nonetheless, there may be a little something to it.) In markets and regions where people are more restrained, it is sometimes the vendor who initiates negotiations by offering a reduced price; your best bet is to wait for that to happen and then take it from there.

Always keep in mind that bargaining is essentially a game, which is most successfully conducted if treated as a form of entertainment. It is also invariably counterproductive to get too involved or to take things too personally. In fact, a tactic occasionally employed by vendors is to pretend to be outraged by an offer, so that the embarrassed purchaser will feel compelled to raise it. Try to convey the impression that you can happily walk away from the item you cherish (even if you are prepared to cave in and pay the full price).

It is not a good strategy to make an offer that is ridiculously below the asking price. Not only will you not succeed, you also risk incurring the real and legitimate indignation of the vendor, who may not hesitate to denounce you to all within hearing distance. Generally, an offer of much less than two-thirds of the asking price is probably a bad idea; if that's all you want to pay, you should probably forget about it altogether. (Also, as was stated earlier in this chapter, if you have succeeded in bargaining the price down significantly, avoid paying with a large bill, since otherwise you risk provoking a sarcastic remark.)

All of this is not to suggest that, no matter how reasonable the asking price, you are required to haggle. Sometimes the price quoted is eminently fair; nothing compels you to try to get it reduced, although I do have friends who argue that, in the interest of *chineurs* generally, tourists should always bargain, to help keep the practice alive. My response is that the tradition of haggling is so solidly entrenched that it is in no danger of extinction.

Language barriers are going to somewhat adversely affect your ability to successfully bargain. Any efforts you make to learn French, or at least familiarize yourself with some important words and phrases—especially numbers—will help. However, unless you are close to fluent, these efforts will only take you so far; this sad truth must simply be accepted as part of the game. And possibly, occasionally, appearing obtuse (whether true or not) may even be to your advantage.

If your command of French is not great, make sure that the price you think you have been quoted is right; if in any doubt, do not hesitate to ask that it be repeated (or written down, if necessary). Also, if more than one item is involved, be sure to clarify whether the price quoted is for one only or for all. (I have made this mistake myself a few times. Once, at the Nice market, I thought I was buying a few Depression-era plates for what the vendor understood to be the price of one; this embarrassing misunderstanding only came to light when she was wrapping them up.)

FACILITIES AT THE MARKET

You will find a wide disparity in the level of facilities (cafés, restaurants, and washrooms) at and nearby the markets. Not surprisingly, urban markets generally have much better amenities nearby than markets located outside town or in small villages. Some of the more nitty-gritty markets are quite deficient in this respect, with primitive washrooms and limited food and drink facilities, at best. Others are much better equipped, offering appealing restaurants and cafés nearby, and reasonable washrooms, either on-site or at the cafés. You will also sometimes see two-franc stand-alone washrooms, which have the advantage of self-cleaning after each use. The best strategy, however, wherever you're going, is to plan ahead, so that you don't arrive at a market desperate for either sustenance or a washroom.

As for bank machines, unless the market is in the center of a town or city, you will have difficulty finding one, so make sure that you have sufficient cash on hand before you go.

Finally, consider stopping, at least for a drink, if you spot a congenial-looking café after scouring the market. Months later back home, you may be surprised to find that the times spent sipping a coffee or a glass of wine, while watching the crowds stroll through the market, are among the best memories of your trip.

TRANSPORTING YOUR MARKET FINDS

Clearly the easiest way to transport your purchases back home is to carry them yourself in your luggage. As long as you don't exceed the baggage allowance of your airline (and you might want to check with a number of airlines before you book your ticket, to note any differences in that regard), you will pay nothing to bring your finds home. Since you did not likely pay a lot for the treasures you have accumulated, you will no doubt be loathe to have to shell out large sums for transport.

Be careful, however, in your packing (since, as you have no doubt often observed, baggage handlers do not treat luggage like delicate objects). Decide which of your purchases are the most fragile and the most important to you. Pack these items in your carry-on bag. You must still wrap these things up carefully, since even in the cabin of the plane they are vulnerable to breakage.

Special precautions must be taken with purchases packed in your checked luggage. If you can, bring solid suitcases, with firm edges, rather than duffel bags, which, although lighter, provide less protection. If you are very organized, bring some bubble wrap from home; although you can find packing materials in France, you won't want to spend time looking for them.

Otherwise, use the next best thing, which is your clothing. Wrap up each item individually, reserving the softest, thickest materials for your most fragile, or cherished, purchases. Before beginning to fill your bag, place a few layers of clothing on the bottom, and on the sides. Then begin putting in your purchases, the heavier items closest to the bottom. Make sure that they are well protected from each other. Do not put sharp-edged or hard objects in with your valuables. Pack heavy, nonbreakable items in a separate bag. Do not put one breakable item inside another, unless necessary for space reasons, and only after protectively padding both.

Fill the bag; some people do not realize that a snug, well-stuffed bag is safer than one with space left inside, allowing things to jiggle around in transit. Also, put a thick layer of clothing along the top of the bag before you close it. If you run out of things to use, stuff any remaining spaces with newspaper.

If you cannot carry all your luggage and purchases with you, think about mailing some things home, such as books (which enjoy a reduced mailing rate) and things that take up space but are not breakable or heavy. (Reserve heavier items, other than books, for your luggage allotment, which is generally quite generous in terms of weight.) The French postal system provides good, solid boxes at a small fee. Note the customs section below, regarding the treatment of items mailed back home.

If even mailing is not going to solve your transport problems, you can explore and weigh a number of other options while in France. Airline freight services (such as Air France), while not inexpensive, are convenient; they are easy to locate and your goods will often arrive home within a few days. (Bear in mind, however, that if you are not returning home right away, you may be charged a storage fee after a few days, which can rapidly add up.) You can also ship through an air-freight shipping company, which may arrange pickup and delivery. (Look in the French telephone book under *transport aérien.*)

Surface shipping arrangements, while perhaps cheaper, will take longer. The best way to make a decision is to call a number of companies and explore the different services and fees, once you know what kinds of shipping needs you have. Try to ascertain the total cost, including all fees.

U.S. CUSTOMS

If you are a U.S. resident returning from France, you are entitled to bring in duty-free up to $400 of otherwise dutiable purchases, provided that you have been away at least 48 hours. This applies to purchases for your personal or for household use (and gifts) brought with you upon your return. This exemption only applies if you have not used the $400 exemption, or any part of it, in the preceding 30-day period. Otherwise you must wait another 30 days before being entitled to another exemption, except for a $200 exemption. (Some limitations apply to certain articles.) Some items are not subject to duty, such as fine art (not handicrafts) and antiques over 100 years old; consult U.S. Customs about the requirements regarding these exemptions.

The head of a family can make a joint declaration for all members of the family, provided they live in the same household and are returning to the United States together. Family members making a joint declaration are permitted to combine their personal exemptions. Children are allowed the same exemptions as adults. Those restricted to a $200 exemption are not entitled to pool their exemption with that of other family members in one declaration.

Dutiable purchases in excess of the allowable exemptions are treated as follows: the next $1,000 worth (fair retail value) is assessed at a flat rate of 10 percent, and any remaining amount is then assessed based on the rates applicable to the purchases involved. The flat-rate provision can only be used for articles purchased for your personal use or for gifts and cannot be used more than once every 30 days (not counting the day of your last arrival).

Different provisions apply to goods that are mailed or shipped; they are not included in your exemption and are subject to duty when received in the United States. Mailed gifts to a person are duty-free where the value of the gift package does not exceed $100. Mailed purchases for personal use are duty-free, if the value of the packaged items does not exceed $200.

CANADIAN CUSTOMS

If you are a Canadian resident, returning after an absence of at least seven days, you are entitled to an exemption for otherwise dutiable purchases of up to $500 (for an absence of at least 48 hours, the amount permitted is $200). If you use only part of the $500 exemption, you cannot save the balance for a subsequent trip. To qualify, the goods must generally be for your personal or household use, or gifts. Personal exemptions cannot be combined with those of anyone else, and while parents can make a declaration for a child, the goods declared must be for the child's use. A fixed rate of duty may be applied to goods of up to $300 more than your personal exemption, for any trip of 48 hours or more, where those goods accompany you. No duty is applied in the case of certified antiques (at least 100 years old) and original works of art. Consult Canada customs about these items.

While goods claimed in the $200 exemption must accompany you, with limited exceptions goods claimed in the $500 exemption need not and can precede or follow your return, by mail or otherwise. You can also send gifts from abroad tax and duty-free, if the gift does not exceed $60 (with certain very limited exceptions).

CAUTION

The customs information provided above is general in nature (it also does not address any French export restrictions); for specific advice, consult the appropriate customs authorities. Also, of course, the amounts of the applicable exemptions, as well as the provisions and conditions, are subject to change at any time.

WHAT ELSE IS AVAILABLE TO READ

Unfortunately, unless you read French, you will not find a lot of recently published books on either French flea markets or the collectibles you will find there. (One book, published in 1987, is *Manston's Flea Markets, Antique Shows and Auctions of France,* by Peter Manston.) Even the number of books in French is limited. While there are numerous books on individual collectibles, few guides to the flea markets are available. The situation, however, seems to be changing; for example, a book published in 1998, *Un Grand Week-end pour Chiner* (*chiner,* again, means to scour around looking for interesting finds), published by Hachette, is a guide to periodic (rather than regular) flea markets throughout France. Another book, the *Guide du Chineur Parisien,* also published in 1998 (by Parigramme), and written by Catherine Vialle and Béatrice de Goutel, canvases the flea markets of Paris.

A number of books in English on French decoration and design will give you some ideas about what you might be interested in looking for in the markets. A few examples are *Pierre Deux's French Country: A Style and Source Book,* by Pierre Moulin, Pierre Le Vec, and Linda Dannenberg, and published by Clarkson Potter; *Provence Interiors,* by Lisa Lovatt-Smith, and published by Taschen; *Living in Provence: Interior Styles and Decoration,* by Sara Walden, and published by Stoddart; and *Bringing France Home,* by Cheryl MacLachlan, and published by Clarkson Potter.

The best general book that I have found about the collectibles in France is the *Guide de la Brocante et des Antiquités,* by Laurence Albert, and published by Éditions de Vecchi. This book identifies and discusses numerous collectibles of all sorts (from canes and pipes to dolls, buttons, and tobacco jars); it also provides information on dealers, associations, and museums for further research. Also of interest is a series of attractive and colorful books, published by Éditions Alternatives, on different collectibles— enamel advertising plaques, tins, phone cards, and Camembert labels, for example. One book in the series—*Le Guide des Collections,* by Vincent Vidal—is a general guide, listing and briefly describing over 100 collectibles and providing information on other sources. Another general book of interest to collectors of everyday objects is *Les Objets de Charme de la Maison Française,* by Chris O'Byrne, and published by Éditions du Chêne.

Your best bet, if you want to find out what else is available, is to visit a FNAC when you arrive. (FNAC is a large bookstore chain, with outlets in many cities.) There, you will find numerous books on individual collectibles.

Currently, at least four regular magazines are devoted to *brocante* and the flea markets. Three—*Aladin, Le Chineur,* and *Antiquités Brocante*—appear monthly, while *La vie du collectionneur* comes out every week. In addition to articles featuring French collectibles, these magazines include lists of both regular markets and special *brocante* fairs taking place in the coming weeks.

What to Look for in the Markets

The great thing about the flea markets of France is that you can find just about anything in them, from old porcelain bathtub fixtures or paintings of wild boars to art deco figurines and silver wine tasters. There is that wonderful moment of infatuation, when you spot something for the first time and start, from that point on, to become a collector of it. So many of the things I now collect started that way—whether it was old *boules,* ceramic foie gras terrines, or the little *fèves* that the French put in their *galettes des rois* during Epiphany.

Collecting is, of course, a very personal and subjective activity, which is part of its great appeal. One person's passion—linens, dolls, pens, tin toys—may leave another cold, not to mention entirely mystified. Learning a little about an item's history or role leads to its understanding (especially important in the case of a different culture, such as that of France); it may also provide the impetus to its appreciation.

In many cases, the things that people collect in France are the same as those people collect elsewhere (except, of course, that the particular examples are the product of France's own history and cultural traditions). A long list of items falls into this category; to name just a few—coins, stamps, dolls, toys, postcards, books, records, jewelry, pens, pewter, oil lamps, military memorabilia, marine items, silver, radios and phonographs, cameras and photographs, paintings and prints, old magazines, scientific and medical implements, weights and measures, glassware, picture frames, posters, sports gear, knives, lighters, clocks, clothing accessories (hats, purses, pipes, canes, umbrellas, watches), figurines, and vases. For many collectors, the thrill of the French flea markets is the opportunity they afford to add an international touch to collections already under way.

Many other collectibles, either unique to France or closely connected with it, constitute symbols or icons of that country's popular culture and traditions. In the first category, for example, are the Provençal *santons* (ceramic folk personages); *indiennes* fabrics and bedspreads; the polka-dotted, or marbled-looking, ceramics from the Savoie; the old wooden, nail-studded *boules* used for playing the game of the same name throughout France; Quimper ceramics from Brittany; and the sturdy, striped linens from the Pays Basque.

Symbolic, if not unique, are old coffee mills; café au lait bowls; enamel coffeepots, utensil holders, and trivets; and the beautifully crafted *échantillons de parfums,* or perfume samples.

It is collectibles of this sort—either unique to France or emblematic of it—that are featured below. And the items selected—which include a mix of rustic and decorative, modest-priced and more rarefied—are all things you can find in the flea markets (albeit some more easily than others).

The 30 or so items featured, in alphabetical order, are *barbotine,* basket ware, *boules,* café au lait bowls, Camembert labels, ceramics of Alsace, ceramics of the Savoie, champagne capsules, chocolate molds, coffee mills, copperware, corkscrews and wine tasters, dish towels, enamel coffeepots, enamel plaques, Epiphany *fèves,* garden bells, garden tools, garden watering cans, irons, linens, mustard pots, perfume bottles and samples, Provençal fabrics, Quimper ware, rattles and baby bottles, *santons,* telephone cards, tins, travel luggage, and yogurt pots. These items are only some of the things that could have been chosen; there are so many collectibles of this sort that a book could be written on this subject alone.

It is impossible, here, to even begin to delve into other vast areas, such as furniture, and the many different regional styles and periods. Nor can all of the different ceramics produced in France possibly be fully explored; a small sampling of some of the ceramics most collected in the markets is, however, included. For these purposes, below are a few simple definitions with respect to ceramics.

The word *ceramics* is used as the generic term that refers to all heated clay objects, which includes terra-cotta, glazed earthenware, faience, stoneware, and porcelain. Terra-cotta, the earliest ceramics used, was based on ordinary clay heated to not very great temperatures, of between 600° and 800°C. A glaze could not be applied before firing, and any decoration was applied after cooling, with a brush.

Glazed earthenware, called *terre vernissée* in French, is the term generally used for works created in clay fired at a temperature of 1,000°C. This form of ceramics is also characterized by the use of a shiny and transparent glaze. Much of the pottery produced in the Savoie, Provence, and Alsace, for example, falls into this general category.

Faience is made from a lighter colored clay and is heated to a temperature of between 800° and 1,000°C. An opaque white glaze is applied and decorative and colorful motifs painted on. Ceramics from Quimper, Rouen, and Moustiers are examples of faience.

Stoneware is made from clay and sand, but of a composition that allows it to be heated up to 1,200°C., making it very hard and solid; appealing finishes can also be applied. Stoneware was the type of ceramics produced, for example, in Betschdorf in Alsace.

Finally, porcelain is made from a mixture of very white clay—called kaolin—feldspar, and quartz. Its characteristic hard and translucent qualities are achieved in part because of the high temperature at which it is fired (1,400 degrees). There have been many porcelain centers in France, including Limoges and Sèvres.

Flea Market Collectibles

BARBOTINE

You have, no doubt, seen those colorful old dishes with different shapes in relief—such as asparagus or grapes—that seem to jump out at you. Considered too kitsch and too garish by some, *barbotine* is an appealing collectible to many. It was produced mostly between the end of the 19th and the early 20th century. This ceramic style is characterized by hand-painted, brilliantly colorful designs in relief. Many different images were used—fruits, vines, animals, and vegetables, for example.

The age of a *barbotine* piece is not easy to tell, nor is its origin, as many did not have markings. One clue to age, apparently, is that the older piece have motifs which are in higher relief. Also, not surprisingly, in older examples, color tones of individual pieces in a set may not completely match. *Barbotine* was made by a number of producers—in Sarreguemines, Longchamps, Monaco, Menton, and elsewhere. Monaco and Menton *barbotine* are characterized, appropriately, by lemons, oranges, and flowers in brilliant colors.

You will see examples of *barbotine* fairly often at the flea markets. It was made for many different uses, many of which are quite practical—pitchers, garden pots, asparagus servers, oyster plates, dessert plates, gravy boats, vases, etc. Prices vary greatly, based on the origin, age, rarity, color, condition, and the nature of the piece. However, as an example, expect to pay about 200 francs for a plate in good condition. More exotic items will be much more expensive.

BASKET WARE (LA VANNERIE)

Old baskets, in all different shapes and sizes, were one of the first things I started to collect in France years ago. At some of the more rural and down-home markets, I would find really appealing ones, in good condition, for as little as 10 to 20 francs. Such bargains are harder to find now, as more and more people recognize the charm, and collectible interest, of these symbols of rural and everyday life.

Since starting my own small collection, I have learned that, given their utilitarian role, and ultimately somewhat fragile nature, the baskets you will find in the flea markets usually only date back to the late 19th century and are often from the first part of this century. They were made in different parts of France—two big basket-making centers, for example, were Cadenet, in the Vaucluse, and Villaines-les-Rochers, in the Loire valley. I went to Villaines-les-Rochers recently, to watch baskets being made in the village cooperative, established by the townspeople in the middle of the 19th century. Some baskets were the product of an even more "local" cottage industry—made by farmers and fishermen in their spare time, for their own use.

Baskets were designed for many different, and very practical, purposes—for holding or handling eggs, chickens, cheese, apples, bread, fish, oysters, grains, linens, bottles, etc. They were made from different materials, depending somewhat on what was locally available—osiers, blackberry bushes, bulrushes, reeds, and both hazel and chestnut tree stems. The size and shape of these baskets varied according to the uses they served. For example, baskets to carry young chicks were shaped in the form of cages, while winegrowers had large baskets with shoulder straps to carry heavy grapes on their backs.

The best places for finding baskets at reasonable prices are the more down-home rural flea markets, where the value of this item as a collectible—as opposed to a functional object—may not be fully appreciated. Prices will vary enormously, based on shape, condition, and just plain chance. Age is, apparently, not a huge factor, probably because it is difficult to determine and because the potential range (usually between the late 19th and early to mid-20th century) is not great. Count, generally, on spending between 20 and 100 francs (and more for the larger baskets).

BOULES

Boules—the word describes the game itself, as well as the balls used to play it—are a big collectible in France and one of my passions. There is something extraordinarily pleasing about holding an old, textured, nail-studded, wooden *boule*—or a more recent vintage, smooth, bronze *boule*—in your hand. And perhaps nothing more symbolizes French cultural traditions than the game of *boules*—similar to curling, but without the ice and brooms— played in towns and villages throughout France, but especially in the south.

While the game is extremely ancient, the term *boules* apparently dates back to the 13th century. This pastime was so popular in the 14th century that for a time it was banned, on the grounds that it caused people to neglect more serious matters. Most in vogue, initially, among the *paysans,* the aristocracy caught on as well, and by the 19th century, *boules* enjoyed a huge following. Individual regions had their own variants of the game, and in 1910, a new Provençal version, *la pétanque,* was created near Marseille, rapidly eclipsing its predecessor.

Before metals were used, *boules* were simply dense, round, wooden balls and then, for about 50 years between 1880 and 1930 (roughly speaking), wooden balls studded with nails of different shapes, depending on the region. The finicky job of covering the *boules* evenly with nails was mostly performed by women, who, we are told, could usually only complete five pairs in a day. Some of the nail-studded *boules* produced were made to order and quite decorative; designs were created by mixing nails of different colors.

In 1923, bronze *boules* appeared on the scene, which had the distinct practical advantage of not warping. Pleasing designs of different sorts were produced by etching lines on the surface of the *boule.* A few years later came the earliest examples of *boules* made of steel, the much less attractive material still used today.

Boules are often found in the flea markets—sometimes dirty and rusty at the bottom of old crates of tools (in low-end rural markets), or well shined and prominently displayed (at high-end urban markets). The range in price is huge—between 50 and 400 francs for old burnished wooden ones; from 50 to 600 francs for nail-studded ones; between 20 and 100 francs for bronze ones; and from 10 to 50 francs for the more recent steel ones. (These fluctuations have to do with condition and appearance, of course, but also, to a significant extent, just plain chance.)

The best places to look for *boules* are the more low-end and rural markets in Provence. (One of my most prized ones was bought at the junk market in Montfavet, near Avignon.) Several years ago, old *boules* were quite cheap, but not really easy to find; now they are more plentiful (as vendors have recognized the interest in them), but also more expensive.

CAFÉ AU LAIT BOWLS *(LES BOLS DE CAFÉ AU LAIT)*

Few things symbolize everyday life in France more than the lovely little bowl —used every morning in French households—for drinking café au lait or hot chocolate. Writers wax eloquent on the subject of childhoods spent dunking their *tartines* (toasted baguettes spread with jam or chocolate) in their own, jealously guarded, bowl. Larger versions, for also drinking the midday soup, were apparently used by *paysans,* in Provence.

The big interest these days in collecting café au lait bowls is not attributable simply to sentimentality. They are also aesthetically pleasing, relatively inexpensive, and easy to find. Moreover, the collecting potential is large and extremely varied. Collections are often based on design themes (geometrics, florals, or landscapes, for example), historical periods, and regions. Regional differences are notable: for example, you can find Savoyard bowls, in green or rust polka dots on a straw-colored background; bowls from southwest France, in geometric patterns in navy and burgundy against a white background; Provençal bowls, in the yellow and green glazes typical of that region; Alsatian bowls, with naive floral patterns in green, dark brown, straw yellow, and blue; and Brittany bowls, decorated with the trademark Breton couple in traditional dress.

Prices of café au lait bowls vary widely, from around 10 to 60 francs. The range is attributable to age, condition, and design—apparently bowls with a Moorish pattern are quite desirable—but also to the nature of the market itself. The best places to find a good deal are junk markets in urban areas, where it is not unusual to find quite nice bowls for as little as 10 francs. I recently discovered an old one, in a lovely geometric pattern in dark green on white, for 5 francs in the Porte de Montreuil market in Paris.

CAMEMBERT LABELS *(LES ÉTIQUETTES DE CAMEMBERT)*

Those whose collecting passion is the round labels from Camembert cheese —the cheese so symbolic of Normandy—even have a name in French. They are called *tyrosémiophiles,* and they are numerous, both in France and in other European countries.

Apart from being visually pleasing, Camembert labels provide a remarkable chronicle of significant events over the last century and a quarter, from war to space travel. The first round label is said to have appeared in the second half of the 19th century, on a cheese called—appropriately—Sans Rival, or "without rival." Since then, several thousand examples have been produced, with images of all kinds—from cows, monks, and healthy-looking farm women to Mickey Mouse. Collectors tend to focus on particular themes, such as scenery, religion, animals (cows, birds, cats, dogs, etc.), and historical events.

I was surprised to learn why Camembert is sold in boxes. I had always assumed that there was a uniquely French reason for packaging the cheese in this manner—a secret French twist for ensuring the cheese ripened to perfection. To the contrary, a cheese exporter apparently developed the box in

1890 so that he could transport the cheese to America; this supple container helped maintain the proper humidity levels during the voyage.

You will occasionally see Camembert labels at the flea markets. Prices are often quite reasonable, starting at just a few francs (although the more rare ones are expensive). If you really become hooked, try to visit the Musée du Camembert, in Vimoutiers, southeast of Caen. There you will see not only many tools used in the production of Camembert, but also over 5,000 examples of the Camembert labels that have been produced over the last century and a bit. Lest you might think otherwise, you won't be alone when you go; the museum receives over 10,000 visitors a year.

CERAMICS OF ALSACE (LA CÉRAMIQUE ALSACIENNE)

Glazed earthenware pottery used to be made in a number of towns in Alsace, but a prime center is Soufflenheim (northeast of Strasbourg), where it is still produced. This pottery was designed for practical purposes—both for cooking and as dishes for the table. The colors used were generally straw yellow, green, an orangy rust, and dark brown. The images were simple and naive—flowers, roosters, hearts, fish, or primitive geometric designs.

Ceramic molds in different shapes and designs were also made for baking certain Alsatian desserts and pastries—for example, kugelhopf cakes (made in a round, undulating mold), Christmas treats, and Easter cakes (cooked in molds in the shapes of lambs or fish).

Less porous stoneware was used for containers for conserving food (grease and pickled eggs or beans, for example) or serving drinks (beer, wine, and water). These gray-colored pieces, often decorated with blue blotches, apparently began to be made in Betschdorf (north of Strasbourg) in the early 18th century.

You will sometimes see Alsatian ceramics (especially not very old pieces) in the flea markets; the Strasbourg market is a good place to look, but so is the huge monthly flea market in Belfort, in neighboring Franche-Comté. While you will find table pieces in other parts of France, the molds are harder to locate outside this region (although I did buy a kugelhopf mold in Rouen recently for 50 francs). Lamb Easter molds are not cheap, usually selling for about 250 francs. The colorful table pieces span a wide price range, but I have often found them cheaper outside the region (for example, in Paris) than in Alsace itself.

CERAMICS FROM THE SAVOIE (LA CÉRAMIQUE SAVOYARD)

One of the most charming styles of glazed earthenware is that found in the Savoie. The 19th century marked an important period in the production of this traditional style of ceramics (still made today by a small number of people). Characterized by simple and classic shapes and designs, this style of ceramics reflects the rustic and rugged nature of this region. Milk pots, bowls, and plates personify this simple style, but perhaps most of all the milk pots (not surprising, given the dairy focus of this region). Either straight or slighty indented in shape, they were made in all different sizes.

The colors used were also rustic and appealing—straw yellow, green, dark brown, and rust. (Blue, apparently, only made an appearance in this century.) In addition to the trademark polka dots, the classic, simple motifs include naive geometric designs (like squiggly lines), mountain flowers (such as edelweiss, tulips, narcissus, and anemone), and also a marbled effect, called *jaspé*.

Savoyard ceramics are widely collected and not inexpensive. You will find them most easily in the region itself, notably at the large monthly flea market in Annecy, but also in Grenoble (and, if you are lucky, elsewhere, such as in Paris). Old milk jugs in reasonable condition are usually sold for at least 300 francs. I bought a small *jaspé* pitcher in Grenoble for just over 100 francs, but failed (stupidly) to snap up a small, attractive jug in Cannes that was only 80 francs. (Sometimes a hot regional collectible will be found at a much lower price at the opposite end of the country, simply because the vendor doesn't know much about it.)

CHAMPAGNE CAPSULES *(LES CAPSULES DE CHAMPAGNE)*

In the 17th century a monk named Dom Pérignon had the idea of using corks to bottle champagne. However, not until almost a century later did the champagne capsule first appear. And it was later still before these capsules evolved into the form we are familiar with today—a round metal piece tied to the bottle with a wire, called the *muselet*.

While the collection of champagne capsules (called *plaquomusophilie*) was initially confined generally to the champagne-producing centers, such as Reims and Épernay, it has spread in recent years throughout France. Initially, it was mostly the capsules of the big producers that were coveted, but the interest has grown to include capsules of all kinds. Collections are often based on different decorative motifs or themes—portraits, churches, monuments, cars, commemorative events, etc. There are, reportedly, now over 8,000 different champagne capsules, and new releases, such as to commemorate the year 2000, are always keenly anticipated.

Champagne capsules are easy to collect; they take up little space in your luggage and are usually reasonably priced, often between 5 and 20 francs each. You will frequently see them in flea markets throughout France, usually being sold by vendors who specialize in them.

CHOCOLATE MOLDS (LES MOULES À CHOCOLAT)

Chocolate molds are a not infrequent feature in the flea markets. Usually found in metal, they were also apparently made in Bakelite. The variety of motifs is impressive—little animals of many kinds, of course, but also more interesting shapes such as lady's slippers.

While chocolate is a big product in France, and the molds thus have a special significance here, they have only recently become the subject of much interest among collectors, unlike in the United States, for example. However, enthusiasm for this collectible has grown quickly, so that now you are unlikely to spot a mold in good condition for under 50 to 100 francs. You can find them throughout the country; I have seen them in the flea markets in Nîmes, Annecy, Paris, and Bayonne (in the Pays Basque), for example. (Apparently, cocoa beans were first introduced into France in Bayonne, a town noted for its chocolate.)

COFFEE MILLS (LES MOULINS À CAFÉ)

One of the biggest collectibles in France is the coffee mill; indeed, as in the case of several items, there is a name in French for coffee mill collectors—*molafabophiles*. These practical gadgets first appeared in France at the end of the 17th century, with the arrival of coffee beans imported from Abyssinia.

Coffee was originally a drink of the upper classes for a simple reason—cost. The story behind the democratization of coffee goes back, it is said, to the Napoleonic Wars, when Napoleon imposed a blockade on England. The British, not surprisingly, retaliated by firing on ships bound for France with spices and coffee beans, causing shipments to halt. However, after the battle of Waterloo, the colonial growers unleashed their accumulated stock on France. Prices plummeted, thereby allowing the ordinary person to adopt the ritual of the *petit noir* in the local café.

Coffee mills were based on the mills used to grind spices. While in different shapes and sizes, they were made in essentially three forms—portable (with a metal handle and a little drawer to catch the grinds); wall-mounted (with decorated porcelain); and *de comptoir* (the large counter models, weighing up to 70 kilograms, which graced the cafés and *epiceries*, or grocery stores). They were also crafted from different materials (iron, wood, and in some cases, even silver). The degree of decoration varied enormously, from the most simple and classic versions to mills that were finely carved and decorated.

Although you are not likely to unearth really old coffee mills in the flea markets, you will find attractive 19th- and early 20th-century models (by such makers as Peugeot and Japy). While some 19th-century models may run as much as 1,000 francs, you can find quite attractive mills of more recent vintage starting at around 100 francs (although many are around the 200-franc range). Both condition and degree of decoration, as well as vintage, are important factors in determining a mill's value. Given the wide variety of models and designs available, this is an interesting and attractive item for collectors.

COPPER COOKWARE (LES CUIVRES DE CUISINE)

Copper is noted for its ability to evenly and effectively transmit heat, thus making it an ideal material for cooking pots and utensils. While copper has been made in Europe since before the Middle Ages, copper cookware apparently began to be "mass produced" in France in the 17th century—in Paris and Lyons, but also in the Auvergne and in Normandy (notably, Villedieu-les-Poêles). Villedieu-les-Poêles (the name combines the three essential notions of city, God, and frying pans) was apparently already making other metal items in the 11th century and is still an important center for the production of copper cookware.

Copper cookware became widespread in France in the 18th century. Surprisingly, it was used by ordinary people as well as by the well-heeled, although the quality would vary. From the 18th century, these pieces were also lined with tin to prevent poisoning. Many different kinds of cookware were produced—pots, casseroles, frying pans, fish poachers, kettles, jam makers, strainers, and pastry molds of all kinds, for example.

Old copper pots and other copper cookware can be found at flea markets throughout France. You are not, however, likely to find anything that dates back further than the mid-19th century. Prices vary greatly, depending on form, size, condition, and age. The price of copper molds, and copperware in unusual and decorative shapes, is quite high; on the other hand, you can find old copper pots and frying pans in the markets at fairly reasonable prices. A friend who is a chef buys all of her copper pots in the flea markets. She has managed to find large frying pans and casseroles in good condition for as little as 100 or 150 francs, although you can also pay much more than that. With a retinning (if necessary), these items are not only decorative but also functional.

CORKSCREWS AND WINE TASTERS
(LES TIRE-BOUCHONS ET LES TASTE-VIN)

Admired for their attractive shapes (as well as their useful qualities), corkscrews are a big collectible in France and often found in the flea markets.

Not surprisingly, perhaps, the French and the English dispute who first invented this handy implement, with some French authorities claiming that it was in France, in the latter half of the 17th century. Whatever its origins, the corkscrew has been subject to many design innovations over the years. The simple T-shaped gadget could be quite detailed, for practical as well as aesthetic reasons (practical, because detailing and texture offered the user a better grip). In the 17th and 18th centuries, popular motifs were bunches of grapes and fish, while in the first half of the 19th century bone handles were the rage.

A number of practical little accessories might also be attached to the corkscrew handle—for example, little brushes to dust off the bottles, boot-lacers, pipe materials, nutmeg grinders, tiny knives, and whistles. Expensive materials were occasionally used, such as gold, silver, and precious stones.

While you will not see many of the more valuable or exotic corkscrews at the flea markets, you will find many attractive ones, in both the T-shape and other shapes and designs, for between 50 and 250 francs. (Check especially the glass cases some vendors use to display smaller items.)

Taste-vin—the little round receptacles with a small handle used (as the name suggests) to taste wine—were produced everywhere in France. Silver wine tasters first appeared in the 16th century, but less valuable materials have, of course, also been used—silver plate, porcelain, and less expensive metals. Designs have varied enormously, depending in large part on the region. Markings might be etched on the center or on the little handle, and might include the name of the owner or the town in which the wine taster was made.

You will quite often see wine tasters in the flea markets throughout France. Naturally, prices vary enormously, depending on the material used, the form, the engravings, and age. For example, silver ones from the 18th century may cost a few thousand francs, while metal ones (which still make a good souvenir of France) can be found in the markets for between 10 and 50 francs.

DISH TOWELS *(LES TORCHONS)*

I have to confess that French dish towels (or *torchons*) are one of my true passions. There is something pure and comforting in their crisp simplicity, whether all white with tiny red initials modestly cross-stitched in the corner or with a colored stripe as in the Pays Basque.

The notion of the *torchon* first appeared in France, we are told, around the 13th century, in the form of a multipurpose cloth used, variously, to do the dishes, polish the furniture, and clean the floor.

While other items falling within the rubric of household linens became more and more refined and segregated (such as tablecloths and napkins), the poor *torchon* did not really come into its own until the 19th century. Then, it began to even be recognized as an important part of a young woman's trousseau. Girls would take the trouble to embroider their initial in red cross-stitch in the corner of the *torchon* and then stitch in their fiancé's once their domestic future was secured.

Torchons were made of different materials depending on their role. Finer linen would be used for more delicate objects, such as glassware, while the more workmanlike *chanvre*, or hemp, would be used for rougher materials. Often, a different torchon would be dedicated to each potential use—for glasses, plates, pots and pans, and even for handling vegetables.

As is often the case in France, there are even regional dimensions to this functional item. Older cloths from the Pays Basque (and Béarn), for example, often had a wide navy stripe against a white background. (More recent examples have different combinations of red, blue, green, or yellow stripes, in conformity with the style of linens from this area.)

You will often see old *torchons* at the flea markets, and the prices will vary widely depending on age, condition, fabric, and the nature of the market itself. I have found really nice ones at the more down-home markets for as little as 10 francs, but you can also pay well over 50 francs for a fine old linen one in pristine condition.

ENAMEL COFFEEPOTS *(LES CAFETIÈRES ÉMAILLÉES)*

Like café au lait bowls, enamel coffeepots evoke much nostalgia among the French, recalling days spent in the kitchen while the adults sat around drinking coffee and gossiping.

Enamel coffeepots first appeared in about 1870, usually composed of three parts—a bottom section, with a handle, for receiving the water; a top part, also with a handle, for holding the ground coffee; and a lid. Shapes and sizes would vary; in addition to small household models, much larger ones could hold up to five liters of water. The spouts on the earliest models were apparently made in two parts, joined together vertically. The production of enamel coffeepots was relatively short-lived; in the early 20th century, they were supplanted by the arrival of aluminum pots.

The pots you will find in France may be from the north of France, or from Belgium, Holland, eastern Europe, or even Finland. Many different decorative motifs are found—birds, floral patterns, stencil-like images, and geometric designs of all kinds (squares and diamonds, for example). The pots come in many colors, with red and yellow said to be the most desirable.

Enamel coffeepots have become a popular collectible in France in recent years, and prices in the flea markets and *brocante* stores have increased significantly. Prices, however, vary widely (based in part upon the level of awareness about the collectibility of this practical item), with flea markets outside of Paris and the large cities the best places to find a bargain. Cost also depends, of course, on the condition of the enameling, the age of the pot, whether the pot has all of its parts, color, and pattern. Generally you will pay between 100 and 400 francs for an attractive model in reasonably good condition.

ENAMEL PLAQUES (LES PLAQUES ÉMAILLÉES)

A big collectible in France is the enamel advertising plaque, which first appeared about a century ago. It was used to advertise all sorts of products, but most notably food and alcoholic beverages. (For example, around 300 plaques were dedicated to the subject of beer alone.) A primary manufacturer of these plaques in France was an Alsatian company, l'Émaillerie Alsacienne de Strasbourg.

As in the case of many collectibles, there is a name in French for collectors of these colorful and appealing hard posters—*plaquophiles*. Although plaques had been in existence for many decades before, not until the 1970s did collectors start to become really interested in them. The biggest production of enamel plaques occurred from the end of World War I to the end of World War II, when plastic materials started to come onto the market. By the mid-1960s, plastic had essentially taken over, because of its various production advantages.

Enamel plaques are now so entrenched as a collectible that aficionados are familiar with the work of individual artists, who are discussed and studied with great reverence. Many of the designs are clever as well as appealing and colorful; the most popular subjects used, apparently, were children, followed by animals of all kinds (giraffes, storks, roosters, etc.). Prices for enamel plaques vary enormously—depending on age, image, and condition —from a few hundred (300 to 600) francs for plaques that have a simple image (rather than just lettering), to several thousand francs for the most sought-after designs. If this is a collectible you are interested in, you are best advised to consult one of the books available on the subject, to find out which are the most desirable and valuable.

You will find enamel plaques fairly often at flea markets throughout France. I particularly noticed them at the big monthly Belfort market (which is not surprising given its proximity to Strasbourg and l'Émaillerie Alsacienne de Strasbourg).

EPIPHANY FÈVES (LES FÈVES DE L'ÉPIPHANIE)

For hundreds of years, Epiphany—the Christian event celebrating the trek to Bethlehem of the Three Wise Men bearing gifts for the baby Jesus—has been observed in France by the *galette des rois*. This cake, made of layers of thin pastry, conceals inside a little *fève*—originally a real bean, but subsequently made of various materials (ceramics, plastic, or metal). The idea is that the person who finds the *fève* in his or her portion of the *galette* must wear the paper crown that is also provided with the cake.

Up until the beginning of this century, we are told, it was a custom of bakers to offer a *galette des rois* as a gift to their customers, and prior to the French Revolution, their guild would make a giant cake for the king. During the Revolution, when practices related to the monarchy were, not surprisingly, forbidden, bakers produced instead *galettes de l'égalité*, which concealed the politically acceptable *fèves* of the revolutionary *sans culottes*. Also, instead of a crown, these *galettes* had the revolutionary symbol, a floppy hat.

With the return of the monarchy in the early 19th century, the *galette des rois* reappeared. It remains a well-entrenched custom today, with the *galette* sometimes substituted for in the south by a brioche garnished with red- and green-colored candied fruit.

In recent years, the collecting of Epiphany *fèves*—called *fabophilie*—has become quite popular in France. The oldest *fèves* were simply beans—the symbol of life. Between 1870 and 1880, the vegetable *fève* was replaced by ceramic ones in the form of babies, either nude or wrapped in swaddling clothes (symbolizing, of course, the baby Jesus). Later, figures in all shapes and varieties appeared. Not only figures were popular as *fèves*, however; animals, symbols, and objects commemorating public events, such as the expedition to the North Pole, were also produced. For a time after the Second World War, *fèves* were often made of plastic, but in recent years there has been a return to ceramic, as the material of choice. The 200th anniversary of the French Revolution in 1989 sparked the creation of entire new lines with revolutionary themes.

You will often see vendors at the flea markets in France specializing only in *fèves*. Given the huge range of subjects available, collectors tend to focus on certain themes—animals, objects, current events, etc. The price of *fèves* is generally reasonable: plastic ones for under 10 francs, ceramic *fèves* for between 5 and 15 francs, and metal ones for around 25 francs. Older *fèves* are, of course, much more expensive, but it is often difficult to tell the age of a *fève*. Generally an older *fève* is decorated in a more primitive fashion than a more modern one, but this is not a foolproof test since new ones have been produced to look old. Your best bet is to buy based on appeal, rather than supposed age.

Fèves are a truly charming collectible that will serve as a permanent reminder of your trip to France. Their other attractions, of course, are that they are inexpensive and will take up very little room in your luggage.

GARDEN BELLS (LES CLOCHES DE MARAÎCHER)

Collectors of garden ware of all kinds—watering cans, wrought-iron plant holders, old terra-cotta pots, garden tables and chairs, and tools—will have a field day in France. Not only are these items widely found in the flea markets, they can also be picked up at quite reasonable prices, particularly in the more down-home rural markets.

One highly sought-after item that you see occasionally is the glass garden bell. This beautiful object was also functional, serving the dual purpose of protecting plants from frost and providing a microclimate to encourage rapid growth. They first appeared, we are told, at the end of the 16th century; over the next three centuries they were produced, to an increasing extent, for the market gardens supplying France's growing towns and cities. (By the 19th century, it is said, some of these operations employed several thousand bells.)

Garden bells were made primarily in eastern France, where many of the glassworks were destroyed during World War I. The bells were also done in by other, more practical, concerns: their fragility and the time-intensive nature of their use.

You are more likely to find old garden bells in regions with a tradition of market gardens. I have seen them particularly in the flea markets of the Loire region, for example, in Orléans and Angers. They will sometimes be slightly damaged, and you will have to decide whether you want to purchase them nonetheless. Prices are fairly high; expect to pay at least 400 francs for a garden bell in reasonable condition, but I have seen them for much more in Paris, for instance.

GARDEN TOOLS (LES OUTILS DE JARDIN)

The French revere the tools that have facilitated all of the activities and trades of their extraordinary social history, but perhaps the tools they cherish the most are those relating to agriculture and gardening. Indeed, a book that appeared in 1996, *Outils de Jardin,* by Guillaume Pellerin, chronicles the author's 25 years of garden-tool collecting, during which he amassed around 4,000 examples.

The 17th century in France witnessed a dramatic proliferation of garden tools, forged out of iron. Given the cost of this material, tools past their prime would be melted down and made into new ones, often by farmers themselves. The biggest increase in the number of tools took place in the next two centuries, however, due to the arrival of a whole new variety of plants, techniques of mass production, and sales through advertising catalogs.

You will often find old garden tools at the flea markets—pitchforks, rakes, spades, hoes, trowels, shears—in every size and shape. Sometimes, they will be dirty and rusty, piled in boxes on the ground, while at other times you will see them all cleaned and beautifully presented; this alone will contribute to the huge range in prices you will find. As in the case of all rustic items, the best place to find bargains is at low-end markets in rural parts of France, where the vendor still views the tool as a functional—as much as a collectible —object. If you buy a tool simply because you are struck by its appearance, try nonetheless to get a description from the vendor of its use, if possible.

GARDEN WATERING CANS (LES ARROSOIRS)

Long ago, containers for watering plants were made of terra-cotta, later replaced by metal, usually copper. As the cost of copper rose, however, watering cans began to be made in iron, zinc, and galvanized iron. Sadly, since the 1950s, even these metals have given way to that ubiquitous material, plastic.

In the flea markets you will see old watering cans in all shapes and sizes and at all prices. Shape, as well as age, is a factor in pricing, for those in the know. I once bought a pretty little one with the image of Betty Boop (I think) on the front for 5 francs in Provence, but that was a really lucky find. Your best bet in finding a bargain is, again, to go to the more down-home markets in rural areas.

IRONS (LES FERS À REPASSER)

Historians tell us that the Chinese were the first to work out a method of using heat to get wrinkles out of clothes, many centuries before irons appeared in Europe in the 16th century. The Europeans, however, have been active on this front since, coming up with a wide variety of different types of irons, particularly in the 19th century. Innovations were aimed both at exploring different means of heating the iron and at responding to the evolving fashion (and hence pressing) requirements of the period.

Until the arrival in France of the electric iron in the early 20th century, the search for the best heating method led to putting the iron directly in the fire; placing coal embers or heated metal ingots in the cavity of the iron; and experiments with alcohol, gas, and water.

Old irons are highly collectible in France; there is (yet again) even a word for iron collectors—*pressophiles*. While earlier models are expensive and not likely to turn up in the flea markets, you will often see irons of more recent vintage, from the late 19th and early 20th century, at fairly reasonable prices.

Also quite collectible are the *repose-fers,* or iron-rests, with their attractive cutout designs.

LINENS *(LE LINGE)*

Tourists in France are always attracted to French linens, whether made from linen itself, *métis* (linen and cotton), or cotton—sheets, large square pillowcases, tablecloths and napkins, handkerchiefs, little doilies, and other small decorative pieces. Linen is considered the finest fabric, given its durability, texture, appearance, and versatility (cool in summer, comfortable in winter); it is also the one most desired by collectors.

France has long been a major producer of linens. An important center historically for the production of linen was Brittany, particularly in the 17th and 18th centuries. The north of France, around Lille, has also been a big producer of linens (both cotton and linen), as have other parts of the country.

Up to the Second World War, young women in France would apparently spend a great deal of time carefully preparing a trousseau, sewing and embroidering linens of all kinds—sheets, pillowcases, tablecloths, napkins, handkerchiefs, and even dish towels (see above). Remnants of these endeavors have found their way into the flea markets of today, where you will often see linens of quite fine quality. Prices vary greatly, but you can, for example, find linen sheets in good condition starting at around 200 francs, with *métis* ones somewhat less and cotton the cheapest of the lot. Better bargains can occasionally be found by scouring the more low-end markets. Be careful, however, for while discolorations can often be removed, this is not always the case. Also, take note that French bedding dimensions differ from North American ones (older sheets, for example, are generally longer and narrower).

Some regional linens are of great interest—for example, high-quality and durable sheets, tablecloths, and napkins from the Pays Basque. Examples of older Basque linens are increasingly rare, but can sometimes be found in flea markets in Southwest France, and occasionally elsewhere. Another area with distinctive linens is Catalonia, with its colorful napkins and place mats in bright blue, red, green, yellow, and white. Sometimes, ironically, these linens can be found at lower prices outside their region of origin; for instance, I recently bought a Basque tablecloth and four napkins in Paris for only 60 francs.

MUSTARD POTS *(LES POTS À MOUTARDE)*

A really fun little collectible, especially for aficionados of French cuisine, is the mustard pot. While the seed is thought to date back 3,000 years to the Chinese, France has been a major mustard producer for a few centuries, with

Burgundy (and its city Dijon) as the center. By the early 20th century, there were, we are told, close to 40 producers of mustard in Dijon, including the well-known Maille and Amora, both established in the mid-18th century. Dijon still produces much of the mustard in France.

At one time, mustard merchants *(moutardiers)* would apparently go door-to-door selling mustard in bulk. As the varieties of mustard increased in the 17th century, so did the need for different labels and containers to store them. The production of mustard pots is said to date back to this period, with the first faience pots with advertising symbols and decorative markings appearing in the 18th century. The pots were sometimes attractively decorated with little flowers and painted patterns. Around 1920, mustard pots took a new turn, as glass became the primary material used (although a few producers have resumed selling specialty mustards in attractive ceramic containers).

Mustard pots were made in a few shapes (although often short, round, and small). In addition to floral motifs and other patterns, they would sometimes bear trademarks and symbols identifying their producer. They often have matching ceramic lids, with a little indent for the insertion of a wooden spoon. Some of the mustard manufacturers whose pots are sought by collectors today are Maille, Amora, Yvetot, and Bornibus.

You will often see mustard pots at the flea markets. You can sometimes find 19th-century examples, in faience, for between 150 and 400 francs, while many 20th-century models can be purchased for between 100 and 200 francs.

PERFUME BOTTLES AND SAMPLES *(LES FLACONS ET LES ÉCHANTILLONS DE PARFUMS)*

The use of perfume is ancient, but started to spread in Europe, apparently, in the late Middle Ages. Perfume served as a kind of hygiene replacement—we all recall being told that the aristocracy would douse themselves with it to disguise the odors resulting from not bathing. By the 18th century, lighter sweet scents came onto the scene, replacing the previous musky perfumes.

Apparently, in the middle of the 19th century what could be termed a perfume "industry" began in France. Until the early 20th century, perfume *flacons,* or bottles, though beautifully crafted by crystal manufacturers, had a fairly uniform shape. The renowned crystal-maker René Lalique got things rolling on this front by creating aesthetically pleasing bottles to reflect the image promoted by the perfume itself. Changes in technology also got into the act, facilitating both this flowering of creativity and the production of bottles at a much more affordable price.

The period between World War I and World War II is considered the high point in the design of perfume containers. Aesthetically innovative pieces were created by famous designers and artists (even Salvador Dalí), mirroring the artistic movements of the time, such as art deco. Many couturiers began to develop their own perfume lines, especially after World War II, a trend that continues today.

Échantillons are *flacon* miniatures (or sometimes different forms or tubes), given away by perfume companies to advertise their products or as a gift for their customers. Some companies created samples of great refinement in very whimsical packaging.

Perfume samples are often found in the flea markets, with bottles appearing less frequently. Prices for *échantillons* vary enormously, from 20 to 200 francs and even more, depending on age, design, and rarity. (Samples with their packaging are also more valuable than those without.) Not surprisingly, the *flacons* are often much more expensive, and contrary to what one might think, whether the bottle contains perfume or not is, apparently, not a significant factor. Popular in France are such brands as Guerlain, Nina Ricci, and Christian Dior.

PROVENÇAL FABRICS (LES INDIENNES)

In the 17th century, printed cottons from India (called *indiennes*) were imported through Marseille and caused a huge stir in France because of their elaborate designs and brilliant colors. French silk and wool manufacturers, however, were less impressed as their businesses began to suffer. They complained to the appropriate officials, and in 1686, the council of state banned all *indiennes*, whether domestic or imported.

As might be expected, the ban only fanned the flames; the forbidden material continued to be brought in or produced surreptitiously. In the 1750s, when the ban was lifted, domestic producers were already well entrenched.

However, the industrial revolution and textile machines took their toll on the hand-printing industry and on the *indiennes;* although the fabrics continued to be made in southern Provence, they lost their popularity, apparently used mainly for regional costumes.

All of this began to change in the 1930s when Charles Deméry took over a fabric company in Tarascon—in Provence—calling his business Souleiado. The company grew as the interest in this style of fabric was rekindled (due in large part, no doubt, to design and product innovations). While hand-blocking was initially used, it was eventually replaced by industrial printing—and vegetable dyes by synthetic ones— although traditional motifs were retained. Souleiado has certainly revived interest in this style of fabric design, both in France and elsewhere, and has also sparked an interest in Provençal fabrics among collectors.

You will sometimes find items made from, or decorated with, old Provençal fabrics in the flea markets—bedcovers, clothing, scarves, fabric boxes, and *santons,* for example. While many of the things you will see date from after this fabric's revival in the 20th century, older examples, particularly bedspreads, can also sometimes be found. Often in colorful prints, these were worked using different techniques—stuffing, quilting, and cording, in which corded material was drawn through parallel lines stitched into two pieces of fabric, using a long, flexible needle, called a *boutis;* this way, a puffed, quilted effect was produced. (Sometimes the word *boutis* is used broadly to describe various kinds of Provençal quilts, made in different manners, not just by cording.)

You are not likely to find old Provençal bedspreads made with the *boutis* needle in the flea markets; you will, however, see colorful quilted Provençal bedcovers of different kinds, and with a varying degree of detailing, particularly at the more high-end flea markets in Provence (L'Îsle-sur-la-Sorgue, for example). They are, however, fairly expensive and have become increasingly so in recent years.

A much less costly collectible is fabric boxes in *indiennes* prints. A friend who collects these nice little objects has found them for as little as ten francs in the flea markets in Provence.

To see fine old Provençal quilts, and many other examples of Provençal fabrics, as well as old hand-blocks, visit the Musée Deméry, at Souleiado, in Tarascon. Call ahead for an appointment at 04-90-91-08-80. I was shown here how to distinguish bedcovers made with the *boutis* needle; just hold the piece up to the light—if it was made using a *boutis,* you will see all the undulating little lines that process produced.

QUIMPER WARE *(LES FAÏENCES DE QUIMPER)*

Over three hundred years ago, faience ware began to be produced in Quimper, in Brittany. Jean-Baptiste Bousquet, who was from Provence, set up operations in 1690, and his descendants carried on the business, with the help of talented people who married into the family. Because of one, Antoine de la Hubaudière, the business later became known as La Grande Maison HB (*H* for Hubaudière and *B* for Bousquet).

Two other companies entered the scene in the late 18th century. One subsequently came to be called Porquier-Beau, and the other, which was taken over in the late 19th century by Jules Henriot, became known as the Henriot Faïenceries. Although the Henriot Faïenceries became quite prominent, it merged with HB in 1968. The new name was Société des Faïenceries de Quimper (although some autonomy was maintained, including separate marks). This entity, however, failed in 1983 and the operation closed. The *faïencerie* reopened in 1984 under the name Société Nouvelle des Faïenceries de Quimper HB-Henriot, or HB-Henriot, under the ownership of an American couple, Sarah and Paul Janssens, long associated with Quimper as its American importers.

These developments, apart from being of historical interest, are important to Quimper collectors (many of whom are Americans) in understanding the various marks used on Quimper ware over the years. However, it is, of course, the Quimper style, and the development of that approach, which is of primary significance.

Quimper faience ware has managed to survive, in part, because of its talent for adaptation. In the late 18th century, when the faience industry in France went into decline, it was saved in Quimper by the creation of the Quimper style. Early on, it consisted of reinterpreting traditional designs with the use of brilliant and exuberant colors. Probably around 1850, the *à la touche* technique was adopted, in which the design was boldly created by a stroke of the brush.

In the 1870s, Alfred Beau—of Porquier-Beau—used lively scenes of Breton life as the subject of decoration. The motifs for which Quimper is now most famous came into great vogue—the Breton couple in traditional dress, with the man sporting a wide-brimmed hat and baggy pants (called *bragou braz*) and the woman wearing a long dress, apron, and headpiece. At the 1878 World Fair, these folkloric Breton scenes were apparently a huge success.

Flowers, animals, and other motifs are also frequent subjects of Quimper pottery; you may also see fruits or vegetables and geometric patterns. Quimper ware is usually quickly recognizable; apart from the use of naive subjects, colors are bright and cheerful, and the pieces are often rimmed with blue and yellow lines or a garland of red and blue flowers with fernlike green leaves.

You will often see Quimper ware at the flea markets throughout France. Prices vary wildly based on age, condition, color, rarity of the item, and chance. In addition to plates, you may spot pitchers, soup tureens, bowls, eggcups, nursing bottles, vases, candlesticks, cider jugs, etc. The marks are critical to the value of these pieces; there are many examples, based on the different producers and periods. If you are interested in becoming a collector of Quimper, you are best advised to consult books available on the subject and familiarize yourself with these marks, among other things.

While you will see many examples of Quimper at flea markets in Brittany, you may well find them at more reasonable prices elsewhere. I bought my first piece at the place des Carmes flea market in Avignon—a covered dish, for 100 francs—while a friend recently bought a bowl, in perfect condition, for 50 francs, at the low-end place d'Aligre market in Paris. Another friend has had very good success in the Dordogne and the Côte d'Azur. The best deals are often found where a vendor has only one Quimper piece mixed in with other items, rather than when he or she specializes in Quimper, or in faience, and is well versed in the value of individual items.

RATTLES AND BABY BOTTLES (LES HOCHETS ET LES BIBERONS)

A collecting theme that interests a fairly large audience is the world of babies, and specifically old baby bottles and rattles.

Baby rattles have apparently been around for a very long time. In the 16th century, rattles made of ivory, crystal, and silver appeared in France, with quite ornate versions—limited to the well-heeled classes—arriving on the scene over the next two centuries. In the 19th century, the use of rattles became more widespread and rattles were made from less expensive materials. Also, the whistle of the older models came to be replaced by an ivory ring (in the 20th century, cheaper materials such as plastic were used).

Rattles from the late 19th to early 20th century can be found occasionally in the flea markets (look for these appealing objects at stalls where the vendors have wooden, glass-topped cases to display smaller objects). Prices vary widely, but you can find rattles from the late 19th or early 20th century for around 150 francs.

Baby bottles are also an interesting collectible. Over the centuries, they have been made of different materials, such as, at one time, little terra-cotta vases with spouts or pierced animal horns or, in more recent times, pewter and faience. Glass bottles, we are told, appeared in the 18th century and were often shaped in a weird flattened form, like a gourd. About a hundred years ago, a glass bottle whose use apparently made cleaning difficult earned the grisly nickname le biberon qui tue ("the bottle that kills"). Then a new type of bottle appeared, called, appropriately, le sauveur ("the savior"), which could be sterilized to prevent germs from developing, followed after World War I by Pyrex bottles, which could withstand high temperatures.

You will not often see old baby bottles in the flea markets; however, you may occasionally spot an old faience or glass one mixed in with other things. (Unless you are lucky, they are likely to be fairly expensive.) Early- and mid-20th-century glass bottles, in shapes similar to those used today, can more readily be found, for under 100 francs.

SANTONS

Santons are the small clothed figures that, at first, peopled the Nativity crèches of Provence and elsewhere. In more recent times, *santons* have been made as decorative objects depicting everyday Provençal life and traditions —farmers, fishermen, women performing everyday chores, old people, etc. Their symbolic importance to Provençal culture was enthusiastically recognized by the great patron of that tradition, Frédéric Mistral.

First made in wood (and wax), *santons* in the 18th century were produced in spun glass, wax, papier-mâché, and faience. Clay *santons* appeared in Marseille at the beginning of the 19th century and production soon spread to other Provençal towns—Aix-en-Provence, Avignon, Apt, Aubagne, Carpentras, and Toulon. Dressed in traditional Provençal costumes, *santons* continue to be produced today, and in the last several weeks of the year, a number of Provençal towns host fairs to display recent works. Aubagne is particularly well-known for its creations.

You will occasionally see *santons* in the flea markets, especially in Provence. Since it is difficult to tell their age, or to ascertain their value, the best advice, if you are in doubt, is to buy based on your affinity for the piece, as well as on condition and the detail of both the figure and its costume. You will find some fine old examples for as little as 100 francs, but the price can also be much higher, depending on age, provenance, and rarity. I bought my first pair in Paris a number of years ago, for 120 francs.

TELEPHONE CARDS *(LES TÉLÉCARTES)*

Telephone cards first appeared in France about two decades ago, introduced to address the vandalism problems posed by coin-operated telephones. The initial test of the cards took place in 1980, in the Gare de Montparnasse, in Paris, and in a few other places (following a brief earlier trial in 1978).

The first telephone cards were not asethetically pleasing, but that changed dramatically during the 1980s. In 1986, France Télécom requested submissions from a number of artists of potential designs; some of the cards produced were even numbered and signed. The marketing potential of *télécartes* was quickly recognized, as companies of all kinds ordered cards to advertise their products. Many cards were also issued to mark special events. Telephone cards were assured a respected spot among the club of collectibles in 1990, when an auction of them was held in Paris and a catalog produced.

And this collectible keeps on going, given that approximately 100 million phone cards, with all kinds of designs and images, are sold every year in France. As you leave a phone booth, you will sometimes be approached by a collector asking you if your card is finished, or *épuisée*, and if so, whether you'll give it up.

Vendors specializing in phone cards can be found at most of the flea markets. This collectible has the big advantage of being generally inexpensive and easily transportable. Given the enormous supply available, collections are often based on particular themes—for example, nature, sports, animals, cars, films, celebrities, particular products, Disney, etc. Phone cards from other countries are also sought-after—Japanese, Belgian, and Italian cards, for example.

You can find phone cards in the markets for as little as 5 francs, while some rare cards are valued at as much as several thousand francs. Factors influencing the value include appearance, age, rarity, and condition (unused cards are more valuable than used). It is difficult in some cases to tell the age of a card; however, starting in 1990, cards issued state the date of release and the number of cards produced.

TINS *(LES BOÎTES)*

Tins are a huge collectible in France. Over the years, they have been used as packaging for various products—candies, cocoa, cookies, rice, tea, and phonograph needles, for example. Appealing motifs have appeared on many of these tins, thanks partly to a printing process known as chromolithography, perfected near the end of the 19th century and used until the mid-20th century. This process facilitated a high degree of detailing as sharp images were produced.

Candy tins, for example, are popular. Usually they were made of tin, although aluminum (or even cardboard) was resorted to during the war. The images produced were often colorful and appealing, with a variety of subjects —naive depictions of a particular region and its folkloric traditions, or pictures of famous people or historical figures. Candy tins can quite easily be found in the markets and range in price from 10 or 20 francs to around 250 francs.

One cannot talk about tins without a special mention of the biscuit-maker LU, the company established in 1887 in Nantes. Tins from this company, which appeared in different shapes and sizes, are finely decorated and highly sought-after. LU packaging and design have varied a lot—some containers were in cardboard rather than metal; some were illustrated by the famous designer Mucha; some designs were produced by chromolithography, while others were done on paper labels; and some tins celebrated famous historical events while others showed romantic scenes. LU tins are highly collectible and can be quite expensive.

Old tins from Banania, a company created in 1914 that made a breakfast product, feature the smiling face of a Senegalese gentleman, now so well recognized in France. Banania tins are enormously popular among collectors, but are now almost impossible to find at reasonable prices.

Generally, however, tins can often be found at a fairly moderate price in the markets. I recently purchased two, with lovely Breton themes, for 10 francs and 50 francs, as well as an appealing candy tin featuring a portrait of Napoleon for 20 francs. Being both small and evocative of the regions of France and its history, tins are a popular collectible among tourists, as well as the French themselves.

TRAVEL LUGGAGE (LES VALISES DE VOYAGE)

Who is not transported and delighted by the sight of a large, old traveling trunk, revealing when opened all of those wonderful little compartments for storing all sorts of accessories thought necessary for a long voyage during the 19th and early 20th centuries? Given the length of time needed to travel by boat across the Atlantic (or across Europe by train), for example, all kinds of belongings would be taken along. These things would be stored in a variety of cases designed for different purposes—trunks, smaller suitcases, vanity cases, hatboxes, shoe cases (maybe with separate compartments for each pair), travel bidets, cases for holding champagne glasses, picnic cases, containers for silverware, and even cases for storing books and writing materials.

The high point, in terms of refinement of design in travel luggage, was this period, from the mid- and late 19th century to the mid-20th century. Luggage, not surprisingly, was often aimed at a fairly well-heeled minority who could afford to take such journeys and buy beautifully crafted travel cases. As a result, prices now asked for vintage pieces by such producers as Vuitton, Lancel, and Hermès are high. (In fact, since makers like Vuitton are sometimes copied, you should be dubious if a piece you see is inexpensive.)

Luggage in good condition by the most renowned firms is not likely to be found at the flea markets (although you may see it at very high-end markets, such as the Puces de St-Ouen in Paris). On the other hand, you will occasionally come across less rarefied—but still interesting—trunks and cases by less fancy producers. The flea markets on the Côte d'Azur—such as in Nice and St-Tropez—are good places to look.

Because travel cases were often stored away in musty corners for many years, their condition is often not pristine. However, they are an appealing collectible and you can sometimes find nice pieces for not too much money if you're lucky.

YOGURT POTS (LES POTS DE YAOURT OR YOGHOURT)

One hot and sunny Sunday afternoon I went to visit the monthly flea market just outside Opio, a small town in the hills behind Antibes. It was a slow day, I was told, because of the confluence of Mother's Day and the 1997 legislative elections. I saw nothing at all to tempt me until my eyes suddenly fixed on two simple white porcelain pots, bearing the logo *Yoghourt Leon*. For a mere ten francs the two gleaming little pots were mine, and I was thus introduced to the world of yogurt-pot collecting. Some fans of this collectible boast of having over 300 pots, made in different materials, colors, and designs, and bearing names such as Danone, Sultan, Maggi, and Ofco.

In France, yogurt was originally sold in small stoneware or faience pots, until porcelain was used, followed by glass. The pots, which could at one time be purchased from pharmacies because of the health benefits yogurt was thought to possess, did not always have a logo identifying their contents. Accordingly, sometimes it is difficult to tell if a pot was in fact used for yogurt or for some other product. One helpful bit of information is that while faience yogurt pots might be in white, blue, brown, or green, the inside would apparently always be white.

Like mustard pots, old yogurt containers make a nice, easily transportable, and generally inexpensive collectible, of special attraction to those interested in French culinary habits.

Other Things to Collect

A list of some of other collectibles not included in the above discussion might also be useful, to give you additional ideas about what to look for as you browse through the markets. Here are a few suggestions of other items—again, either unique to France or emblematic of it—in no particular order: café tables and chairs, ceramic spice-canister sets, ceramic tobacco jars, ceramic pharmacy pots, foie gras terrines, wooden shoes, *boîtes à sel* and *boîtes à allumettes* (the ceramic containers with wooden lids, used to store salt and matches), religious statues and other religious objects, *pelles d'absinthe* (the flattened utensil with holes, used for the consumption of absinthe), wire baskets and utensils, beer coasters, bistro items, alcohol miniatures (a big collectible in France), siphon bottles, *Tintin* books, Asterix books, Becassine books and dolls, World War I and II memorabilia, advertising ashtrays, cheese-making items, wine-making items, cutlery holders (*égouttoirs*), bread holders (*panetières*), bread boards, metal bottle carriers, butter molds, sugar cube wrappers, Pin's (the pins often released for advertising purposes), olive oil jars, lace curtains, porcelain cooking pots, mortars and pestles, and so on.

Since the kinds of things that are collected in France are, as elsewhere, ever-expanding, if you see something that appeals to you and it's not expensive, buy it. Who knows? Ten years from now it may become a hot French collectible, and you can tell people how clever you were.

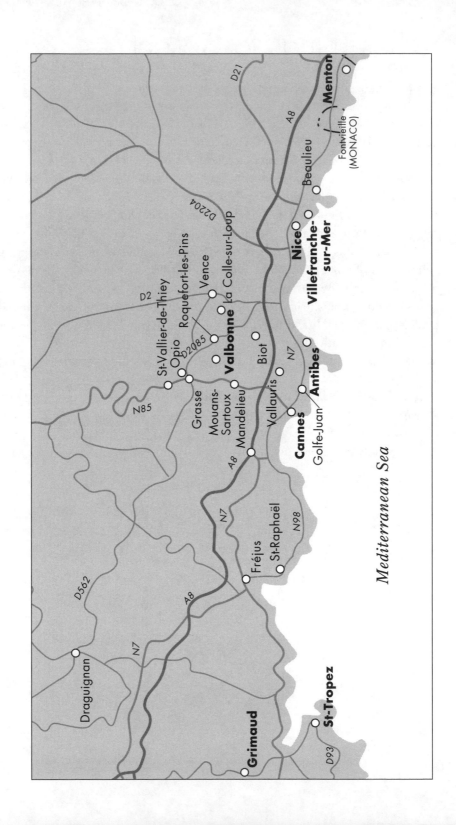

The Flea Markets
of the
Côte d'Azur

Monday   *CANNES (Marché Forville), [60 vendors]
(8 A.M. to 6 P.M.)

*NICE (cours Saleya) [180 to 200 vendors]
(9 A.M. to 6 P.M., but some vendors leave earlier)

Tuesday   ST-RAPHAËL (pl. Coullet) [40 to 50 vendors]
(8 A.M. to 5 P.M.)

*ST-TROPEZ (pl. des Lices) [25 to 30 vendors]
(8:30 A.M. to 1 P.M.)

Wednesday   MANDELIEU (boul. Ecureuils) [20 vendors]
(first and third Wednesday of month)
(8 A.M. to 3 P.M.)

VENCE (pl. du Grand Jardin) [20 vendors]
(7:30 A.M. to 4 P.M.)

Thursday   *ANTIBES (pl. J. Audiberti and pl. Nationale) [60 vendors]
(9 A.M. to 6 P.M.)

CANNES (La Bocca) [20 vendors]
(8 A.M. to 5 P.M.)

Friday   FRÉJUS (pl. Formigé) [50 vendors] (first Friday of month)
(8 A.M. to 6 P.M.)

GRASSE (cours Honoré Cresp) [30 vendors] (first Friday of month)
(8 A.M. to 6 P.M.)

MANDELIEU (287 av. de Cannes) [25 to 30 vendors]
(last Friday of month)
(8 A.M. to 5 P.M.)

*MENTON (pl. aux Herbes) [20 vendors]
(8:30 A.M. to 6 P.M.)

Saturday   *ANTIBES (pl. J. Audiberti and pl. Nationale) [60 vendors]
(9 A.M. to 6 P.M.)

*CANNES (Les Allées) [70 vendors]
(8 A.M. to 6 P.M.)

FONTVIEILLE (Monaco) (Port de Fontvieille) [20 vendors]
(8 A.M. to 6 P.M.)

MOUANS-SARTOUX (pl. Jean Jaurès) [15 vendors]
(9 A.M. to 6 P.M.)

ROQUEFORT-LES-PINS (Jardin des Décades–rte. de Grasse)
[25 to 30 vendors] (fourth Saturday of month)
(8 A.M. to 7 P.M.)

ST-RAPHAËL (vieille ville) [20 vendors] (second Saturday of month)
(8 A.M. to 6 P.M.)

*ST-TROPEZ (pl. des Lices) [30 vendors]
(8:30 A.M. to 1 P.M.)

Sunday   *CANNES (Les Allées) [40 vendors] (first Sunday of month)
(8 A.M. to 6 P.M.)

LA COLLE-SUR-LOUP (av. de l'Ancienne Gare) [15 to 20 vendors]
(second Sunday of month)
(8 A.M. to 6 P.M.)

FRÉJUS (port) (last Sunday of month, from May to September)
(8 A.M. to 6 P.M.)

GOLFE-JUAN (Parking du Vieux Port) [25 vendors]
(last Sunday of month)
(8 A.M. to 6 P.M.)

*GRIMAUD (Jas des Roberts) [50 to 75 vendors]
(6 A.M. to 1 P.M.)

GRIMAUD (pl. Neuve) (first Sunday of month)
(8 A.M. to 6 P.M.)

*MENTON (Mail du Bastion, pl. F. Palmero) [30 vendors]
(second Sunday of month)
(9 A.M. to 6:30 P.M.)

OPIO (Centre Cial. Champion) [15 vendors] (fourth Sunday of month)
(8 A.M. to 5 P.M.)

ST-VALLIER-DE-THIEY (Grand Pré) [50 vendors] (second Sunday of
month, from March to October)
(8 A.M. to 6 P.M.)

*VALBONNE (center) [40 to 50 vendors] (first Sunday of month,
except February and August)
(8 A.M. to 6 P.M.)

*VILLEFRANCHE-SUR-MER (pl. A. Pollonais) [35 vendors]
(8:30 A.M. to 6:30 P.M.)

*VILLEFRANCHE-SUR-MER (pl. de l'Octroi) [30 vendors]
(8:30 A.M. to 6:30 P.M.)

Regional Overview

GETTING ORIENTED: ABOUT THE REGION

For many, the words "Côte d'Azur" are like an elixir to the imagination. They evoke images of rocky cliffs, turquoise sea, luxuriant vegetation, and lemon yellow sun. Despite the occasional blight of rampant and ugly development, the Côte d'Azur really does feel like paradise. Surely few stretches of land and sea are more remarkable than that part of this region extending along the coast from Menton, on the Italian border, to St-Tropez on the west. The Côte d'Azur's less well-known area, the *arrière-pays*, or hinterland, stretching above the coast west from Italy to Draguignan, has its own quite different charms.

I recently lived in Menton for six months and never tired of that route along the Basse Corniche (or the Corniche Inférieure as it is also called) to Nice—across luxurious Cap Martin with pines tilting toward the sea, through the ornate and unreal Monaco, past the pastel villas of Beaulieu-sur-Mer and the exquisite bay of Villefranche-sur-Mer, and descending into Nice, with its impossibly blue Baie des Anges bordered by the Promenade des Anglais. The route southwest from Cannes along the Corniche de l'Esterel, beside red, rocky cliffs sloping to the sea, is almost as impressive.

The seemingly endless parade of flowers along this coast—mimosa, flowering aloes, jacaranda trees, oleander, hibiscus, and especially the brilliant deep red and purple bougainvillea—provides a continual feast for the senses. Palms, parasol pines, cypresses, olive trees, and eucalyptuses fill the landscape with every imaginable shape and shade of green. Add lemon and orange trees, with their ripe fruit even in January and February, and you would truly say that this is nirvana.

The *arrière-pays*, rising above the sea toward the mountains, provides a sharp contrast to the colorful and lavish coastal towns. Here villages, sometimes perched precariously on rocky slopes, are constructed of stone in neutral colors that seem to blend into the surrounding countryside. Panoramas stretch far down to the sea, and the brilliance of the sun conspires with pines and other trees to produce a powerful, sweet scent.

The human landscape of the Côte d'Azur is similarly rich, if sometimes overwhelming. It feels more Mediterranean than French, which is not surprising given the region's historical and geographic proximity to Italy. The towns are lively and crowded, with people strolling about and sitting year-round in outdoor cafés.

These are not shy or reserved folks. Indeed, at times they seem a bit hard-edged, although more often effusive and expressive. They are tanned, toned, and stylish; not a lot of *paysans* to be found in this region, where the number of topless women on the beach rivals those in traditional bathing gear (older women not excluded).

The Côte d'Azur does have its detractors. Yes, it is sometimes gaudy, far too expensive, and overdeveloped, and the drivers are surely the worst and most aggressive in France (which, some would claim, is saying quite a lot). And it is true that garbage can be seen floating in the sea, and that the poodle population has reached alarming proportions. But what a place to be on a winter day, especially for those whose consciousness is etched with the memory of a lifetime of snow and sleet. No wonder that, until the 1930s, winter was the season most favored by visitors from Britain and other European countries. Only in the last fifty years or so, with the advent of mass tourism, has summer replaced winter as the preferred time to visit. If you come other than in the summer, you will find that the Côte d'Azur is, in fact, a real place, where ordinary life does go on without fanfare and glitter.

MARKET RHYTHMS: WHEN THEY'RE HELD/WHEN TO GO

One often has the feeling that the Côte d'Azur is a bit of a world apart, where normal concepts about days and hours—and even seasons—have only a tenuous place. The flea markets of this region reinforce this impression.

In the Côte d'Azur no huge gulf separates weekdays and weekends, unlike in some other parts of France where *brocante* is essentially a Saturday/Sunday phenomenon. In this region, you can find a market to visit, somewhere, every day of the week. The biggest one by far takes place on Mondays in Nice along the cours Saleya. And there is also the Marché Forville in Cannes on Mondays, the Tuesday markets in St-Raphaël and St-Tropez, Vence's market on Wednesday, Antibes' Thursday market, and the monthly markets in Fréjus and Mandelieu (near Cannes)—as well as the weekly Menton market—on Friday, to mention a few.

One also has the sense of time being suspended while browsing in these markets. Strolling among the crowds at the Monday market in Nice, for example, you do wonder when people actually work in this city. There are lots of foreign tourists, to be sure, but many more are locals who seem in no hurry at all. Maybe it is because nature is so kind in the Côte d'Azur, making the days —and the hours available for doing things—appear kind of amorphous.

Many of the markets in this region carry on all day; you get the sense that a half-day market would generally be considered too hectic here. Things usually start out slowly and get much more lively as the morning progresses. After a fairly lengthy lunchtime lull, for vendors and purchasers alike, the markets pick up again in the midafternoon as locals venture out for a stroll and a browse. Some vendors will start to pack up between 4 and 5 P.M., but on lazy sunny afternoons, many will stay around until much later. Morning-only markets usually wind down by 12:30 or 1 P.M., the vendors slowly packing up their wares in the midday sun while chatting with late browsers.

Perhaps the greatest feature of these markets, in terms of their rhythm, is their truly year-round character (with a few exceptions), in every sense. You will find just about as many vendors in winter as at other times of the year. Winter is often wonderfully mild, with an average daily maximum temperature in January and February of around 12°C. (53.6°F.), and it is often sunny, with little or no wind. The summer (July and August) is hot and sunny, with the average daily maximum at around 28.3°C. (83°F.). The autumn is often very pleasant, although late fall is prone to rain, while the spring is generally glorious, albeit with some occasional showers.

While the region's mild and generally sunny climate neutralizes the effect of the seasons on its markets, the weather is a guide in deciding what time of day to come. In winter, browsers often do not arrive until after the sun has burned off the morning chill; by late morning it can feel quite balmy, and you will often be able to sit outside for lunch. And since there are generally fewer bargain-hunting opportunities here than in other regions of France, such as Provence, there is no great incentive to arrive really early. By contrast, in summer, you should plan to come early in the morning or later in the afternoon (in the case of the all-day markets), to avoid the sometimes brutal midday sun and heat.

While the seasons are not much of a factor in the rhythms of these markets, tourism is. Winter is the least hectic period and, hence, the best time to come to find bargains and avoid crowds. The fall and the spring are busy but not oppressive, while the summer can pose a challenge to those suffering from claustrophobia or an aversion to traffic jams; it is also the least desirable season to come for bargain hunters. August, in particular, should be avoided if at all possible; that is when the French usually take their holidays and the Côte d'Azur remains a very popular vacation destination.

MARKET FLAVORS: HOW THEY LOOK/HOW THEY FEEL

Not surprisingly, the flea markets of the Côte d'Azur are a bit of a microcosm of the region itself—colorful, animated, overwhelming, and generally (though not always) upscale.

Because of their truly picturesque nature, these markets are of as great an interest to general tourists as they are to collectors. With a few exceptions—such as the Sunday weekly market in Grimaud (near St-Tropez) and the markets in Mandelieu and Opio (near Grasse) and—the markets are located in quite stunning settings. Often they are held by, or nearby, the sea—as in Nice, Cannes (Les Allées market), Villefranche-sur-Mer, Antibes, Menton, and Fontvieille (in Monaco). Occasionally they are set in the hill towns north of the sea, as in Valbonne and Mouans-Sartoux, not far from Antibes. Whatever their surroundings, the markets are almost always located in the quaintest and most historic parts of town.

When I am sitting in North America and I try to visualize these markets, it is the dazzling kaleidoscope of colors that I see. They are of a vividness unimaginable to North Americans and northern Europeans (and unfamiliar to other regions in France). Every shade of yellow, pink, and orange blends with deep ocher and green. And the beauty of the Côte d'Azur seems magnified through the prism of the markets, with their stalls heaped with every kind of decorative object and topped with brightly colored parasols.

The sun does its part to contribute to the brilliance of these markets. In six months of browsing through them, I can only remember one time when it rained in any real way, and hardly any days when the sky was not clear and bright blue. In fact, on the rare occasions when the sun is not shining, it is as if the lights have gone out onstage; the coast suddenly looks like an unfamiliar and even somber place.

These are lively and entertaining spots. Above the buzz of voices and laughter, you sometimes hear music, as street musicians serve up old favorites like "La Vie en Rose" and other classics. In a few markets, mimes and other artists perform for the crowds, while vendors sit together over a game of chess or cards. And, as is typical of this region, a frequent market-side activity is to lounge at outdoor cafés, watching the proceedings and chatting with friends. You almost feel the stress and cares of the world draining from your body. How can life seem other than easy and good in a place like this?

But all is not gaiety and frivolity. Lunch, for example, is an important business and a serious affair in the Côte d'Azur markets. In Nice and Cannes, for example, waiters from nearby restaurants sometimes carry trays of food back and forth to vendors. The fare is impressive—fish and seafood in the spring and summer or maybe pasta and thin Mediterranean pizza in the winter. Some vendors sit down like old-fashioned *paysans* to hearty and hot meals brought from home, which they consume under the curious and admiring eyes of browsers. A bottle of wine stands on many tables, and it is evident that this lunchtime ritual is one to be carefully observed.

THE COLLECTIBLES: WHAT YOU'LL FIND/WHAT TO LOOK FOR

The emphasis in the Côte d'Azur markets is generally on the decorative, rather than on rustic or everyday items. The wares are also often high quality, in pristine condition, and tastefully displayed. Vendors tend to specialize in a limited range of collectibles and are usually quite knowledgeable about their wares, except those outside the scope of things they normally sell.

At these markets, you will typically find ceramics of all kinds, glassware, silver, jewelry, paintings, prints, antique cameras and phonographs, perfume samples, old books, Limoges boxes, fine linens, and a wide variety of accessories, such as purses, fans, hats, canes, etc. The things for sale are often not intrinsic to this region, but rather come from all parts of France, as well as from Italy and occasionally other countries.

Although the markets are eclectic in the origins of the things they sell, there are some regional items to look out for; for example, yellow- and green-glazed dishes and pots from Vallauris (the town near Antibes where Picasso spent a few years doing ceramics in the late 1940s), large jugs and pots from Biot (also near Antibes), the decorative faience ware from Moustiers-Ste-Marie (up in the mountains northwest of Grasse), and the brightly colored *barbotine* ceramics, decorated with fruits and flowers, from Menton and Monaco. Marine collectibles of all kinds and old traveling trunks—emblematic of this part of France if not intrinsic to it—are often spotted here. Occasionally, posters, and other tourist items, advertising Côte d'Azur travel or special events such as the Cannes Film Festival, are also found at these markets.

BUYING: PRICE LEVELS/BARGAINING OPPORTUNITIES

These markets are not as noteworthy for bargain hunting as they are for sight-seeing and entertainment, although there are some exceptions. Prices are often quite high, which is not surprising given the upscale and touristy nature of this place. However, bargaining is as acceptable here as in other parts of France; the vendors can not be described as reticent, and haggling seems to be deeply embedded in the Mediterranean psyche. Many vendors, particularly in the big markets, speak a little English so that you can often negotiate, at least to some extent, even if you do not speak French. Occasionally, you may find vendors a bit abrupt, particularly if your offer does not impress them. Do not be offended; this will likely have more to do with the somewhat theatrical style of the region than with any offense you may have caused.

Unlike in some other parts of France, you are not likely to make a great discovery here for only a few francs. Luckily for bargain hunters (like me), exceptions do exist. The best strategy is to search out stalls where the goods are particularly eclectic or piled out on blankets or stacked on the ground or in boxes. This is where you may discover that attractive old café au lait bowl for 10 francs.

GETTING AROUND: HOW TO TRAVEL/WHERE TO GO

One great thing about the Côte d'Azur is that you do not need a car to get to many of the flea markets. Most of those along the coast are easily accessible by local trains, which run regularly between Menton and St-Raphaël, and many of these trains stop at all the little towns along the way. Also, since most markets are located in the center of town, you can get usually reach them from the station within a few minutes by foot. Train travel in this region is scenic, pleasant, and relatively inexpensive. Even if you have a car, the train is often the best way to go, since it will save you the time and hassle of finding a parking space (not to mention the cost). For those markets west of St-Raphaël and Fréjus, or north of the coast, however, a car is the easiest and best option.

When planning your itinerary, be aware that a number of vendors come to sell at more than one market. While not peculiar to the Côte d'Azur, this phenomenon is more pronounced here than elsewhere in France. It is likely the product both of proximity and of the many days of the week on which markets are held. For this reason, don't be concerned if you do not have the time to visit all of the markets, especially the smaller ones. Focus on seeing the significant ones and then take in others that fit into your overall travel plans.

Apart from the Nice market, which is large, all of the markets in the Côte d'Azur are moderate, or small, and may be visited in an hour or so. You can simply include a stopover at them in your sight-seeing plans for the day. The

Nice market, on the other hand, is an important tourist attraction on its own and merits a couple of hours' visit. However else you organize your stay in the Côte d'Azur, plan your time so as to be sure to be in Nice on Monday.

Market Close-Ups

The markets of eight towns in this region are featured below—Antibes, Cannes, Grimaud, Menton, Nice, St-Tropez, Valbonne, and Villefranche-sur-Mer. They have been selected based on a number of criteria—scenic value, size, range in quality, and variety in scheduling. Together, they generally comprise the most significant and interesting flea markets in the Côte d'Azur.

ANTIBES (Thursday and Saturday)

No. of Vendors: 60
Price/Quality Range: ★★ – ★★★★
Scenic Value: ★★★
Amenities Nearby: ★★★★

Featured Items: Ceramics, paintings, linens, books, garden ware, silver, small decorative objects, kitchenware

WHEN, WHERE, HOW: Antibes has an all-day *brocante* market twice a week, on Thursdays and Saturdays, from 9 A.M. to 6 P.M. The market takes place in two locations close together in the center of town—the place Nationale and the place J. Audiberti.

If arriving by car, meter parking can be found in the port area or along the ramparts, where some sections are also free. If arriving by train, the market is less than a ten-minute walk southeast from the station. Follow the avenue Robert Soleau south to the boulevard du Président Wilson and then head east a few blocks on the rue de la République to the place Nationale. The place J. Audiberti is just a couple of blocks farther east, near the ramparts.

Tourist Office: 04-92-90-53-00

LIKE "CANNES," THE word "Antibes" conjures up images of the rich and chic, although you might wonder why if you enter this town from the autoroute past the unappealing boxlike superstores. Even if you arrive from the coast, you may feel disappointed because Antibes does not have the kind of spectacular setting you would expect from such a famous and trendy place. There are high-rise apartments here, just as elsewhere along the coast, and it is virtually impossible to get a decent view of any of the stunning villas you know must exist on Cap d'Antibes at the southern end of town. Indeed, Antibes— named Antipolis by the Greeks, meaning "the city opposite" Nice, some think—seems a bit in the shadow of its big neighbor to the northeast.

Antibes, however, soon grows on you as you spend a little time wandering through its charming narrow streets or along its seaside ramparts. It does not, however, really feel like a Côte d'Azur town. Rather, Antibes is more reminiscent of a Provençal center like Aix-en-Provence; its muted and neutral colors are quite unlike the brilliant pastels that you find, for example, in Menton, Nice, and Villefranche-sur-Mer. Perhaps this reflects that Antibes was an important military post of the kings of France for a couple of hundred years beginning in the 15th century, on the border of the Savoy holdings to the east; its Fort Carré, not far from the harbor, is testimony to Antibes' strategic role.

THE MARKET

Antibes is somewhat unusual in having a *brocante* market twice a week, on Thursdays and Saturdays. This medium-sized market, with about 60 vendors, takes place at two locations close together in the center of town—the place Nationale, with its rows of carefully pruned plane trees, and the smaller place J. Audiberti, just north of the covered food hall. They feel like separate markets, in that the things you will find at the place J. Audiberti are somewhat more rustic and everyday, as well as lower-priced, than the high-quality and decorative collectibles you will see at the place Nationale.

Start your visit at the place J. Audiberti. Any finds that you are likely to make will happen here, and the earlier you arrive the better your chances. In this part of the market you will see kitchenware, tools, linens, garden ware, small decorative items, regional ceramics, etc. I have occasionally spotted English porcelain and kitchenware here, reflecting the large British presence in the area. While a number of the vendors specialize in certain items, others sell a hodgepodge of things, sometimes laid out on the ground or piled in boxes. A close examination may occasionally net you a find.

After visiting this part of the market—and perhaps after stopping for a drink at the Café des Chineurs at the end of the square (if only just because of its name)—move on to explore the place Nationale. There you will find paintings, prints, silver, antique books, high-quality linens, porcelain dishes, glazed earthenware pots, small decorative objects of all kinds, garden tables and chairs, and some other furniture. Prices are quite high; vendors here specialize in certain collectibles and are well aware of the value of the things they are selling.

While real bargains are not easily found at either part of the Antibes market, friends living part-time in this town swear that they have made some great discoveries at the place J. Audiberti and have regaled me with stories of old garden pots, and dishes from Vallauris, bought for a song. They've also proudly shown me old glass wine jugs and odd-looking garden tools of all kinds and descriptions, which they allege to have found at great prices. The best day to come, they claim, is Saturday, when space vacated by sellers who go to Les Allées in Cannes is occupied by more casual vendors. Not surprisingly, bargains are also more plentiful during winter than in spring and summer, when tourists descend upon Antibes in droves.

OTHER THINGS TO DO

After seeing the *brocante* market, be sure to visit Antibes' wonderful morning food market, in the cours Masséna just south of the place J. Audiberti; few can match this one for the variety and freshness of the produce. On Thursday mornings, a large and colorful general market also takes over several of the surrounding streets.

While you are in this part of town, make sure to see the Musée Picasso, housed in the Château Grimaldi just east of the place J. Audiberti. (Open from mid-June to mid-September from 10 A.M. to 6 P.M., and the rest of the year from 10 A.M. to noon and 2 P.M. to 6 P.M. Closed Mondays. Phone: 04-93-57-72-30.) Apart altogether from the works displayed, the views of the sea from here are pretty staggering.

If it's Saturday and you are keen to visit another flea market, head to Les Allées market in nearby Cannes, held all day in the center of town across from the *vieux port* (see Cannes, below).

Collectors interested in regional ceramics should be sure to visit the town of Vallauris, a few kilometers west of Antibes. Long a pottery center, this town's ceramics tradition was reinvigorated in the middle of this century when Picasso came to work here. Some of the pottery shops in the town are fairly gaudy, although there are exceptions. The Galerie Madoura, where Picasso worked, apparently has the sole rights to reproduce his designs.

Another village that may be of interest to collectors is Biot, a few kilometers north of Antibes toward Nice. This town, historically a prominent ceramics center (famous for its large pots or *jarres*), is now also devoted to glassblowing, as a visit to its boutiques will demonstrate.

CANNES (Saturday, first Sunday of the month)
(Monday)

LES ALLÉES
No. of Vendors: 70 on Saturday, 40 on the first Sunday of the month
Price/Quality Range: ✦✦✦ – ✦✦✦✦
Scenic Value: ✦✦✦
Amenities Nearby: ✦✦✦

Featured Items: Silver, porcelain, paintings, books, glassware, toys, vases, figurines

MARCHÉ FORVILLE
No. of Vendors: 60
Price/Quality Range: ✦✦ – ✦✦✦
Scenic Value: ✦✦ – ✦✦✦
Amenities Nearby: ✦✦ – ✦✦✦

Featured Items: Household items, tools, cameras, scientific/marine items, ceramics

WHEN, WHERE, HOW: Two *brocante* markets are held each week in the center of Cannes. One takes place on Saturdays, from 8 A.M. to 6 P.M. (and the first Sunday of the month), at Les Allées de la Liberté, just across from the *vieux port*. The other is held on Mondays, from 8 A.M. to 6 P.M., at the Marché Forville, the market building at the corner of the rue du Marché Forville and the rue Louis Blanc (about a two-minute walk northwest of the Les Allées market).

If you are arriving by car, parking can be found near the port or in the covered lot just northwest of the Marché Forville (follow signs indicating Parking Forville).

If you are traveling by train, both markets are only about a ten-minute walk southwest from the train station. For the Les Allées market, head south on the rue des Serbes, then turn right (west) on the rue d'Antibes, which leads to Les Allées de la Liberté (just west of the rue du Maréchal Joffre). For the Marché Forville, continue along the rue Félix Faure (the western extension of the rue d'Antibes), then turn right (north) on the rue Louis Blanc to the rue du Marché Forville.

Other Markets Described: Mandelieu (last Friday of the month)
Tourist Office: 04-93-39-24-53, 04-93-99-19-77

CANNES IS A city which arouses strong emotions. Many criticize it for its hype and fashion obsession, most evident during the Cannes Film Festival in May and the summer, when the city is teeming with visitors. Expensive boutiques dominate the narrow streets of its inner core, and its strip, along the boulevard de la Croisette, boasts one chic hotel after another. My experience of this town, however, has been mostly during the winter, when Cannes almost feels like a quiet provincial city.

Ironically, Cannes' growth into a city symbolizing wealth and luxury had rather inelegant origins. In the 1830s, the threat of a cholera epidemic resulted in the closure of the road farther east, prompting an English traveler, Lord Brougham, to stop at Cannes, which was then a small fishing port. He eventually set up winter residence here, returning for over 30 years. His wealthy compatriots soon joined in, as did Russians, Germans, and Swiss, and by the 1920s, Cannes had become the place to be for the well-heeled of Europe.

LES ALLÉES MARKET

The Saturday *brocante* market at Les Allées (also held on the first Sunday of the month) reflects, in a way, the elegance and wealth of Cannes' past. It is a high-quality market, where beautiful and expensive objects are displayed at tables arranged in a serpentine fashion at the east end of the *place*. The shaded square is dominated by an impressive wood and metal gazebo, sometimes surrounded on Saturdays by a small arts-and-crafts fair (not to be mistaken for the flea market).

The spot is pleasant, with a section at the edge of the *place* set aside for *boules* players. From the market, or from one of the many benches at its periphery, you can see the pleasure boats in the port and the sea beyond. Cafés and restaurants, offering all varieties of fish and seafood, line the streets to the north. In the market area itself, snack bars selling *pan bagnats* (large round rolls, filled with various things—tuna, olives, and crudités) offer an opportunity to refuel while browsing. (Some of the vendors, however, favor more refined fare; I have seen a few sit down to heaping plates of oysters and langoustines, at tables laid with linen cloths. Much as I have wanted to, I have not dared to photograph these scenes; the atmosphere at this market is a bit frosty.)

About 70 vendors are here (on Saturday, with about 40 on the first Sunday of the month), generally offering small decorative objects of high quality, such as silver, jewelry, crystal, porcelain, vases, Limoges boxes, figurines, and paintings. You will also find fine linens, old books, and toys. Christofle (a renowned name in silver-making) is much in evidence, as are some of the well-known names in crystal, such as Baccarat. You will not see many rustic items, and as in Nice, those you do find will be well polished and expensive.

Vendors are serious; they usually specialize in a few things, and while they are prepared to bargain somewhat, great deals are not likely to be found. These vendors seem prepared to wait for someone to come along who will pay the amount asked or close to it. Prices are generally quite high, perhaps even higher, in some cases, than those you will find in Nice and Antibes.

There are, however, exceptions. The last time I visited, I saw a woman leafing through a box of framed original paintings and sketches. She asked the price of two small but attractive watercolors of local scenes. They were 20 francs for the two, and the vendor added that another one, of flowers, was 10 francs. Needless to say, the woman scooped them up and I was consumed with jealousy. A man who witnessed this scene said admiringly, *"C'est comme ça, la chine"* (That's what collectibles hunting is like).

This is particularly true in the northeast corner of Les Allées market, where you are more likely to find vendors selling a hodgepodge of things laid out on blankets or piled in boxes. If you are looking for bargains, it's best to arrive early. You are also more likely to encounter vendors selling more inexpensive items in the winter than in the summer, when the tourists abound.

MARCHÉ FORVILLE

Although much less picturesque than Les Allées, the Monday flea market at the Marché Forville is of potentially greater interest to collectors of everyday items and those hopeful of finding a bargain. It takes place all day inside the market building, whose ugly rust-colored exterior conceals a classic art deco interior. A large clock in the center, bearing the logo *Claudel—Beurre, crème, fromage de Normandie,* serves as a reminder of the building's usual function.

The ambience at this spacious market is pleasant and relaxed. Around 60 vendors are here—perhaps more in winter than in summer, when *brocante* vendors may share space with fruit and vegetable stands. The scene is much more "down-home" than at Les Allées, as is reflected in both the things for sale and the prices.

As at Les Allées, some of the vendors deal in particular collectibles, such as antique cameras, scientific and marine equipment and instruments, tools, paintings, toys, etc. However, others—such as the woman in the northeast corner who makes periodic trips to her truck to replenish her stock—simply bring a jumble of odds and ends to sell. One of the best features of this market is the ever-present potential to make an interesting discovery, at a good price. I have found some wonderful, and inexpensive, kitchenware from the 1940s and 1950s. I have also bought some great sheets in both linen and *métis* (a mixture of linen and cotton), at prices lower than most other places in France, let alone the Côte d'Azur. I could, however, kick myself for passing up other things, such as an old polka-dotted Savoyard jug, which was only 80 francs.

The Marché Forville ranks up there as one of my favorite flea markets in the Côte d'Azur. The last time I visited, it was to take notes for this book; I instead fell immediately into that trancelike state characteristic of collectors on the scent of some great find, the book entirely forgotten. If I lived in Cannes, I would consider an early-morning visit here an indispensable part of my Monday regimen.

OTHER THINGS TO DO

If it's Monday and you have not yet seen it, be sure to also take in Nice's wonderful all-day market along the cours Saleya. If, on the other hand, it's a Saturday, Antibes' all-day *brocante* market is only about 20 kilometers away and well worth a visit.

If you are in the vicinity of Cannes on the last Friday of the month, and you have a car, consider stopping in at the modest-sized, all-day market in Mandelieu, a few kilometers northwest of Cannes, just off the A8 autoroute. This market is of some interest to bargain hunters, and those who collect rustic and everyday objects. Some dealers also specialize in certain collectibles, such as marine items and photographic equipment.

GRIMAUD (Sunday morning)

No. of Vendors: 50 to 75
Price/Quality Range: ✿ – ✿✿
Scenic Value: ✿✿
Amenities Nearby: ✿ – ✿✿

Featured Items: Kitchenware, tools, baskets, ceramics, hardware, linens, second-hand clothes

WHEN, WHERE, HOW: This market takes place every Sunday morning, from 6 A.M. to 1 P.M., in a field (Jas des Roberts), alongside the D14, about four kilometers east of the village of Grimaud. If arriving from the coast on the N98, head west on the D14 at St-Pons-les-Mûres for a few kilometers in the direction of the village of Grimaud. You will know when you have reached the market by the cars parked along the road and off to the right up a slight hill.

Tourist Office: 04-94-43-26-98

THE VILLAGE OF Grimaud (not to be mistaken with Port Grimaud, the 1970s experiment on the coast nearby), lies on the edge of the surprisingly rugged and unsullied Massif des Maures. The village, with its narrow streets and pristine flower-bedecked buildings, is picturesque and warrants a short visit.

It is not, however, a spot that will appeal much to those seeking a lively, and "real," travel experience.

By contrast, the weekly flea market—held in a field a few kilometers east of the village of Grimaud—has a distinctly real feel. The setting is plain and undramatic; it also provides a contrast to the usual landscape of this region where, except right along the water, one often has the impression of being on an angle. With its soft, green grass and fairly flat ground underfoot, this spot is a bit reminiscent of the eastern United States, central Canada, or southeast England.

THE MARKET

I have to confess that, somewhat perversely, this is one of my favorite markets in the Côte d'Azur. What a surprise it was to find such an unabashedly low-end scene in this upscale part of France. The number of cars here attests to the market's popularity—at least among bargain hunters—and reinforces the feeling that you have a decent chance of unearthing something interesting. While definitely not to everyone's taste, for those who not only don't mind, but relish, a bit of a "down and dirty" collecting experience, the weekly Grimaud market is a good one to visit along this coast. This is definitely more a for-ager's market than a stopover on a tourist's itinerary. However, coming here will give tourists an excuse to visit a part of the Côte d'Azur that they would probably not ordinarily see.

The 50 to 75 vendors at this market generally display their wares on blankets on the ground or heaped in boxes. Little attention is paid to presenting items in their best light, and often no attempt at all is made to clean or shine things up. The "almost new" is mixed in with the old in a somewhat chaotic fashion, with secondhand clothes sold alongside real collectibles.

At this market, you will primarily find rustic objects and practical household items, such as linens, bowls, pots, enamelware, buckets, baskets, garden implements, hardware, and tools. I could kick myself for passing up some solid, and inexpensive, old *torchons* (or dish towels, a popular collectible in France) made of *chanvre*, or hemp. However, I did unearth a lovely French ivory container for only ten francs. Sure, remnants of face powder were still in it, but that almost enhanced its appeal to me and it was otherwise in pristine condition.

All in all, this market is worth making a short detour for collectors, and if you are a bargain hunter like me, a bit of a find.

OTHER THINGS TO DO

After you've looked around the flea market, check out the stone buildings at the far end of the field, housing permanent—and surprisingly upscale—

brocante shops. Then, sit down for a drink and a snack at the pleasant and shady *terrasse* of the café next door, before you head back out to rejoin the hectic scene of the coast. If it's the first Sunday of the month, there is also an all-day flea market in the village of Grimaud itself, in the place Neuve.

MENTON (Friday)
(second Sunday of the month)

PLACE AUX HERBES
>   No. of Vendors: 20
>   Price/Quality Range: ✦✦✦
>   Scenic Value: ✦✦✦
>   Amenities Nearby: ✦✦✦
>
>   Featured Items: Ceramics, books, silver, cameras, Limoges boxes, small decorative objects

PLACE F. PALMERO
>   No. of Vendors: 30
>   Price/Quality Range: ✦✦✦
>   Scenic Value: ✦✦✦ – ✦✦✦✦
>   Amenities Nearby: ✦✦✦
>
>   Featured Items: Ceramics, paintings, militaria, tools and hardware, kitchenware

WHEN, WHERE, HOW: There are two flea markets in Menton, both all day—one on Fridays, from 8:30 A.M. to 6 P.M., at the place aux Herbes, and the other on the second Sunday of the month, from 9 A.M. to 6:30 P.M., at the place F. Palmero. Both markets are held in the center of town. If you are traveling by car, meter parking can be found without difficulty along the street or in the lots near the covered food market.

If you are arriving by train, the place aux Herbes market is a 15-minute walk southeast from the station. Head east on the avenue de la Gare, turning right (south) on the avenue Boyer (on the east side of the Jardins Biovès). Turn left (east) on the avenue Félix Faure, which then becomes the rue St-Michel. The place aux Herbes borders the rue St-Michel near its eastern end. Follow the same route for the place F. Palmero—which is located near the Cocteau museum by the sea—continuing south from the place aux Herbes.

>   Other Markets Described: Vallecrosia Alta (Italy)
>   Tourist Office: 04-92-41-76-76

MENTON DESCRIBES ITSELF as the *"perle de la Côte d'Azur"* (pearl of the Côte d'Azur), and I think that is apt. Apart from its spectacular setting, with the steep slopes of the rugged Alpes Maritimes behind and its wonderful stretch of the blue-green Mediterranean, Menton is among the least spoiled of the towns and cities along the coast.

Menton does not really feel French and is widely considered the most Italian-looking of the Côte d'Azur towns. Its old quarter is an amazing jumble of buildings, in all shades of pastel and ocher, that appear to be spilling down to the long promenade that winds its way along the sea. The lower part of town is dominated by a colorful pedestrian street (albeit lined with far too many tourist shops selling Provençal fabrics and lemon-shaped soaps for my taste).

Lemons are a big thing in this city, which holds its renowned Fête du Citron every February. The Jardins Biovès are filled with sculptures formed from oranges and lemons (which I confess to finding a bit garish). The extraordinary thing (at least to those who hail from northern climes) is that, because of Menton's particularly mild winters, lemon trees thrive all year.

And there is sun, sun, sun, almost all the time, and little wind, which makes this place truly spectacular. No wonder Menton was one of the preferred haunts of the British and the Russians in the late 19th and early 20th centuries and is a favorite of the retirement set today. It is true that Menton is pretty square and stodgy, especially compared to such towns as St-Tropez and Antibes. Its old-fashioned character—which is evident everywhere including in the age of its residents—may make it less appealing to some and more so to others. I like its genteel quality, although the ratio of dog-grooming shops and tea salons to trendy clothing stores is pretty staggering.

PLACE AUX HERBES MARKET

The place aux Herbes, site of the Friday flea market, is a perfect little square, surrounded by yellow and ocher buildings, and edged at the southern end by a graceful arcade through which you can see palm trees and the sea beyond. At its other end, the *place* backs onto Menton's main pedestrian street, the rue St-Michel.

The Friday market is small, with just 20 vendors, but it is a pleasant and relaxing place to visit. Perhaps it is the Italian influence—the border is just a few minutes away—but I find vendors here more laid-back, and easygoing, than at other markets in the region. You will also often find yourself in the company of as many Italians as French; vendors can frequently be heard conversing in Italian and negotiating in lira.

As is perhaps fitting for this pristine little square, the things for sale are almost exclusively small decorative items—fine porcelain and glassware, Limoges boxes, silver, linens, and dolls. You will also see old books, paintings, and cameras. You will not find much in the way of rustic or everyday items. Look out for the brilliantly colored *barbotine* ware from Menton and nearby Monaco; it is difficult to find and will likely be expensive if you do come upon it. Prices in this market are moderate to fairly high, generally, although vendors are willing to bargain to some extent.

Sit down for a drink in the *place* after you spend a few minutes (which is all you will likely need) looking through the market. You will find your market experience relaxing, if not productive.

PLACE F. PALMERO MARKET

Menton's other *brocante* market, in the place F. Palmero on the second Sunday of every month, is somewhat larger than the Friday market, with about 30 vendors. Until recently, this market was held in the place Lorédan-Larchey, a particularly unaesthetic modern square. Its move to the place F. Palmero, a dramatically more appealing spot near the Musée Jean Cocteau, by the sea, was a very welcome development.

This monthly market has traditionally offered a wider range of wares than the Friday market, including a greater variety of everyday and rustic items. In addition to the things found at the place aux Herbes, this market has tended to feature such things as military memorabilia, hardware and fixtures, kitchenware, and tools. As is generally the case in this region, prices are not cheap but bargaining is possible and expected.

OTHER THINGS TO DO

While you're in town, be sure not to miss Menton's wonderful food market, which takes place every morning except Monday in and around the colorful market building just below the place aux Herbes. Here, you can pick up some pizza or *pissaladière* (like pizza, topped with anchovies and onions) for a picnic lunch by the sea. I especially recommend the bread sold at the booth by the middle door at the north end.

If you have a car, and some time, a really pleasant spot for lunch after visiting the *brocante* markets is the Auberge du Village (04-93-35-87-83) in the center of Gorbio, a tiny village in the hills high above Menton. The food here —from lightly tossed salad greens and stuffed tomatoes to garlic-flavored lamb—is fresh and nicely presented; it is also not expensive. If you're lucky, your host will also entertain you on the piano, and after lunch you can stroll along the little roads that go from village to village, with dizzying views down to the sea.

If it's Friday, you might instead consider heading to the huge weekly general market in nearby Ventimiglia, about 15 minutes' drive along the coast into Italy. This is mostly a clothing, leather, linens, and kitchenware market. While the quality of things is sometimes questionable, some good buys are to be had and it's also fun. On your way, stop in at the spectacular Hanbury Gardens; they are about two kilometers inside Italy, on the upper route from Menton, via Garavan (a part of town with wonderful old villas overlooking the sea). In Garavan, there is also a great pizzeria-restaurant, called La Braise (06-93-57-24-16), where you can eat beautifully thin wood-fired pizzas while gazing out at the spectacular coastline below.

If it's the second Sunday of the month, and you'd like to see an Italian flea market, head for Vallecrosia Alta, a few kilometers east of Ventimiglia. This eerie-looking, tiny village hosts a fairly interesting low to midrange market; you'll find mostly Italian collectibles but also some French items. The prices here are not cheap but bargaining is possible.

Two things not to miss in Menton have to do with Jean Cocteau, the prolific artist. The Salle des Mariages, or Marriage Room, in Menton's Hôtel de Ville, is a bizarre place decorated by Cocteau in 1957, with scenes depicting jealousy and revenge—odd images for a wedding room. (Open Monday to Friday, from 8:30 A.M. to 12:30 P.M., and 1:30 P.M. to 5 P.M. Phone: 04-92-10-50-50.) The Musée Jean Cocteau, by the water, houses tapestries and ceramics by this versatile individual. (Open Wednesday to Monday, 10 A.M. to noon, and 2 P.M. to 6 P.M. Phone: 04-93-57-72-30.)

Finally, leave some time for walking along the Promenade, along with everybody else in Menton. If you can, continue your stroll to the far side of Cap Martin, facing Monaco; it's right up there with the great walks in France.

NICE (Monday)

    No. of Vendors: 180 to 200
    Price/Quality Range: ✱✱ – ✱✱✱✱
    Scenic Value: ✱✱✱✱
    Amenities Nearby: ✱✱✱✱

    Featured Items: Silver, ceramics, paintings, kitchenware, cameras, phonographs, advertising items, antique clothing, linens, militaria, art deco, books, tools

WHEN, WHERE, HOW: The Nice flea market is held on Monday, all day from 9 A.M. to 6 P.M. The market takes place along the cours Saleya and the adjacent place Pierre Gautier, in the old town, parallel to and just north of the Quai des États-Unis, the eastern extension of the Promenade des Anglais. If you are traveling by car, try to find parking along the Quai or in the lot by the place Guynemer, a few hundred meters farther east, by the port.

If you are traveling by train, the market is about a 20-to-25-minute walk southeast of Nice's central train station. Head south on the avenue Durante (and its continuation, the rue du Congrès) until you reach the Promenade des Anglais. Turn left (east) and follow the Promenade until it becomes the Quai des États-Unis, and then turn left (north) on one of the little streets to the rue St-François-de-Paule, which leads into the cours Saleya. For public transit, take the #15 or the #17 bus from the station (inquire at the tourist office).

Tourist Office: 04-93-87-07-07 and 04-93-87-60-60

WHEN I THINK of my favorite flea market towns in France, Nice comes quickly to mind, right up there with Paris, Annecy, and Toulouse. While Nice suffers from a case of multiple bad publicity, regarding everything from crime and corruption to pollution and incessant traffic, it is still a mesmerizing place. For a glimpse of real life in the Côte d'Azur, Nice, blemishes and all, is the spot to be.

The city, with its ornate, pastel-colored buildings lining the Baie des Anges, has a strong Italianate feel; Nice was only returned to France in 1860, following close to 500 almost continuous years in the hands of the Italian House of Savoy. You also sense here, as in other places along the coast, the presence of the British, who began frequenting the area in the late 18th century and whose efforts contributed to the Promenade des Anglais. Queen Victoria was particularly fond of this region and would apparently wander about in a buggy pulled by donkeys.

Vieux Nice, the city's most colorful and charming quarter (although I'd be careful here at night), is overlooked by the landmark Château park, site of Nice's Greek origins as Nikea, and of the old château, which was destroyed in 1706.

The centerpiece of the old quarter is the cours Saleya. In the 19th century, the *cours* was a chic spot and it is no wonder: the yellow, orange, pink, and ocher buildings that line it, with the Chapelle de la Miséricorde in the center, create a feeling of intense harmony, particularly in the bright light of the Mediterranean sun. The cours Saleya is also the site of Nice's Monday flea market (and on other days of the week, its wonderful food and flower market).

THE MARKET

This is one of the great flea markets of France and, with between 180 and 200 vendors, by far the biggest along the Côte d'Azur. In this lively and vibrant place, large numbers of visitors from all over mingle with the locals in some serious *chine*. On any given day you will hear people speaking English, German, Japanese, and especially Italian as you make your way through the crowds; some vendors will even accept payment in lira instead of francs.

General tourists will enjoy the Nice market almost as much as collectors. It's a great place for strolling along, watching the live entertainment, and sitting at one of the many outdoor restaurants and cafés soaking up the scene. It is also a good market for both "serious" collectors—who know exactly what they're looking for—and the more eclectic kind, like me, who are easily attracted to all sorts of things. When I lived in Menton for six months, I would come to this market almost every Monday. It was an hour drive each way along the Corniche Inférieure, and I could not wait to drop off my kids at school and get moving.

The market fills the cours Saleya and spills into the adjacent place Pierre Gautier, with its former Palais du Gouvernement decorated with rows of stately columns. Given its setting, the majestic and dramatic feel of this market is not accidental. You sense that you are in a special place, and that the experience is one to savor. Not that the things on display in the long rows of stalls at this huge market are of a particularly rarefied or ancient nature. On the contrary, part of what is wonderful about this market is that it spans a wide range in terms of the level of goods, from expensive silver and porcelain to bits of old crockery and pots. To me, it is close to being the ideal flea market, where things are not too pristine and where there is something for every range of taste and purchaser. One of my friends, a flea market addict and expert with an uncanny ability to scent a great find, swears by the Nice market. She almost always manages to find something great—both unexpected and inexpensive—here.

You will find the higher-end and higher-priced merchandise along the rows that run the length of the cours Saleya, while the less expensive and more modest, everyday objects are more likely to be found in the adjacent place Pierre Gautier (which is the area I always check out first in hopes of a real find). Along the *cours,* vendors specializing in linens and lace, advertising items, silverware, Limoges boxes, Provençal ceramics, jewelry, books, antique cameras, weights, ceramic tobacco jars and spice containers in descending sizes, coffee mills, gramophones, radios, and old telephones mingle with those selling art deco ware, telephone cards, seltzer bottles in colored glass, perfume bottles, antique clothing, and military memorabilia. A fair selection of regional ceramics is to be found at both the easternmost and the westernmost ends of the *cours.*

In the place Pierre Gautier, in addition to the stalls selling more low-end items, you will find paintings and prints, glassware, toys, more ceramics, some rustic items, and postcards. Furniture—there's not a lot here but more than at many markets in this region—is to be found in the center, where the *cours* meets the *place*, or at the east end of the *cours* under the archway leading to the sea.

Since the same vendors come to the Nice market each week and generally set up their stands in the same spot, you will begin to recognize them if you visit a few times. One vendor along the *cours*, whose approach I find particularly amusing, sells books by the kilo. Another woman nearby oversees her collection of hundreds of ceramic *fèves* (the figures and shapes that are hidden in the *galettes des rois*, sold during Epiphany). A woman in the center of the *cours* specializes in linens and 19th-century Provençal clothing. A couple of tough-looking guys at the end of the *place* preside over somewhat-the-worse-for-wear kitchenware spread out on a blanket and sold for a few francs, while an English vendor nearby expounds authoritatively on the subject of botanical prints. At the eastern end of the *cours*, you will often see a man with a large number of military hats laid out in a pile on the ground.

Vendors at the Nice market will bargain, but don't expect to get the price reduced by more than 20 to 25 percent. Also, do not expect to find a lot of inexpensive rustic items, as you will at other markets in France. Most of the tools, wrought-iron ware, wooden utensils, and garden implements you see will be in pristine condition and well polished, a clear signal that the price is going to be a bit steep. I collect 19th- and early-20th-century *boules*—the balls used in playing games like *pétanque* all over Provence and the Côte d'Azur—which were made out of wood, nail-studded wood, and bronze. The *boules* that I have found at the Nice market were polished and in good condition; they were also quite a bit more expensive than those I have picked up at nitty-gritty flea markets in Provence, such as Jonquières, Montfavet, and Mornas.

A notable feature of the Nice market is that you can occasionally find British and American collectibles (owned, no doubt, by some of the many expatriates from those countries) at quite reasonable prices. I have often remarked that, while the vendors know a lot about French and Italian wares and prices, they are much less plugged in when it comes to the English-speaking world. One of my most treasured, and surprising, finds here was a nice old American baking bowl, by the renowned McCoy company. The person selling it had no idea what it was and asked me if I thought it might be Fiesta ware, perhaps the one North American name he had heard.

A similar phenomenon can be observed regarding collectibles generally from the 1940s and 1950s. While things from this period are keenly sought by collectors in North America, they have not yet become the rage in France (although it is definitely starting). I recently bought a beautiful old blue glass reamer at the Nice market, in perfect condition, for 30 francs and a lovely pink Depression glass pitcher for 40 francs.

It is best to arrive at this market in the morning. Late morning is when it is at its liveliest, and given the intensity of the sun in this region, coming later can be a bit brutal. Also, if you arrive at noon (which is announced by a blast from a cannon nearby, so don't be alarmed), you are likely to find that things look a bit dead. Vendors are rigorous about sitting down to a leisurely and fairly elaborate lunch, which they consume at tables set up behind their stalls. While they are technically available during their meal, it is not really a good time to make a purchase if you are planning to bargain.

OTHER THINGS TO DO

If you find yourself at the Nice market at midday, the best idea is to follow the vendors' example and sit down for lunch at one of the many outdoor cafés and restaurants lining the market. My favorite place is Le Safari (04-93-80-18-44), at 1 cours Saleya, which serves fresh fish and wonderful niçoise pizza on a thin crust with a basil-flavored oil dribbled over it. While I always prefer to sit outside and take in the market while eating, the inside of this restaurant is also pleasant and a good alternative on a bad day. If you are not looking for a meal, you can snack on the street on some *socca*, which looks like a crepe and is made from chickpea flour and served to you in a paper cone. Or try *pissaladière*, another regional specialty, which is like pizza, garnished with onions, olives, and anchovies.

You should also be sure to sit down at one of the outdoor cafés along the cours Saleya for a drink. While a café au lait or a Coke can be quite expensive, it is well worth it, given the entertainment value thrown in, and no one will pressure you to leave. My spouse, who has absolutely no interest in flea markets other than as a congenial spot for writing and reading, has spent many an hour at the cafés along the *cours* while I comb the market.

Those who are keen, and particularly bargain hunters, should also try to squeeze in a visit to the flea market at the Marché Forville in Cannes, also held all day on Mondays (see Cannes, above). The drive is about 45 minutes along the coast (shorter, but less scenic, by autoroute), or you could take one of the frequent local trains (although it is about a 20-to-25-minute walk from the cours Saleya to the Nice central train station).

If you are in Nice other than on Monday, for an inexpensive light snack try the Bar René Socca, at 2 rue Miralhetti in the old quarter. Here you can sit outside on one of their picnic tables and sample not only their great *socca*, but also fried zucchini flowers and stockfish, a regional specialty.

Another great niçois spot is La Merenda (sadly closed on Mondays), at 4 rue de la Terrasse, just west of the cours Saleya. This little, crowded restaurant—which at least until recently had no phone and took no credit cards—displays its daily menu on a chalkboard. The *pistou* pasta is delicious and there are also often *poutines* (a small fish) and stockfish. Also closed on Mondays, but nearby at 14 rue St-François-de-Paule, is Alziari, a haven for olive oil, olives, and wonderful olive soaps.

Finally, if you have a car and some money to spend, treat yourself to lunch at Jacques Maximin (04-93-58-90-75), at 689 chemin de la Gaude, just outside of Vence, northwest of Nice. (You guessed it: this place is also closed on Mondays.) Not only is the food at this Michelin two-star restaurant wonderful, it's hard to beat lunch outside on the *terrasse* on a sunny day, surrounded by greenery and flowers.

ST-TROPEZ (Tuesday and Saturday morning)

No. of Vendors: 25 to 30
Price/Quality Range: ✦✦✦✦
Scenic Value: ✦✦✦ – ✦✦✦✦
Amenities Nearby: ✦✦✦✦

Featured Items: Marine items, paintings, books, silver, glassware, some furniture, vases, figurines, art deco, linens

WHEN, WHERE, HOW: The St-Tropez *brocante* market takes place every Tuesday and Saturday morning, from 8:30 A.M. to 1 P.M., as part of the town's general market. It is held in the place des Lices in the center of town. If arriving by car, parking is difficult to find and your best bet is to park in the lot by the port. If you don't have a car, there is unfortunately no rail linkup with the towns to the east. You will have to get off the train at St-Raphaël and then take a bus from there to St-Tropez. From the bus station, head northeast, past the place A. Blanqui, to the boulevard Louis Blanc, which leads into the place du XVième Corps and the place des Lices beyond.

Other Markets Described: St-Raphaël
Tourist Office: 04-94-97-45-21

ST-TROPEZ IS ANOTHER of those mythical towns (one of many in this region). I confess that when I first came here years ago, I was disappointed. The immediate area is pretty flat and lacks the natural splendor of many other places along the coast. My initial reaction quickly changed, however, when

I saw the town's port, which has a wonderfully languid feel, despite the tourist joints.

For no obvious reason, what was once a tranquil fishing village became, in the late 19th and early 20th centuries, a magnet for artists and writers and then a major hot spot when Brigitte Bardot was filmed here in a movie in the mid-1950s. Ever since, St-Tropez has symbolized a kind of chic and trendiness (as well as topless and nude bathing, which has been going on along its beautiful sandy beaches for many years). The numerous upscale boutiques lining its streets attest to St-Tropez's continuing cachet.

THE MARKET

Though quite small, the flea market in St-Tropez's place des Lices is well worth a detour to this famous town. It is not that the market's physical surroundings are so remarkable, but that the extraordinary denseness and color of the scene are overwhelming.

Between 25 and 30 *brocante* sellers share the place des Lices on Tuesday and Saturday mornings with many general-market vendors selling fruit and vegetables, flowers and new Provençal fabrics and clothing. Giant plane trees provide a kind of cathedral ceiling over the market, enveloping the *place*. (Sadly, it was found several years ago that some of the trees were diseased and had to be removed, and massive efforts have been made to save the rest.) The *place* is also surrounded by cafés and restaurants, which protrude right into the market area.

Do not assume that because the *brocante* market shares space with fruit and vegetables, and new goods, there is anything modest or pedestrian about its wares, or its prices. To the contrary, this is a high-end, high-quality market, perhaps the most high-end of all the markets in this region. I was first struck by the fact that price tags were not openly displayed at some of the booths. I was also awed by the quality of the displays, a number of which are like little theatrical sets; some are so appealing that you just want to move in.

The things for sale are impressive. Appropriately, maritime and travel motifs are particularly evident, in prints and paintings of ships, wooden ship models, old oars, travel luggage, and books on maritime themes. Silver abounds at this market, in both art deco and art nouveau designs. You will also find some furniture—including classic examples of what North Americans would call porch furniture—ceramics, perfume bottles, glassware, old books, paintings, Provençal fabrics, and fine linens.

While this is a fun market to look around, looking is probably all you will do unless your budget is fairly large. That prices are high should, however, come as no surprise since just about everything is expensive in St-Tropez. Here, you will also be able to converse in English with many of the vendors.

Be warned that there are often long traffic jams getting into St-Tropez during the high tourist season from June to September, so that, if you come then, you should definitely try to arrive early if at all possible. There is really only one route into town from La Foux to the west, and that short stretch can be brutal. Needless to say, this is a much easier place to visit during cooler times of the year.

OTHER THINGS TO DO

If it's Tuesday, and you are heading east from here along the coast, consider a short stopover at St-Raphaël's medium-sized, all-day flea market. While its site, the place Coullet, is not particularly quaint (and is also sorely lacking in shade), you might chance upon something of interest.

If it's a Saturday, plan to include a visit to Cannes' all-day flea market at Les Allées or the all-day market in Antibes (see Cannes and Antibes, above).

VALBONNE (first Sunday of the month)

No. of Vendors: 40 to 50
Price/Quality Range: ✦✦✦
Scenic Value: ✦✦✦
Amenities Nearby: ✦✦ – ✦✦✦

Featured Items: Ceramics, glassware, linens, books, decorative items, some furniture

WHEN, WHERE, HOW: The Valbonne flea market is held all day, from 8 A.M. to 6 P.M., on the first Sunday of the month (except in February and August). The market takes place in the center of town, along the rue du Cours and in the main *place* in the heart of the village.

Other Markets Described: Opio (fourth Sunday of the month) and Mouans-Sartoux (Saturday)
Tourist Office: 04-93-12-34-50

VALBONNE IS A pleasant little oasis, hidden up in the *arrière-pays* north of Cannes and northwest of Antibes. I like making the trek up here, even if just to take a break from the crowds and hectic pace of the coast. The village has a nice sleepy feel and a lovely, colorful large central *place*, shaded by oak trees, with arcades dating from the 15th to 17th centuries. Coming here reminds me of riding into a quiet, dusty town in the Old West.

THE MARKET

Apart from serving as a welcome respite from the glitter of the coast, Valbonne's flea market is good both in terms of ambience and the kinds of things sold. The 40 to 50 vendors put up their stalls in the central *place*—a congenial setting for browsing and for watching the proceedings over a cold drink—and on the nearby rue du Cours (a somewhat less appealing spot), just above the *place*.

Strolling through the Valbonne market, an activity that would appeal to both tourists and collectors, is strangely calming and restorative. Tourists will get a sense of the gentleness and beauty of the *arrière-pays*, while collectors have a good chance of finding something interesting. As elsewhere in the Côte d'Azur, the focus here is on high-quality decorative items of all kinds, as well as linens, books, and paintings. But this is also an especially good place for finding a wide variety of Provençal and regional ceramics, including dishes and pots from nearby Vallauris in those beautiful shades of green and yellow.

Not surprisingly, the generally high quality of the goods is reflected in the prices. You will also not see many vendors laying out odds and ends on blankets and selling them for only a few francs. However, I once bought, for 50 francs, an attractive ceramic pitcher in blue and white checks, which I have seen several times since for four times that price. The rue du Cours is the best spot for bargain hunters and people interested in more low-end and inexpensive everyday objects, such as kitchenware, hardware, and tools.

I would certainly frequent the Valbonne market if I were staying in this area. No doubt its sedate feel is less in evidence in July, during the high tourist season, than at other times of the year, but it would still be a good spot to escape to if you want a little break from the beach and promenade scene of the coast.

OTHER THINGS TO DO

A few other flea markets are close by, which you might want to check out if you plan to be in this area for a little while. For example, in Mouans-Sartoux, a few kilometers southwest of Valbonne, there is a small *brocante* market all day on Saturdays, at the place Jean Jaurès. When I was here, there were not many vendors, perhaps because the market had only recently been established and was then held on Wednesdays. The much bigger town of Grasse, famous for its perfume industry, also has a flea market, on the first Friday of the month. It takes place on the cours Honoré-Cresp, in the center of town near the casino and the public gardens.

A quite small market takes place on the fourth Sunday of the month just outside the village of Opio, a few kilometers northwest of Valbonne. The setting of this market—a shopping center outside the village—is dramatically less pleasing than that of Valbonne, but you might stumble upon something you want at a reasonable price.

VILLEFRANCHE-SUR-MER (Sunday)

PLACE A. POLLONAIS
   No. of Vendors: 35
   Price/Quality Range: ✦✦✦
   Scenic Value: ✦✦✦✦
   Amenities Nearby: ✦✦✦

   Featured Items: Silver, glassware, ceramics, phonographs, jewelry, linens, high-end kitchenware, some furniture

PLACE DE L'OCTROI
   No. of Vendors: 30
   Price/Quality Range: ✦✦✦
   Scenic Value: ✦✦✦
   Amenities Nearby: ✦✦ – ✦✦✦

   Featured Items: Porcelain, glassware, vases, paintings and prints, books, some furniture

WHEN, WHERE, HOW: There are two all-day *brocante* markets every Sunday in Villefranche-sur-Mer—one at the place de l'Octroi (from 8:30 A.M. to 6:30 P.M.), alongside the Corniche Inférieure, the N98, between Nice and Menton, and the other at the place A. Pollonais (also from 8:30 A.M. to 6:30 P.M.) in the lower part of town by the sea.

If you have a car, parking for the place de l'Octroi market can be found in a small lot just past the Office du Tourisme next to the *place,* while parking for the place A. Pollonais is available in the fairly large lot across from it. If you arrive by train, both markets are within easy walking distance south (place A. Pollonais) and southwest (place de l'Octroi) of the station.

Tourist Office: 04-93-01-73-68

VILLEFRANCHE-SUR-MER is one of the most picturesque towns along the Côte d'Azur and, like Menton, one of the most unsullied. Set in a large bay across from the humped peninsula of Cap Ferrat, the town was an American naval base before France left the command structure of NATO during the 1960s. Warships, as well as many cruise ships, can still be spotted dropping anchor here.

Despite Villefranche's pretty chic reputation, the old town has managed to retain some of the character of a fishing village, with its harbor under the protective eye of the little medieval Chapelle de St-Pierre. The interior of the *chapelle* was decorated by Jean Cocteau in 1957 with scenes of robust fishermen whose eyes are shaped, appropriately, like tiny fish.

PLACE A. POLLONAIS MARKET

It is hard to imagine a nicer setting than Villefranche's waterfront for a *brocante* market, and here, in the place A. Pollonais opposite the Chapelle de St-Pierre, one of the town's two Sunday markets takes place. About 35 vendors set up their tables in the *place*, which, surrounded by two-century-old Italianate buildings in every shade of yellow, rose, orange, and ocher, is one of the prettiest along the coast. Sunday is especially pleasant here, as people sit outside at cafés and restaurants watching others stroll through this small but appealing market.

Here, you will find some furniture, but primarily small decorative items of fairly high quality—silver, jewelry, glassware, ceramics, old phonographs, pristine kitchenware and linens, etc. The atmosphere is laid-back and relaxed. This is a spot for lazy Sunday-afternoon browsing, while casting an occasional glance at the sea through the palms and flowering trees. It is, however, not a place where you are likely to find many bargains.

PLACE DE L'OCTROI MARKET

Once you've seen the place A. Pollonais market, head up to the place de l'Octroi, by the main road. While not nearly as stunning a setting as the place A. Pollonais, it has its own charms, including an elegant carousel and impressive statues of a couple of large and languorous nudes. This market, which has about 30 vendors, is set in a congenial, shaded little garden, a good place to be on a hot day. The market also extends along the wide sidewalk by the main road, under the protection of palms and plane trees.

The kinds of things sold here are similar to what you will find at the place A. Pollonais, although the range of items is somewhat narrower, with less of an emphasis on small decorative objects. You may find the prices for some things somewhat less expensive than in the other market, but it's really just a question of hit-and-miss.

OTHER THINGS TO DO

After looking through Villefranche's markets, come back to the waterfront and join the "beautiful people" at one of the cafés or restaurants in the place A. Pollonais. It won't be cheap but the experience will be well worth it. Or, for a taste of a truly regional specialty, try some *socca* (a crepelike snack made of chickpea flour) from La Socca de Villafranca, a vendor who sells from a little mobile wood oven in the parking lot opposite the *place*. The *socca* here, cooked on large round trays, then scraped off in arclike shapes and served to you hot in paper cones, is the best I have tasted.

If you have time, and it is the first or third Sunday of the month, you should also check to see if there is a *brocante* market in nearby Beaulieu-sur-Mer. This market has been interrupted from time to time. (The last time I checked it was temporarily suspended, so call beforehand to see if it has been reinstated.) The site is beautiful—beside the Corniche Inférieure just above the town's port, with a backdrop of huge cliffs jutting into the sea and boats in the harbor below.

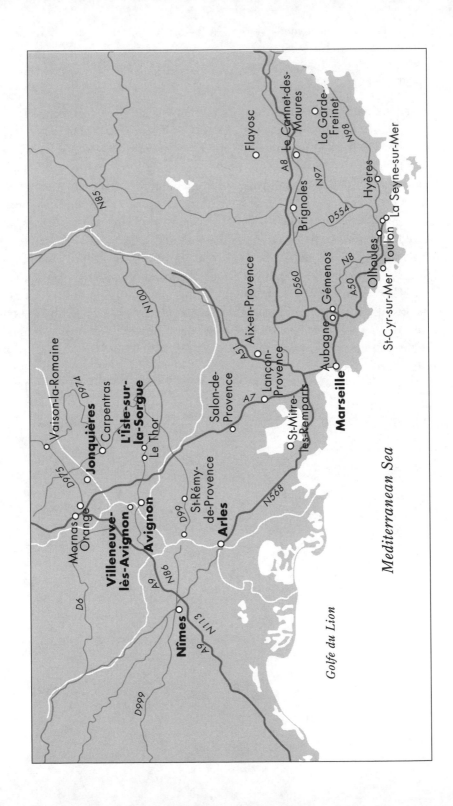

Vaison-la-Romaine

N85

Flayosc

A8 Le Cannet-des-Maures

La Garde-Freinet

N98

N97

Brignoles

Hyères

La Seyne-sur-Mer

D554

Aix-en-Provence

D560

N8

Gémenos

Olioules

A50

St-Cyr-sur-Mer

Toulon

N100

Aubagne

Marseille

Carpentras

D974

Jonquières

L'Isle-sur-la-Sorgue

Le Thor

Salon-de-Provence

Lançon-Provence

A51

A7

St-Mitre-les-Remparts

D975

St-Rémy-de-Provence

Arles

N568

Mornas

Orange

Villeneuve-lès-Avignon

Avignon

D99

D6

A9

N86

Mediterranean Sea

Nîmes

N113

A6

Golfe du Lion

D999

The Flea Markets of Provence

Monday   AIX-EN-PROVENCE (pl. Jeanne d'Arc) [30 to 60 vendors]
(last Monday of month)
(8 A.M. to 5 P.M.)

          *NÎMES (av. Jean Jaurès) [80 vendors]
(8 A.M. to 6 P.M. but many vendors leave by noon)

Tuesday   *AIX-EN-PROVENCE (pl. de Verdun) [35 vendors]
(8 A.M. to 12:30 P.M.)

          APT-EN-PROVENCE (pl. St-Pierre) [20 to 30 vendors]
(8 A.M. to 7 P.M.)

Wednesday   *ARLES (boul. des Lices) [80 to 100 vendors]
(first Wednesday of month)
(8 A.M. to 6 P.M.)

          PERNES-LES-FONTAINES (pl. F. Mistral) [15 to 20 vendors]
(7 A.M. to 1 P.M.)

          LE CANNET DES MAURES (Parking Intermarché) [20 vendors]
(8 A.M. to 6 P.M.)

Thursday   *AIX-EN-PROVENCE (pl. de Verdun) [35 vendors]
(8 A.M. to 12:30 P.M.)

          ORANGE (cours A. Briand sud) [10 vendors]
(8 A.M. to noon)

Friday   TOULON (pl. du Théâtre) [15 to 20 vendors]
(9 A.M. to 5 P.M.)

Saturday *AIX-EN-PROVENCE (pl. de Verdun) [35 vendors]
(8 A.M. to 12:30 P.M.)

ARLES (boul. des Lices) [15 vendors]
(8 A.M. to noon)

CABANNES (pl. de la Mairie) [30 vendors]
(second Saturday of month)
(8 A.M. to 1 P.M.)

LA CADIÈRE D'AZUR (rue Max Dormoy) [12 vendors]
(second Saturday of month, from March to November)
(8 A.M. to 6 P.M.)

LE CANNET-DES-MAURES (center) [75 vendors]
(8 A.M. to noon)

LANÇON-PROVENCE (Big Bazar, Z.I. les Combes) [100 vendors]
(6 A.M. to noon)

MONTFAVET (rue des Écoles) [75 to 100 vendors]
(6 A.M. to 1 P.M.)

ST-CYR-SUR-MER (pl. Portalis) [40 vendors] (last Saturday of month)
(9 A.M. to 6 P.M.)

ST-MÎTRE-LES-REMPARTS (ZAC des Étangs, rte. de Martigues)
[150 vendors]
(7 A.M. to 6 P.M.)

SANARY-SUR-MER (pl. Cavet) [20 to 25 vendors]
(last Saturday of month)
(8 A.M. to 6 P.M.)

TARASCON (center) [25 to 30 vendors] (second Saturday of
month) (9 A.M. to 6 P.M.)

TOULON (Quartier Ste-Musse) [200 vendors]
(6 A.M. to noon)

*VILLENEUVE-LÈS-AVIGNON (pl. C. David) [80 to 100 vendors]
(6 A.M. to 2 P.M.)

Sunday AUBAGNE (Departmentale 43c), [40 to 50 vendors projected]
(7 A.M. to 6 P.M.)

AUBAGNE (Marché de Gros de la Tourtelle) [100 to 120 vendors]
(last Sunday of month)
(8 A.M. to 6 P.M.)

*AVIGNON (pl. des Carmes) [100 vendors]
(6 A.M. to 12:30 P.M.)

BESSE-SUR-ISSOLE (around lake) [50 vendors] (first Sunday of
month from April to October)
(8 A.M. to 6 P.M.)

BRIGNOLES (Parc Mini-France) [60 vendors]
(7 A.M. to 6 P.M.)

FLAYOSC (center) [40 vendors] (fourth Sunday of month from
March to October)
(8 A.M. to 6 P.M.)

LA GARDE-FREINET (center) [35 vendors] (third Sunday of month
from May to September)
(7 A.M. to 7 P.M.)

GÉMENOS (pl. du Village) [35 vendors] (third Sunday of month)
(8 A.M. to 6 P.M.)

HYÈRES (La Capte, av. de la Pinède) [80 vendors]
(7:30 A.M. to 1 P.M.)

*L'ÎSLE-SUR-LA-SORGUE (av. des 4 Otages) [40 vendors]
(9 A.M. to 7 P.M.)

*JONQUIÈRES (rte. d'Orange) [100 to 150 vendors]
(6 A.M. to 1 P.M.)

LANÇON-PROVENCE (Big Bazar, Z.I. les Combes)
[400 to 500 vendors]
(5 A.M. to 1 P.M., but some vendors stay until 4 P.M.)

*MARSEILLE (av. Cap Pinède, La Madrague, 15th arrond.)
[120 vendors]
(5 A.M. to 1 P.M.)

*MARSEILLE (cours Julien, 6th arrond.) [30 vendors]
(second Sunday of month)
(8 A.M. to 6 P.M.)

MORNAS (R.N. 7, south of Mornas) [100 vendors]
(6 A.M. to 1 P.M.)

NÎMES (Parking du Stade) [80 vendors]
(8 A.M. to 4 P.M., but some vendors leave earlier)

OLLIOULES (Marché Floral Méditerranean) [170 vendors]
(second Sunday of month)
(8 A.M. to 6 P.M.) ($)

ST-MÎTRE-LES-REMPARTS (ZAC des Étangs, rte. de Martigues)
[150 vendors]
(7 A.M. to 6 P.M.)

SALON-DE-PROVENCE (pl. Morgan) [60 vendors]
(first Sunday of month)
(8 A.M. to 6 P.M.)

LA SEYNE-SUR-MER (pl. B. Frachon) [300 vendors]
(8 A.M. to 6 P.M., but most vendors leave by 2:30 P.M.)

LE THOR (pl. du Marché) [50 vendors] (second Sunday of month
from April to September)
(8 A.M. to 6 P.M.)

TOULON (Quartier Ste-Musse) [400 vendors]
(4 A.M. to noon)

VAISON-LA-ROMAINE (pl. Montfort) [35 vendors]
(third Sunday of month)
(7 A.M. to 7 P.M.)

Regional Overview

GETTING ORIENTED: ABOUT THE REGION

If you want to hear people sigh, just mention Provence. It is as if we were all somehow imbued with a collective awareness of the magic of this place, whether we have been here or not, read about it or not. In our imagination, Provence symbolizes not just sun, vineyards, olive groves, and quaint stone villages, but also a kind of life in harmony that seems to elude us elsewhere.

How hard it is to live up to such expectations, and yet the real Provence manages to do it quite well. It has a special, yet undefinable, quality, which adds drama to tall cypresses, fields of wild poppies, tidy rows of vines, and humps of thick lavender. Events also seem to be infused with a heightened significance, whether it's the village *fête*, men playing *boules* in town, farmers working in their fields, or children yelling in the school yard. I have heard it said that in Provence everything is larger than life, while in other places things are smaller than life. Sometimes that seems to be true.

The boundaries of Provence are characterized in many different ways by writers. In this book, the term describes the area from above Orange on the north to the Rhône River on the west (but including Nîmes and Villeneuve-lès-Avignon), the Mediterranean on the south, and just shy of St-Tropez on the east. This region is a strange mixture of traditional and modern, insular and outward-looking. It has always been accustomed to influxes of foreigners; the Greeks came here over 2,500 years ago, followed by the Romans and then others. Today, northern Europeans and North Americans, as well as French from outside the region, flock here in huge numbers. In some villages in Haute-Provence and the Luberon, for example, the population is overwhelmingly non-Provençal.

But while Provence has been altered in recent decades as a result of these influxes and other changes, it still retains a strong connection to its *paysan* roots and a distinct cultural tradition. This quality, despite its fragility, makes Provence so alluring to those who come. Here, small villages and the countryside hold as much appeal for visitors as the large towns and cities.

I lived in a tiny village in Haute-Provence with my family for three years. The large stone house we stayed in was, by all accounts, well over three hundred years old, and from the *terrasse* you could see the remains of a thousand-year-old château high up on a hill beyond the vineyards. Our neighbors were farmers who worked hard in their fields. Nature was central to their lives, but so was the history of this region. They told us that the Romans had come to our village for stone to build nearby Vaison-la-Romaine and showed us the wheel marks of their carts, still visible today.

Even though we were not farmers and not French, we were accepted. Our children went to the local one-room school, played soccer, and participated in the town *fêtes*. We learned about wine-making, beekeeping, olive picking, quince-jelly making, pastis, hunting, irrigation, snakes, scorpions, truffles, *tisanes* (herbal teas), the Provençal language (which some of the older people still speak), *aïoli* (a dish served with garlic mayonnaise), rosemary, and wild-boar stew.

We also learned that, while the people of Provence are generally very friendly, warmhearted, and generous, at the same time they can be wary and inward. But even that seemed to add to the greatness of the place. We were regaled with stories of family feuds, sharp political differences, and scandals. I sometimes think that anyone who has spent any time in this region would soon amass enough material for a book like Peter Mayle's *A Year in Provence*. People you meet sometimes seem like caricatures, and each story you hear is more fantastic than the one before.

MARKET RHYTHMS: WHEN THEY'RE HELD/WHEN TO GO

The rustic nature of Provence helps to make it a prolific region for flea markets; there are far more regular markets here than in most other parts of France. The *paysans* do not throw things out; their possessions collect over generations in the sheds of their old stone houses, sometimes ultimately providing the flea markets with their wares. The plenitude of markets here is also no doubt due to the huge presence of visitors to this region, keen to acquire some much coveted tokens of Provence to take home.

The weather is likely another contributing factor to the markets' abundance. It is usually quite mild and gentle, although the infamous mistral—the cold northern wind that blows down the Rhône River, often for days at a time—can be fierce. I have been to markets in the mistral's path where the wind was strong enough to send plates and glassware flying. Usually, however, the mistral is just an irritant and even has its compensating qualities: mistral days are usually brilliantly sunny and clear.

Although there are many markets to visit in this region, the challenge is in timing your visit to coordinate with their schedules. Most occur on weekends, especially on Sunday, making it difficult for short-term visitors to get to see many of them. Several are also morning-only, starting up around dawn and completely winding down by 12:30 or 1 P.M.

The fall and the spring are the best seasons to come. The weather is mild (albeit sometimes rainy), the markets are quite lively, and prices are generally lower than during the summer high-season. While winter is probably the best time for deals, it can be cold (despite what anyone tells you to the contrary), particularly in the morning; this is apparently also the worst season for the mistral. In summer, the markets are fairly crowded with tourists (with prices often somewhat higher as a result), and the weather can be hot, particularly at midday.

Bargain hunters should try to arrive at the markets early in the day since, unlike in some other regions, real finds can still be had here, particularly at the more basic and no-frills markets. In the summer, arriving early is a good idea for everyone, just to avoid the midday heat and sun. In the winter, on the other hand, unless you are really keen, it is better to come a bit later, after the sun has burned off any early-morning frost. At midday, it can feel quite mild, even in January and February—that is, if the mistral is not blowing.

MARKET FLAVORS: HOW THEY LOOK/HOW THEY FEEL

There is a wide range of markets in this region. While the high-end ones are not as glamorous as some you will find in the Côte d'Azur, for example, the low-end ones are as "down and dirty" as any you will see in France. Many of the markets, particularly the less nitty-gritty ones, are held in the center of towns and cities, in surroundings that, while not always picturesque or brilliantly colorful, are reasonably attractive. Others—usually the more low-end ones—are held in much less appealing spots, outside of town or village centers. But whatever the market's location or its range, you are always conscious of the presence of the rustic Provence countryside; these are truly markets of the *terroir,* or surrounding area.

The markets have a real charm; the atmosphere is noticeably congenial and low-key, just like the region itself. Vendors are generally friendly and down-to-earth; they will usually treat you in a straightforward and good-humored manner, although sometimes slightly amusedly. If your French is good, you will have a better and easier time. While some vendors (particularly in the more high-end markets) speak a little English, generally in this region they do not, or at least not much. If you don't speak French, however, you will not be made to feel uncomfortable; although often rural, people here are well used to foreigners.

These are generally matter-of-fact markets, for fairly serious browsing. Even in the cities and towns, you will not find a lot of cafés and restaurants alongside the flea markets filled with people whiling away the hours; instead, market browsers who want to relax afterward in a café or a restaurant usually head elsewhere.

While not terribly scenic, the low-end markets held in fields or parking lots outside town do reveal a side of Provence that many tourists do not see —different ethnic minorities and social classes, for example. They will be of interest to those who welcome exposure to a broader range of French life when they travel, as well as to bargain hunters. However, these are markets where you will want to drop in, look around, and then take off to visit more picturesque spots, which abound in this region.

COLLECTIBLES: WHAT YOU'LL FIND/WHAT TO LOOK FOR

You will find a large rustic emphasis in the wares sold at these markets— farm implements, tools, baskets, pails, wrought-iron ware, wooden clogs, rustic furniture, glazed earthenware and terra-cotta pots, sturdy linens, etc. Fine antiques are not a big feature, nor are collectibles from outside France. Generally, the focus is on utilitarian and everyday objects of traditional Provençal life, rather than on ornate and high-quality decorative items.

You will also notice a true regional focus in the things sold here— Provençal ceramics in the classic mustard yellow and dark green, colorful Provençal quilts, old *boules* (in wood, nail-studded wood, and metal), *santons* (the ceramic figures dressed in Provençal costumes), baskets, wooden shoes, and Provençal furniture. In addition to other symbols of Provençal agriculture, you may also spot olive oil jugs, truffle jars, and wine-making implements.

BUYING: PRICE LEVELS/BARGAINING OPPORTUNITIES

The markets span a wide range in prices. In recent years, Provençal collectibles of all kinds have been in hot demand throughout Europe and North America and have generally soared in cost. Surprisingly, however, the flea markets are still interesting for bargain hunters; great deals can be found, particularly if you don't mind going to the less pristine markets to look for them. You will notice a tremendous variation in cost, based on whether something was found in a down-home market—such as Jonquières, Mornas, Montfavet, or the place des Carmes in Avignon—or whether it was purchased, all polished and cleaned up, at L'Îsle-sur-la-Sorgue, Aix-en-Provence, Arles, or Nîmes.

Bargaining is accepted and generally friendly in this region. Speaking French is useful, not only in making yourself understood, but to help disabuse vendors of any notion that you are a wealthy foreigner, willing to pay big prices for a piece of Provence.

GETTING AROUND: HOW TO TRAVEL/WHERE TO GO

Having a car is a real advantage in this region; it will allow you to see some of the more out-of-the-way markets (not to mention the wonderful little towns and villages) not easily accessible by train or bus. Also, having a car will permit you to get an early start, as you will want to do here, and maybe catch a few markets in one day. Driving is relatively easy in this part of France, and you will usually have no problem finding parking.

If your objective is to incorporate flea markets into your overall experience of Provence, I would focus on visiting those markets in the more picturesque parts, around Avignon, Arles, Aix-en-Provence, and Vaison-la-Romaine. Though not my favorite town, Avignon is a good base for this purpose, given its proximity to other places and to so many of the interesting markets.

Market Close-Ups

I have selected eight flea market towns to feature in this chapter—Aix-en-Provence, Arles, Avignon, L'Îsle-sur-la-Sorgue, Jonquières, Marseille, Nîmes, and Villeneuve-lès-Avignon. The markets run the gamut in size, range of things sold, and schedules.

AIX-EN-PROVENCE (Tuesday, Thursday, and Saturday morning)

No. of Vendors: 35
Price/Quality Range: ✦✦ – ✦✦✦
Scenic Value: ✦✦ – ✦✦✦
Amenities Nearby: ✦✦✦

Featured Items: Books, paintings, jewelry, ceramics, some furniture, rustic items generally

WHEN, WHERE, HOW: There is a *brocante* market in Aix-en-Provence every Tuesday, Thursday, and Saturday morning, from 8 A.M. to 12:30 P.M., in the place de Verdun, in front of the Palais de Justice. The *place* is located in the center of Aix, in the pedestrian maze of streets to the north of the cours Mirabeau.

If you have a car, meter parking is best found along the streets just south of the *cours*. If arriving by train, the market is about a 20-minute walk northeast from the train station. From the station, head north, along the rue G. Desplaces, turning right on the avenue des Belges to the place du Général de Gaulle. Then follow the cours Mirabeau east, turning left (north) just past the place Forbin at the end of the *cours*, onto the rue Thiers, which leads into the place de Verdun.

Tourist Office: 04-42-16-11-61

AIX-EN-PROVENCE is a much more lively town than either Avignon or Arles—its main rivals for the title of most appealing Provençal city—and a favorite spot of both foreign tourists and the French. Its prominence dates back a long time; for about seven centuries prior to the French Revolution, it was the capital of Provence. It has also enjoyed the reputation as a center of the arts and learning, its popular university dating from the 15th century.

Aix's stature remains pretty much intact today. It is a prosperous-looking town, with many fine and imposing buildings providing solid evidence of its distinguished history. It is also a city of the young, as a stroll down the cours Mirabeau will quickly demonstrate; students crowd the lively cafés, chatting with friends, apparently oblivious to the cares of the world. Perhaps this youthfulness somewhat masks the city's underlying conservatism and makes it seem less stolidly bourgeois than nearby Avignon, for example.

The cours Mirabeau, with its plane trees and fountains, is quite splendid; for a second, you could imagine that you are on one of the wide boulevards of Paris, rather than deep in Cézanne territory. And the winding, narrow streets leading off the *cours* to the north are lively and full of trendy boutiques. However, if you lack a sense of direction, as I do, you'll need a bit of luck or a good map to find your way back to the car in this maze.

THE MARKET

The place de Verdun flea market in Aix is not large. Around 35 vendors share the *place* and the immediate vicinity with a few secondhand-clothing vendors and others selling crafts and new Provençal ceramics. What this flea market perhaps lacks in size it makes up for in frequency, being held on Tuesday, Thursday, and Saturday mornings. The setting is quite appealing. The *place* is colorful and cool at the same time—the contrast makes it a bit of an oasis in this rather dense urban setting. The *place* also gives a nice enclosed feeling without being claustrophobic.

You will find some furniture at this market, as well as old books, paintings, prints, ceramics, silver, and small decorative objects of all sorts. I would describe this as a midrange market—not nitty-gritty, but also not terribly high-end. The prices are generally moderate to moderately expensive, though you can bargain somewhat.

While it is perhaps not worth going far out of your way, I would certainly recommend visiting this market if you happen to be in the vicinity on market days, whether you are a general tourist or a collector. The market has a casual and friendly feel and the *place* itself is pleasing.

OTHER THINGS TO DO

After browsing in the flea market, take a stroll through Aix's popular food and flower markets (especially if it is a Saturday), at the place des Prêcheurs, the place de l'Hôtel de Ville, and the place Richelme.

The best way to explore Aix is to simply wander through the old quarter and along the cours Mirabeau. Be sure to stop for a drink on the *cours,* at Les Deux Garçons (at number 53). This Consular-period café, which apparently dates from 1792, is one of the most famous in France. Then try some of Aix's signature candy, the *calissons d'Aix,* at À la Reine Jeanne, at 32 cours Mirabeau. (There are several places in town to buy this almond-shaped and fruit- and almond-flavored treat.) Unlike many places in France, Aix has quite a good selection of ethnic restaurants—Vietnamese, Japanese, Indian, and North African—so you might want to try one of them here, in the old quarter.

A monthly flea market also takes place in Aix, all day on the last Monday of the month, in the place Jeanne d'Arc, just north of the place du Général de Gaulle.

ARLES (first Wednesday of the month)

No. of Vendors: 80 to 100
Price/Quality Range: ✦✦✦
Scenic Value: ✦✦ – ✦✦✦
Amenities Nearby: ✦✦ – ✦✦✦

Featured Items: Provençal clothing, accessories, fabrics and lace, ceramics, toys, some furniture

WHEN, WHERE, HOW: Arles has an all-day *brocante* market on the first Wednesday of the month, from 8 A.M. to 6 P.M. The market takes place at the south end of town below the Jardin d'Été, alongside the boulevard des Lices. If you have a car, meter parking is available on the boulevard and on nearby streets.

If arriving by train, while the market is at the opposite end of town from the station, the walk is not excessively long (about 25 minutes). Head south on the avenue Talbot and then, near the end, jog a little east and continue south again on La Cavalerie, which turns into the rue Voltaire and leads into Arles' Arena. Continue south, at the other end of the Arena, on the rue Porte de Laure, which leads into the Jardin d'Été. The market is at the south end of this garden.

Tourist Office: 04-90-18-41-20

WHEN I FIRST saw Arles, I understood what people mean when they talk about the light of Provence that so inspired the impressionist painters, such as van Gogh, who came here. Arles has an especially luminous quality, which makes its Roman ruins and its center seem almost disturbingly languid and dreamlike. Even though it has modern shops and streets, Arles feels like a place from the past, bypassed by modern civilization. There is some truth to that impression. Arles was the center of the region during the Roman empire and was also an important town during the Middle Ages. However, in the last couple of centuries it has enjoyed a less prominent position.

Arles is, of course, famous for its large arena, dating from 46 B.C. and accommodating up to 20,000 spectators. Arles is also a center of Provençal folk history; Frédéric Mistral, the great promoter of that tradition, established the Museon Arlaten—the museum celebrating the culture and traditions of this region—here at the end of the 19th century. When people speak of the heritage and culture of Provence, Arles is perhaps the place that most often comes to mind.

THE MARKET

The Arles *brocante* market, which takes place on the first Wednesday of every month along the boulevard des Lices, is interesting to visit, for both collectors and general tourists. While not as picturesque as one might have hoped, its location is not altogether bad either. Although the boulevard des Lices is a busy street and not particularly scenic, the market is bordered on the north by the tranquil Jardin d'Été, which links up with the Théâtre Antique and the Arena itself. There is a nice slow-moving feel here, as there is generally in Arles.

About 80 to 100 vendors set up their wares at this fairly, but not excessively, high-end market. One time when I was here with my adolescent daughter (who usually accompanies me unwillingly, if at all, to these markets), I asked what she found special or noteworthy about this one. Her reply was swift: antique clothing and fabrics, she said, as she rifled eagerly through the racks and racks of surprisingly contemporary-looking black vests and jackets, crisp white blouses, and elegant skirts. You will also find a lot of lace (at prices that seemed high to me), as well as linens and many accessories, such underskirts, sashes, parasols, hats, and hat pins. Anyone interested in antique fabrics and traditional costumes would find this great place to explore.

But many other things are sold at the Arles market. You will see Provençal ceramics, old toys, scientific implements, antique books, household items, and some furniture. Prices are moderate to expensive, although I noticed a few stalls where prices were more reasonable.

OTHER THINGS TO DO

If you want to learn more about Provençal culture and lifestyle, be sure to visit the Museon Arlaten, at 29 rue de la République, just a few minutes' walk from the flea market. (Open daily, except closed on Monday from September to May. Hours from September to March are 9:30 A.M. to 12:30 P.M., and 2 P.M. to 5 P.M.; hours are the same, except until 6 P.M., in April and May; and from 9:30 A.M. to 1 P.M. and 2 P.M. to 6:30 P.M. from June to August. Phone: 04-90-96-08-23.). Here you will find an impressive collection of Arlesian costumes and headdresses, tools, kitchen implements, Provençal furniture—*radassiés* (or rush-seated benches), fine armoires, and *panetières* (for storing bread)—and even a *cabane de gardien,* or herdsman's cottage, from the Camargue region south of Arles.

You may also want to check out the colorful food and general market around the corner from the flea market, on the boulevard Émile Combes. Another, larger general market takes place in this part of town on Saturday mornings, where 15 or so *brocante* vendors also come to sell their wares.

For a delicious, regional, and reasonably priced lunch, try Le Vaccarès, at 9 rue Favorin (04-90-96-06-17), overlooking the pretty place du Forum. Try to get a table out on the flower-bedecked balcony.

If you are leaving Arles and heading in a northerly direction, you might want stop in at St-Rémy-de-Provence, to the northeast. Although it does not boast a regular flea market to speak of, St-Rémy has lots of interesting antique and *brocante* shops to explore. If you plan your route right, you will pass some wonderful sights along the way—the windmill immortalized by Alphonse Daudet in *Les Lettres de mon Moulin* (Letters from My Windmill), in Fontvieille; the eerie, fortified medieval village of Les Baux; and on the edge of St-Rémy, the ruins of the ancient city of Glanum, Les Antiques (the arch and mausoleum built by the Romans), and the monastery where van Gogh spent a year for treatment at the end of the 1880s.

If you are in St-Rémy around midday, stop for a really enjoyable and affordable lunch at Le Bistrot des Alpilles (04-90-92-09-17), located at 15 boulevard Mirabeau, the ring road that circles the town. The decor is warm and appealing; the food is also very good, with, as the specialty, leg of lamb hung to cook over a wood fire.

Tarascon, just west of St-Rémy and north of Arles, is the home of the famous Provençal fabric and design company Souleiado. If you are going to be in this region for any length of time, you should make an appointment to visit this company's impressive museum of Provençal fabrics and culture (see Nîmes, "Other Things to Do," below).

The walled, medieval town of Aigues-Mortes, not far southwest of Arles, has periodically had an all-day Saturday flea market during the summer. To check to see if is on, call Aigues-Mortes' tourist office at 04-66-53-73-00.

AVIGNON (Sunday morning)

No. of Vendors: 100
Price/Quality Range: ✦ – ✦✦
Scenic Value: ✦✦
Amenities Nearby: ✦✦

Featured Items: Kitchenware, tools, hardware, books, records, secondhand clothing

WHEN, WHERE, HOW: A flea market is held on Sunday mornings, from 6 A.M. to 12:30 P.M., at the place des Carmes in the center of Avignon. If arriving by car, park for free just outside the ramparts (at the eastern end), at the Porte St-Lazare, and walk the short distance to the *place* along the rue Carreterie.

If arriving by train, the market is about a 25-to-30-minute walk northeast from the train station, through the center of Avignon. Go north up the cours Jean-Jaurès, which becomes the rue de la République, to the rue des Marchands (near the Hôtel de Ville). Head east on the rue des Marchands to the place Carnot and then continue east on the rue Carnot, which becomes the rue Portail Mathéron and leads into the place des Carmes.

Tourist Office: 04-90-82-65-11

UNLIKE AIX-EN-PROVENCE not far to the east, Avignon gets a lukewarm reaction from some people. I confess that it's not my favorite place; I find it somewhat cramped and claustrophobic. The 14th-century ramparts surrounding the city, while impressive, effectively confine the center to a rather small area. Traffic is busy and there is not much green space to speak of. Avignon also feels a little too coldly bourgeois to me; indeed, its most lively period seems to have been during the 14th century when the popes were in residence and built the remarkable Palais des Papes.

Apart from the principal streets and squares, the city is not a very festive place; it is also much more appealing during the day than at night. After dark, you get the feeling that the business and professional class prefers the privacy it finds behind massive wooden doors framing the imposing stone buildings along Avignon's narrow streets. During the daytime, however, Avignon has a much lighter feel, with shoppers filling the rue de la République and the surrounding pedestrian areas and people relaxing in the large outdoor cafés of the place de l'Horloge.

THE MARKET

There is one regular flea market in Avignon proper, which takes place on Sunday mornings at the place des Carmes. This small square, lined with plane trees, is dominated by a large church in the center. (You can see people arriving for mass as you browse through the market.) About 100 vendors crowd the square, selling generally low-end junk interspersed with some real collectibles. You will find secondhand clothes, linens, books, old records, hardware, tools, kitchenware, etc. I would rank the quality of the things for sale here as a slight step up from the Sunday markets of Jonquières and Mornas to the north, but well below the Saturday market in nearby Villeneuve-lès-Avignon. For a city of the size and renown of Avignon, this is a somewhat disappointing market.

I have, however, occasionally found something nice here—for example, a

Quimper dish complete with lid, in good condition, for 100 francs, and a French ivory brush for 10 francs. As with low-end markets generally, it's a question of hit-and-miss. The advantage is that, when you do find something, it is often quite inexpensive. Bargaining is welcomed, and since most vendors seem to be here casually, you can often be quite successful in haggling.

While bargain hunters will be somewhat interested in this market, not much is here to appeal to either serious collectors or general tourists. The market is not located in a particularly nice part of Avignon, and the cafés nearby are not inviting.

OTHER THINGS TO DO

On Sunday, there are a number of other interesting flea markets to visit in the vicinity of Avignon. Avid bargain hunters should try to take in the down-to-earth markets in Jonquières and Mornas, to the north (see Jonquières, below). General tourists and collectors of more high-end objects should head instead for L'Îsle-sur-la-Sorgue, about 25 kilometers to the east, which has, on Sunday, an impressive, although not large, all-day flea market, and a lively morning food (and general) market (see L'Îsle-sur-la-Sorgue, below). If it's the second Sunday of the month (from April to September), stop in at Le Thor's all-day flea market.

If you have no car, or all of this sounds a little daunting after visiting Avignon's flea market, you could simply head over to the popular place de l'Horloge for a drink, followed by a Vietnamese meal in the pedestrian streets just behind.

If you are in Avignon on a Saturday morning, be sure to get to Villeneuve-lès-Avignon's flea market, just across the Rhône River. This substantial, eclectic market is one of my favorites in France. There is also a Saturday-morning junk market in Montfavet, just east of the center of Avignon. (Both markets are described in Villeneuve-lès-Avignon, below.)

L'ÎSLE-SUR-LA-SORGUE (Sunday)

No. of Vendors: 40
Price/Quality Range: ✦✦✦
Scenic Value: ✦✦ – ✦✦✦
Amenities Nearby: ✦✦✦

Featured Items: Ceramics, paintings, garden ware, Provençal fabrics and quilts, linens, books, kitchenware, silver, some furniture, rustic items generally

WHEN, WHERE, HOW: L'Îsle-sur-la-Sorgue has an all-day *brocante* market, from 9 A.M. to 7 P.M., every Sunday along the avenue des 4 Otages. Parking is difficult to find, but you should be able to get a spot on one of the side streets nearby.

Tourist Office: 04-90-38-04-78

L'ÎSLE-SUR-LA-SORGUE is synonymous with *brocante,* not only in Provence but also elsewhere in France. This town has many antique stores, as well as *brocante* malls housing several dealers. In recent years, the antiques and collectibles business has become a big part of the local economy, helping to fill a void left long ago by a once-thriving leather and textile industry. At one time, the waters of the Sorgue River provided power for these industries, but essentially all that is left from that era (at least to the tourist's eye) are the moss-covered wheels that still slowly turn with the flow of the river.

I really like this town, in large part because it is one of the few places in this dry region that has actual grass and streams running through it. Several branches of the Sorgue, whose source is in Fontaine-de-Vaucluse nearby, meander through the town, providing pleasant spots for café lounging.

THE MARKET

The Sorgue River also provides a perfect backdrop to the Sunday *brocante* market, which takes place along the water's edge beside the avenue des 4 Otages. With about 40 vendors, this is not a large market, but it is a good one. The things for sale, while not inexpensive, are of high quality. Conspicuously absent here are stalls piled indiscriminately with odds and ends for you to rifle through, which you find at so many of the markets in Provence.

You will see many regional items, such as colorful Provençal quilts, rustic Provençal furniture, ceramics, linens, baskets, tools, and *boules.* You will also find collectibles from elsewhere in France, such as paintings, silver, old books and prints, café tables and chairs, wrought-iron ware, weights, coffee mills, enamelware, advertising items, and porcelain. Everything is tastefully displayed and in pristine condition.

People in this town are accustomed to foreigners, and you may find that some of the vendors speak quite good English. They will bargain somewhat, although one gets the impression that they are not desperate to make a sale. Indeed, they sometimes appear rather uninterested in the proceedings, which makes browsing quite stress-free. I have not bought much here; one purchase that stands out was a wonderful circular hooked rug of a gentleman leisurely smoking a cigarette, for 75 francs.

OTHER THINGS TO DO

After you visit the *brocante* market, you can take in some of the many antique and *brocante* stores in the vicinity, in the so-called antiques villages. If it's still morning, take advantage of the giant food and general market here then; next to Vaison-la-Romaine's Tuesday market, it is my favorite in Provence. After all this, sit down for a drink and a snack at the pleasant fin de siècle Café de France, located in the central place de l'Église. You will feel that your visit to L'Îsle-sur-la-Sorgue was well worth it, especially on a hot summer day when the town seems like a lush oasis.

If you want a quiet and relaxed lunch deep in the Provençal countryside, try the Auberge du Beaucet (04-90-66-10-82), about 25 kilometers north of L'Îsle-sur-la-Sorgue in the tiny, out-of-the-way village of Le Beaucet. If you are then in the mood for a little side trip, join the French in a classic Sunday-afternoon activity and make the short expedition to Fontaine-de-Vaucluse (about six kilometers from L'Îsle-sur-la-Sorgue) to see the strange fissure in the cliff from which the Sorgue River flows. Visit the Musée des Restrictions (the Resistance museum), which opened a few years ago. Apart from informing you about the Vichy period in France and the Resistance, the museum's displays show objects of everyday life from the period, which will be of interest to collectors as well as history buffs.

If you want to see another market, and it's the second Sunday of the month between April and September, Le Thor, just a few kilometers west of L'Îsle-sur-la-Sorgue, has an all-day flea market then.

JONQUIÈRES (Sunday morning)

No. of Vendors: 100 to 150
Price/Quality Range: ✦ – ✦✦
Scenic Value: ✦
Amenities Nearby: ✦

Featured Items: Rustic items, tools, hardware, kitchenware, secondhand clothing, some furniture

WHEN, WHERE, HOW: This market takes place every Sunday morning, from 6 A.M. to 1 P.M., about two kilometers west of Jonquières, on the D950 to Orange. If coming from the east, you will see the market in a large, flat field to your left. Parking is available on-site for 10 francs. Do not park on the side of the road, as you will be ticketed.

Other Markets Described: Mornas (Sunday morning)
Tourist Office: 04-90-34-70-88 (Orange)

JONQUIÈRES, LOCATED IN the Rhône valley to the northeast of Avignon and just southeast of Orange, is not a pretty town. Indeed, it often does not appear in tour books of this region. I have come to love Jonquières, though, because one of my favorite junk markets in France is located here.

The Jonquières flea market is actually a few minutes' drive west of town, and while not scenic either, it is lively. You will know when you have reached the market site—which consists of a large, flat paved area next to a hangar-like building—by the cars lining the side of the road or waiting to turn into the parking lot.

THE MARKET

I am a big fan of this market, despite its definitely grimy qualities. I would come here every Sunday morning, whatever the weather, during the years that I lived in this region. In the early morning, a friend and I would leave our little village, the Mont Ventoux looming like a giant black figure behind us as we traveled west past Vaison-la-Romaine toward the Rhône. In the distance we would spot the lights of other cars heading, like us, to the Jonquières market.

You will find between 100 and 150 vendors here, with fewer on cold winter days or during a bad mistral. There may also be slightly fewer now than a few years ago, as more of the space is occupied by a lively North African food market. The flea market vendors set up before dawn under the roof of the hangarlike building close to the road and along a number of rows outside. Their wares are laid out on blankets on the ground, piled in baskets and boxes, or displayed on makeshift tables.

If you are an eclectic collector and a bargain hunter, you will find the Jonquières market fun, fun, fun. This is one of those places that are really properly called a junk market. Even the expression "everything but the kitchen sink" would not be apt, since you will find the kitchen sink here as well, just as you will find rusted tools, cracked pots, beekeeping equipment, old bikes, snorkeling gear, comic books, and Michael Jackson CDs. You name it, one day or another you will see it here.

But the greatness of this place is that you may also come across (as my friends and I have) wooden African sculptures, giant earthenware pots, Quimper vases, Japanese cooking pots, beautifully decorated nail-studded *boules,* valuable old prints and maps, traditional Provençal fabrics, and primitive wooden toys. And sometimes you will find these great treasures at really good prices; it's just a matter of luck and persistence, as well as of being willing to wade through what can only be described as a lot of junk. If you arrive before dawn, you will see dealers, and others, doing just that, armed with flashlights to inspect the goods as vendors unload their trucks.

The Jonquières market is a great place for those with no idea what they want to collect, except a vague notion that they like old everyday French objects of various kinds. This is where I first learned about wooden coffee mills in all shapes and sizes, farmers' baskets, wrought-iron plant stands and garden accessories, handblown glasses, pitchers with advertising for pastis and Ricard, wooden *quilles* (or toy pins), clay marbles, *fèves* (the little figures hidden in the *galettes des rois* during Epiphany), pale yellow terrines, decorated with lions' heads for storing foie gras, etc. You will spot a little treasure that you've never seen before, decide that you like it, and from then on pursue collecting it with a passion.

The atmosphere is laid-back and easygoing. Some vendors just seem to be ordinary folks who have come to unload the contents of their *greniers* and are enjoying themselves doing it. Bargaining is a big part of the scene; I have friends who argue strenuously that one must haggle as a matter of principle, even if the price seems eminently reasonable, just to ensure that Jonquières retains its character.

And prices are low. You should make sure to have lots of change with you here, because you will see things for as little as 5 or 10 francs. The more serious problem you may encounter is finding someone who can give you change. A friend has picked up beautiful old handblown glasses, and Steiff stuffed animals, for 5 francs. I have bought large, old baskets for 10 francs, wrought-iron garden-pot stands for 10 francs, old terra-cotta pots for 5 francs, a very old polka-dotted jug for 20 francs, nail-studded *boules* for between 30 and 50 francs, and a beautiful large wooden milk jug, in tarnished shades of green and yellow, for 80 francs. Although vendors do not usually speak much English, they are accustomed to foreigners and generally very friendly.

If your interest in markets is primarily as a tourist and you prefer aesthetically pleasing spots, this is likely not the place for you. Coming here could well disabuse you of any notion that all of Provence is picturesque and quaintly rustic. On the other hand, the Jonquières market is an adventure that will certainly give you an insight into a different aspect of life in this region.

OTHER THINGS TO DO

If the Jonquières market has whetted your appetite for the less polished side of Provence, then you may want to continue on and take in the Mornas flea market, along the N7, just south of Mornas and north of Orange. This market, also on Sunday morning, is perhaps even more down-to-earth than Jon-quières. You will find around 100 vendors here—seemingly, mostly people trying to make a little cash selling their old belongings, which may include a treasure for you. The prices, especially for old kitchenware, tools, and rustic items generally, are rock-bottom. I paid 5 francs for some dishes here that I had seen for 40 francs at Villeneuve-lès-Avignon. I also saw beautiful old seltzer bottles in lovely shades of green and blue—and going for 250 to 400 francs elsewhere in France—for 100 to 150 francs.

Like Jonquières, the Mornas market is for true bargain hunters and collectors of modest, everyday, and rustic objects. This is definitely not the kind of place for people looking for antiques, or for general tourists who want to browse through beautiful markets offering good photo opportunities.

You will probably be ravenous after visiting both the Jonquières and Mornas markets, and you will also likely feel that your budget has not been much challenged. Rectify this by treating yourself to a great lunch at La Beaugravière (04-90-40-82-54), a much underrated restaurant a few kilometers north of Mornas on the N7, just south of Mondragon. This place is a favorite haunt not only of mine, but of the celebrated restaurant reviewer and writer Patricia Wells, and the vignerons in the area. The reasons are the regional specialties—lamb is always a good choice here as are any dishes with fresh truffles (available in winter)—and the extraordinary Rhône wine list. The service is also impeccable. If you speak French, take the opportunity to talk with the chef, Guy Jullien. This impassioned man may speak to you in apocalyptic tones about the imminent, if not completed, demise of French produce and cuisine. Whether or not you agree—and I don't see how you can since you've just finished one of his fine meals—you will find him fascinating. This restaurant is open for Sunday lunch, but not dinner, so plan your day accordingly.

If it happens to be the third Sunday of the month, consider also going to Vaison-la-Romaine to see its all-day *brocante* market in the place Montfort in the center of town. Vaison-la-Romaine is, in many respects, the quintessential Provençal town. Tourists flock here, perhaps because it manages to retain a reassuringly staid and tranquil feel (despite the fact that a devastating flood wreaked havoc here in September 1992, tragically killing a number of people). The town's huge Tuesday-morning food and general market is my favorite in Provence. If you are in the area for a little while, and you like ceramics, I highly recommend a visit to the pottery studio of Martine Gilles, in the tiny mountainside village of Brantes, along the rugged Vallée de Toulourenc. The faience ware here is beautifully decorated and very whimsical. Call ahead, though, to avoid disappointment (04-75-28-03-37).

MARSEILLE (Sunday morning)
(second Sunday of the month)

AVENUE CAP PINÈDE
  No. of Vendors: 120
  Price/Quality Range: ✤ – ✤✤
  Scenic Value: ✤
  Amenities Nearby: ✤ – ✤✤

  Featured Items: Tools, hardware, kitchenware, old toys, secondhand clothes, North African objects, marine items

COURS JULIEN
  No. of Vendors: 30
  Price/Quality Range: ✤✤ – ✤✤✤
  Scenic Value: ✤✤ – ✤✤✤
  Amenities Nearby: ✤✤ – ✤✤✤

  Featured Items: Books, linens, kitchenware, ceramics, vases, some advertising items

WHEN, WHERE, HOW: There are two regular flea markets in Marseille—one on Sunday morning, from around 5 A.M. to 1 P.M., at the avenue Cap Pinède, and the other on the second Sunday of the month, all day from 8 A.M. to 6 P.M., along the cours Julien in the sixth arrondissement.

The avenue Cap Pinède market is located in the north end of the city, close to the coast. If arriving by car from the center of Marseille, take the Autoroute du Littoral to the St-Louis exit. Veer to the right at the exit and you will soon see cars parked on both sides of the road. Follow suit if you can; parking at this market is limited. If you have no car, you can take #35 bus from the Vieux Port; from the train station take metro line 2, direction Bougainville, and get off at Joliette, and then take #35 bus.

The cours Julien market is in the center of town, southeast of the Vieux Port. It is also south of the train station, the gare St-Charles; from the south end of the station, head south along the boulevard d'Athènes (which becomes the boulevard Dugommier and then the boulevard Garthaldi, after crossing La Canebière). Just past La Canebière, turn left at the rue des 3 Mages, and on your right you will see the cours Julien, which, a little farther along, is the site of the market. On the metro, the closest stop is Notre-Dame-du-Mont, cours Julien, which will drop you right by the market; also nearby is the Nouailles metro stop.

Tourist Office: 04-91-13-89-00

MARSEILLE IS ONE place in France about which opinions are sharply divided. It has been described as both scruffy and appealing, rough and charming. While perhaps not a big tourist attraction, Marseille is a significant cross-roads of many cultures and traditions. This port city (first called Massalia by the Greeks who founded it) has been an important trading center since around 500 B.C.

Architecturally, Marseille is not brilliant, although its Vieux Port, the hub of the city, is colorful and lively, filled with outdoor cafés overlooking the pleasure boats in the harbor. Corny as it may seem, the city's populace, rather than its appearance, is credited as its greatest asset. The people of Marseille have a reputation for vigor, charm, generosity, and expansiveness. (I have to say that the few I have met absolutely conform to that stereotype.) Interestingly, the French national anthem, "La Marseillaise," was named after a group of Marseille volunteers supporting the French Revolution who marched from the Rhine to Paris in 1792 singing this song.

This is a place of high passions, perhaps especially when it comes to soc-cer. The Olympiques de Marseille, the city's team, is revered here, as are the city's legendary soccer stars, such as Zinedine Zidane, who contributed so much to France's recent World Cup victory.

AVENUE CAP PINÈDE MARKET

Even the most intrepid flea marketers may feel, at first, that they may have pushed the envelope a little too far when they visit the avenue Cap Pinède market, held on Sunday mornings (starting very early) in the north end of the city. My spouse and I got off to an inauspicious start here. Not knowing exactly where to go, we headed instinctively for the Vieux Port and started to ask directions from there. We got our first insight into this market when we stopped to ask an elderly gentleman the way. He looked us up and down, glanced at our rental car, then said, "You don't want to go there, *madame*. It is not a place for you." When I persisted and showed him a few pictures I had of the market, he shook his head and responded, "You think you are going to find charming little knick-knacks there, *madame*, but you are wrong. What you are showing me is not real, it is just cinema. The reality is quite different."

I was a litle concerned by this, but insisted that I was going to the market anyway. (My spouse, on the other hand, was much amused, openly cheering on our new friend.) The gentleman reluctantly gave us the directions, but added, "You will never find a parking space. You must not take a purse with you, and you should leave nothing visible in your car. We Marseillais are ashamed of our city, *madame.*" With that, off we went; I was a little shaken, perhaps, but determined.

It turned out that most of what we were told was an exaggeration, although not all of it. This market is, if not the most nitty-gritty of those I have been to in France, certainly right up there. There's also no question that finding a parking place here is extremely challenging, even creative. We managed to park rather precariously on top of the median of the road (as many others were doing), but I don't recommend it, at least if you don't relish damaging the underside of your car.

Off I then went to see the flea market, which is part of a giant general market of just about everything, from cheap shoes and brightly colored fabrics to pizza and North African food. It is a hectic scene. You are simply caught up in the momentum of people weaving their way along the jammed rows, and off you head in directions that are not entirely of your choosing.

The flea market part of the market is not instantly identifiable in this crush of produce and humanity. It is, however, centered around a large hangarlike building in the middle of the market space, housing about 40 dealers of *brocante* of all kinds. These dealers are joined on Sunday mornings, starting very early, by a large group of casual vendors who set up around the building's periphery, usually simply spilling their wares onto a blanket on the ground or tossing them indiscriminately into cartons.

Many of the things for sale outside here are pure junk. Presentation is also clearly not a big concern. Rusted tools are mixed in with old chipped dishes, with a few broken wooden toys thrown in for good measure. But there are exceptions, and that is what will appeal to the true bargain hunter who doesn't mind a little grime. Also, if you do find something interesting in amongst all this, it probably won't be very expensive. Some vendors (mostly in front of the entrance to the building) sell better-quality goods, but their prices are, not surprisingly, higher.

This is definitely not a flea market for most visitors; it's not scenic, it's not in a beautiful part of town, and it is pretty hectic. If none of that deters you, I have just two bits of advice: first, don't carry a purse with you (instead, put some cash in your pocket or in a pouch around your neck), and second, do not carry a camera, as attempts to take photos here are likely to be negatively received.

COURS JULIEN MARKET

The monthly *brocante* market on the cours Julien (held all day on the second Sunday of the month) is in stark contrast to the avenue Cap Pinède scene. The cours Julien is a trendy, upscale spot, in the center of town not far from the Vieux Port. Little pools and fountains decorate the center of this lively street, lined with interesting restaurants, boutiques, and outdoor cafés.

The *brocante* market here is, sadly, not large, but satisfying enough if you combine it with a browse through the numerous antique and brocante stores that are also to be found in the vicinity. Around 30 vendors set up here, selling such things as books, ceramics, jewelry, and household items of different sorts. I was somewhat surprised by the moderate price of some of the wares. While I would not go out of my way to come to this market because of its modest size, if you are in the vicinity on the second Sunday of the month, this would be a pleasant way to spend some time.

OTHER THINGS TO DO

You may well feel inclined to head out of town after seeing Marseille's flea markets. However, before doing so, you must at least have a drink at one of the cafés in the Vieux Port. If you'd like to visit a seaside town of a much more manageable scale, I highly recommend Cassis, about 30 kilometers southeast of Marseille on the D559. This still-unspoiled town's port, surrounded by high hills on either side, has lots of outdoor restaurants for sampling some bouillabaisse, the traditional Mediterranean fish soup, while watching the boats head out to sea.

NÎMES (Monday)

No. of Vendors: 80
Price/Quality Range: ✦✦✦
Scenic Value: ✦ – ✦✦
Amenities Nearby: ✦✦

Featured Items: Ceramics, furniture, Provençal linens, kitchenware, rustic items generally

WHEN, WHERE, HOW: The Nîmes *brocante* market is held all day on Monday, from 8 A.M. to 6 P.M. (although many vendors leave at noon). It takes place along the avenue Jean Jaurès in the western part of town. If arriving by car, you can find meter parking on the street nearby.

If arriving by train, Nîmes' train station, in the eastern part of town, is within walking distance of the market. From the station, take the avenue Feuchères northwest to the esplanade Charles de Gaulle and the Arena beyond. From the Arena, continue west, past the rue Porte de France, until you reach the avenue Jean Jaurès, the site of the market.

Tourist Office: 04-66-67-29-11

NÎMES IS BEST known for its impressive Roman ruins, particularly its beautifully proportioned Maison Carrée temple and its well-preserved arena, built
after the slightly larger one in Arles. Several centuries ago, the Arena became
the site of a tenement, housing a couple of thousand people, a situation that
continued until it was finally removed around the beginning of the 19th
century.

Nîmes is also known as a textiles center, and is credited as the place in
which denim originated; this fabric "de Nîmes" was apparently exported in
the 19th century to the United States. In recent years, this down-to-earth and
bustling city has vigorously attempted to promote itself and its industries and
has been waging a battle to compete with its larger, and more elegant, rival to
the southwest, Montpellier.

Although it is located west of the Rhône River and thus technically falls
within the geographic area of Languedoc rather than Provence, I am including Nîmes in the Provence chapter, as travel guides often do. Apart
from reasons of proximity, in many ways Nîmes really feels more like a
Provençal town.

THE MARKET

Monday is an unusual day for *brocante* markets, but that is when Nîmes' is
held. This market, which, theoretically, continues all day (many vendors
actually pack up around noon), takes place in the space along the middle of
the avenue Jean Jaurès at the western end of the city. The location is not picturesque, but it is spacious and shaded by some large trees. The one disad-
vantage is the mistral, which can blow fiercely here, making life difficult for
vendors and visitors alike.

This is a quite interesting *brocante* market, and good-sized as well, with
about 80 vendors. It is one of the better places for Provençal and rustic
objects of all sorts. You will see colorful Provençal quilts and fabrics,
Provençal ceramics, rustic furniture, old wooden clogs, wrought-iron ware,
and tools. Many other general collectibles are also to be found—glassware,
enamelware, chocolate molds, linens, etc. Prices are not particularly low, but
not terribly high either.

I would certainly recommend this market to collectors, particularly those
looking for rustic items of all kinds. It would also be of some interest to general tourists, giving them an idea about everyday objects of French rural life
from decades past. However, since this is not a good place for café-sitting,
once you've finished here, head to the center of town by the Arena. On the
boulevard Victor Hugo, the boulevard de la Libération, and the boulevard
Amiral Courbet, you will find lots of congenial cafés and restaurants.

OTHER THINGS TO DO

If you are in the vicinity of Nîmes on Sunday, and you are a true bargain hunter, you might want to have a look at the flea market that is held in the parking lot of the Nîmes stadium. For those traveling through, this market—which has about 80 vendors—is conveniently located right beside the A9 autoroute to Montpellier. Montpellier, about 55 kilometers southwest of Nîmes, has its own enormous flea market on Sunday mornings, which is featured in the chapter on the markets of Languedoc-Roussillon.

Those interested in Provençal fabrics will want to head east from Nîmes to Tarascon, just across the Rhône. While a rather forlorn-looking town, Tarascon is the headquarters of the renowned Souleiado company, which specializes in high-quality Provençal fabrics (called *indiennes*), clothing, and household items. Souleiado, at 39 rue Proudhon, has its own museum, the Musée Charles Deméry, where you will see fine examples of traditional Provençal quilts, and the wooden blocks once used to make the fabric's prints, as well as a wonderful collection of Provençal ceramics and household items. Visits are guided and can be arranged ahead of time by phoning the Tarascon office (at 04-90-91-08-80).

Also, for those interested in pottery, not far north of Nîmes is the town of Uzès, famous for its long ceramics tradition. Two members of the Pichon family (which is known, among other things, for its signature *corbeilles tressées,* or braided baskets, and lovely pale-colored dishes with scalloped edges) have shops here—Véronique Pichon, with two stores across from each other on the rue Jacques d'Uzès, and Jean-Paul Pichon, who has a shop on the rue St-Étienne (although when I was here, a sign on the window referred visitors to another location just outside town). A few kilometers farther north is another town long renowned for its ceramics, St-Quentin-la-Poterie.

If you are driving around in this area, be sure to plan your route so as to take in the Pont du Gard, to the northeast of Nîmes. The Pont du Gard is the extraordinary bridge built by the Romans almost 2,000 years ago as part of a 50-kilometer-long aqueduct to bring water to Nîmes.

VILLENEUVE-LÈS-AVIGNON (Saturday morning)

No. of Vendors: 80 to 100
Price/Quality Range: ✦✦ – ✦✦✦
Scenic Value: ✦✦
Amenities Nearby: ✦ – ✦✦

Featured Items: Furniture, ceramics, tools, hardware, kitchenware, glassware, militaria, rustic items generally

WHEN, WHERE, HOW: The Villeneuve-lès-Avignon market is held every Saturday morning, from 6 A.M. to 2 P.M., across the Rhône River from Avignon, in the place C. David (also called the place du Marché), alongside the avenue de Verdun. Parking is available across from the market. If you have no car, take the short trip by taxi from Avignon, or take bus #11, which leaves regularly from the post office near the Avignon train station.

Other Markets Described: Montfavet (Saturday morning)
Tourist Office: 04-90-25-61-33

"VILLENEUVE-LÈS-AVIGNON" means "Villeneuvene near Avignon," which is what this place is, albeit separated from its larger neighbor by the Rhône River. During the late Middle Ages, Villeneuve was a fortress town, when the Rhône was the boundary between Provence and papal areas, on the east, and the territories of the French monarchs on the west. Even then, Villeneuve-lès-Avignon served as a bedroom community; cardinals from Avignon, home of the papacy during this time, were permitted to build their villas in this quiet spot, giving it the nickname City of the Cardinals. Today, this town remains a bit of a haven from Avignon's crowded scene.

Although, like Nîmes, Villeneuve-lès-Avignon technically falls into the geographic area of Languedoc rather than Provence, I am including its market in this chapter, given the town's close proximity and ties to Avignon and to Provence.

THE MARKET

Some *brocante* markets are geared to collectors of decorative objects, while others may appeal to bargain hunters, history buffs, furniture lovers, or rustic types. Few markets manage to embrace all of these groups. The *brocante* market at Villeneuve-lès-Avignon, although not especially large, is such a place; it is also one of my favorite markets in France.

When I was living near Vaison-la-Romaine, I used to come to this market every Saturday morning—a bit of a testimony to its interest, since the drive was about an hour each way. The market is located in the place Charles David just below the town's fort. You are reminded of this every once in a while when you take a break from intense browsing and gaze up at a little bit of medieval France above. The location is spacious and feels quite removed from the hustle and bustle of nearby Avignon.

The market is moderately large, with between 80 and 100 vendors, both casual and more serious. It has a pleasant, laid-back atmosphere. People stroll along, sometimes sitting down at a little snack bar at the end of the market for a coffee. There is not much shade, which is usually not a problem, although it can be somewhat brutal on hot, sunny days. The only real drawback is the mistral; the market seems to be right in this wind's path (as are many places along the Rhône River), which can make this feel like a chilly place on a windy winter morning. I have been here on occasions when gusts have wreaked momentary havoc on tables displaying dishes and glassware.

You will find just about everything here—rustic furniture, old toys, art deco ware, military memorabilia, stamps, coins, scientific implements, pharmaceutical items, hardware, weights, Provençal ceramics, linens, *santons, boules,* farm tools, glassware, kitchenware, books, etc. While the location of the various things in this market is not fixed, you will generally find furniture and larger objects along the back row against the hillside, glassware and porcelain along the row next to the street, and all of the other things interspersed throughout the *place.* There is a nice mix of vendors specializing in particular collectibles and those with a pile of things laid out on the ground for you to forage through.

Prices run the gamut from low to moderate to moderately high, and bargaining is expected. Some of my most prized collectibles were bought here at quite reasonable prices—*boules,* at between 20 and 50 francs, a lovely art deco pitcher for 40 francs, little Depression-era glass bowls in pastel colors and with scalloped edges for 5 francs each, a porcelain plate bearing the picture of Marshal Pétain (from the dark days of Vichy France) for 40 francs, a little wooden stool for 30 francs, and a wooden toy, composed of a row of movable candles, in descending sizes, for 40 francs. Most of the year, the market is frequented essentially by people from Avignon and the surrounding area. However, during the summer months, when Provence is really thick with tourists, you will notice many foreigners, and prices will tend to be a little higher. While vendors generally speak little English, they are usually very gracious and will make every effort to communicate with you if your French is not great.

OTHER THINGS TO DO

If you have some time left in your Saturday morning after visiting the Villeneuve-lès-Avignon market, you might also want to take a look at a market of a very different sort, in Montfavet, an exurban community just east of

Avignon. This is really more like a giant garage sale than a *brocante* market, with most of the things for sale piled haphazardly on blankets on the ground or spilling from crates.

With between 75 and 100 vendors, this very low-end market will not be to everyone's taste. However, I like to come because here you can find, at extremely low prices, such things as kitchenware from the 1940s and 1950s, rustic farm implements, and garden tools. The best find I ever made here was a large nail-studded *boule,* dating from the late 19th century. If you are not a serious bargain hunter, however, this market is likely not for you, and you might find your time better spent, for example, in heading north from Villeneuve-lès-Avignon to visit the vineyards of Châteauneuf-du-Pape.

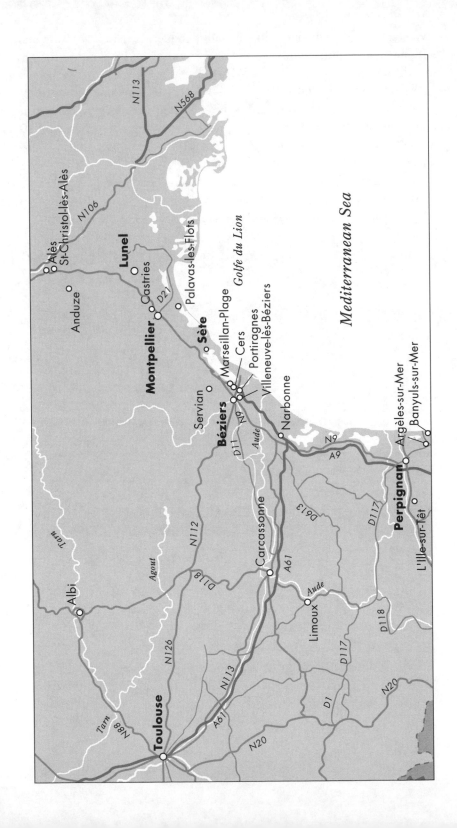

The Flea Markets of Languedoc-Roussillon

Tuesday ARGÈLES-SUR-MER (Parking des Platanes) [40 vendors]
(mid-June to mid-September)
(8 A.M. to noon)

Thursday NARBONNE (pl. Voltaire) [12 vendors]
(8 A.M. to noon)

Friday BANYULS-SUR-MER (Allées Maillol) [30 to 40 vendors]
(mid-June to mid-September)
(8 A.M. to noon)

*TOULOUSE (Allées J. Guesde) [140 vendors]
(first Friday, Saturday, and Sunday of month)
(7 A.M. to 7 P.M.)

Saturday ALBI (pl. du Castelvieil) [30 to 40 vendors]
(8 A.M. to noon)

*BÉZIERS (Allées P. Riquet) [60 to 70 vendors]
(first Saturday of month)
(7:30 A.M. to 6 P.M.)

CARCASSONNE (pl. des Jacobins) [25 to 30 vendors]
(third Saturday of month)
(8 A.M. to 6 P.M.)

*LUNEL (pl. des Arènes) [150 to 200 vendors]
(5:30 A.M. to 12:30 P.M.)

PALAVAS-LES-FLOTS (Parking des Avenues) [200 vendors]
(6:30 A.M. to 1 P.M. in summer; 6:30 A.M. to 5 P.M. other times
of year)

*PERPIGNAN (promenade des Platanes) [30 to 40 vendors]
(8 A.M. to 6 P.M.)

ST-CHRISTOL-LÈS-ALÈS (pl. de la Mairie) [100 vendors]
(6 A.M. to noon)

SERVIAN (Z.I. La Baume) [80 vendors]
(7 A.M. to 5 P.M., but most vendors leave by noon)

*TOULOUSE (Allées J. Guesde) [140 vendors]
(first Friday, Saturday, and Sunday of month)
(7 A.M. to 7 P.M.)

*TOULOUSE (pl. St-Sernin) [80 vendors]
(8 A.M. to 1 P.M.)

VILLENEUVE-LÈS-BÉZIERS (pl. Faren) [50 to 80 vendors]
(7 A.M. to 1 P.M.)

Sunday ALÈS (av. Carnot) [150 vendors]
(8 A.M. to 12:30 P.M.)

ALÈS (Gd. Parking 608, rte. d'Uzès) [40 vendors]
(third Sunday of month from April to September)
(7 A.M. to 6 P.M.)

ANDUZE (Parking du C. Cial. Super U.) [50 to 100 vendors]
(7 A.M. to noon)

CASTRIES (Ancienne Gare) [150 vendors] (first Sunday of month)
(7 A.M. to 5 P.M.)

L'ILLE-SUR-TÊT (pl. du Forail) [40 to 60 vendors]
(7 A.M. to 1 P.M.)

LIMOUX (av. de Tivoli) [30 vendors] (first Sunday of month)
(8 A.M. to 6 P.M.)

MARSEILLAN-PLAGE (Cave Coopérative, R.N. 112) [180 vendors]
(6:30 A.M. to 1 P.M. in summer, 6:30 A.M. to 6 P.M. other times
of year)

*MONTPELLIER (Espace Mosson, La Paillade) [500 to 600 vendors]
(6 A.M. to 1:30 P.M.)

PAULHAN (esplanade de la Gare) [20 vendors]
(8 A.M. to 4 P.M.)

PERPIGNAN (av. du Palais des Expositions) [40 to 80 vendors]
(7 A.M. to noon)

PORTIRAGNES (center) [40 to 60 vendors]
(8 A.M. to noon)

*SÈTE (pl. de la République) [280 vendors]
(7 A.M. to 1 P.M.)

*TOULOUSE (Allées J. Guesde) [140 vendors]
(first Friday, Saturday, and Sunday of month)
(9 A.M. to 7 P.M.)

*TOULOUSE (pl. St-Sernin) [80 vendors]
(8:30 A.M. to 1 P.M.)

UZÈS (boul. Gambetta) [12 vendors]
(7 A.M. to 1 P.M.)

VILLENEUVE-LÈS-BÉZIERS (pl. Faren) [50 to 80 vendors]
(7 A.M. to 1 P.M.)

Regional Overview

GETTING ORIENTED: ABOUT THE REGION

In this book, Lanquedoc-Roussillon describes the long, narrow strip of southern France west from the Rhône River to Toulouse, and south to Perpignan near the Spanish border. The term has both a historical and a current meaning, which do not always coincide. For example, while it is outside the present political region of Languedoc-Roussillon, Toulouse (in the Midi-Pyrénées) is the historical capital of Languedoc and a center of its traditional language (called Occitan) and culture. Toulouse is often included in the Languedoc section of guidebooks and is, thus, also dealt with in this chapter. (By contrast, Nîmes, technically part of Languedoc—although on the dividing line with Provence—is often put with Provence, as it is in this book.)

The word *Languedoc* comes from *langue d'oc*, meaning the "language of yes," in the Occitan language. Languedoc was once the center of a large area called Occitania. In the period up to the 10th century it was apparently a more advanced and culturally developed part of the country than the area to the north. Over the last two thousand years, this region has been the subject of occupations by a variety of forces—Phoenicians, Romans (with Narbonne as the capital of a large Roman province), Visigoths, Saracens, Franks, and then for a few hundred years (from the 9th to the 13th century), the counts of Toulouse, renowned for their cultivated society (and their troubadours).

This region has suffered much religious conflict over its history—the suppression of the Cathars (an ascetic movement in opposition to the Church of Rome) in the 13th century, and from the 16th to 18th centuries, struggles with the Huguenots, or French Calvinists. Not until 1787 were persecutions of the Protestants ended, by act of Louis XVI granting them freedom of worship.

Languedoc essentially lost its independence in the middle of the 13th century with the surrender of the counts of Toulouse to France (although parts of Languedoc were then periodically under the control of the Spanish). Then, after the Revolution, its remaining vestiges of separate status were removed and its area broken up into departments.

Writers on the subject attribute much of the independent spirit of the people of this region, and their historical suspicion of the centralizing force of Paris, to the region's turbulent history. This spirit has continued to manifest itself on occasion in this century, particularly on the part of the region's winemakers, who have periodically felt threatened by lower prices and cheap imports.

After the Second World War, the French government set into motion a number of projects to boost and diversify the economy of this region, including a large seaside resort development. These initiatives were not always looked upon favorably by the locals, but resistance to Parisian authority has declined generally over the years, perhaps influenced by the growth and surge in prominence of both Montpellier (the capital of Languedoc-Roussillon) and Nîmes as high-tech, modern cities.

Roussillon (also known as French Catalonia), in the southwest corner of this large region, was historically part of Catalonia, extending from Perpignan to Barcelona. Catalonia first became a force in the 10th century, with the 13th and 14th centuries marking the height of its fortunes. However, a long period of struggles with France followed, and in the middle of the 17th century Roussillon became permanently subject to the rule of France.

Despite centralizing pressures since, a strong sense of Catalan identity remains in this corner of the country. The Catalan language is still spoken by some, and you will also sometimes see the brightly colored Catalan flag being flown. Perpignan is the central city of this part of the region, where the kings of Majorca had their base several centuries ago; the Palais des Rois de Majorque is a major sight in this town.

Languedoc-Roussillon is characterized by sandy beaches, backed by flat expanses of marshy land dotted with lagoons, and also by rough, stubbly rocky formations called the *garrigue*. In the southwest, around Perpignan, you will also see low-lying plateaus in red rock. At first glance, you might find this landscape a bit shocking, especially if you are driving through along the autoroute. But you will soon appreciate this region's attractions, once you get off the highway and start exploring. Its beaches are long and not crowded (compared to the Côte d'Azur, for example), and its cities—Montpellier and Toulouse, for example—are significant centers, with both a long history and a lively atmosphere.

MARKET RHYTHMS: WHEN THEY'RE HELD/WHEN TO GO

As in many parts of France, the flea markets of this region are usually held on weekends—both Saturday and Sunday—rather than on weekdays, although there are some exceptions. Many are also mornings only (for example, Montpellier's Espace Mosson and Toulouse's place St-Sernin markets, and the markets in Lunel and Sète), which means you will have to time your visits carefully. Markets also tend to start fairly early (particularly the morning-only markets), so that if you are hoping to find a real bargain, you should try to arrive soon after dawn.

The climate in this region (particularly in the south) is generally similar to that of Provence. It is quite dry, hot in summer, often nice in spring and fall, and never very cold in winter; as a result, many of the markets are year-round. However, if you don't like heat and pretty oppressive sunshine, you should avoid the height of the summer (which is, of course, also the height of the tourist season). The average daily maximum temperature for the region is 12.4°C. (54.3°F.) in January, and an average of around 28.3°C. (almost 83°F.) in July and August, while both June and September are also quite warm. All in all, May and June or September and October are probably the best months to come.

MARKET FLAVORS: HOW THEY LOOK/HOW THEY FEEL

Many of the markets of this region are fairly down-home affairs, tending toward the nitty-gritty and eclectic rather than the high-end and pristine. I was pleasantly surprised when I came here for the first time. Long accustomed, and much attached, to some of the down-to-earth markets of Provence, I did not expect to find a similar situation here.

In many of the markets, vendors pile their wares onto blankets on the ground or in crates; you will spend a lot of time rifling through a fair amount of junk to find something you covet. But the scene is not grungy or unpleasant, and if this kind of market appeals to you, you will enjoy yourself. On the other hand, for this reason, some of the markets will be of much less interest to general tourists or to people looking for fine decorative objects.

There are exceptions, of course, to the generally down-home quality to the markets. The monthly market at the Allées J. Guesde in Toulouse, for example, is extremely high-end and one of the most high-quality markets I have been to in France.

This region also has some of the country's biggest flea markets. Montpellier's Espace Mosson may have the largest number of vendors of any single market (not counting the Puces de St-Ouen in Paris, which is made up of several markets). Other substantial markets are in close proximity to Montpellier—Sète, Marseillan-Plage, Palavas-les-Flots, and Lunel, for example. (Nearby Nîmes has a smaller, but still significant, market; see the previous chapter on Provence.) You get the distinct feeling that the collecting bug has taken hold here in a big way.

As well as being down-home, these markets are generally quite friendly and low-key. While not nearly as festive and colorful as those in the Côte d'Azur, for example, they have a pleasant look and feel, similar to that in Provence. And, as in Provence, you will want to look around these markets for a while and then head off in search of more aesthetically pleasing places.

COLLECTIBLES: WHAT YOU'LL FIND/WHAT TO LOOK FOR

The emphasis in many of the markets of this region is on rustic items and modest objects of everyday use. You will find agricultural implements, tools, hardware, and household items of all kinds—coffee mills, enamel coffeepots, copper pots, dishware, etc. You may also find ceramics from this region, in the yellow and green shades found all over southern France, or the light-colored ceramics characteristic of the town of Uzès. You may also spot collectibles from the Camargue and its vicinity—traditional clothing, tools, horseback-riding equipment, or fishing gear, for example. In the southwestern part of this region—such as in Perpignan—look out for the bright, colorful Catalan linens. And in and around Toulouse, you will likely see sports gear and souvenir items from the Pyrénées—old skis and snowshoes, for example, or mementos from Lourdes.

While fine decorative objects are generally not a big feature of these markets, there are of course exceptions. The Allées J. Guesde is one of the best markets in France for finding high-end collectibles of all sorts, including items from Britain. Otherwise, you are not likely to find much in these markets from outside France, except perhaps in Perpignan, where you may spot collectibles from nearby Spain.

BUYING: PRICE LEVELS/BARGAINING OPPORTUNITIES

Generally speaking, prices are quite reasonable in this region. If not the best part of France for bargains, it is right up there. The reason, partly, is that these are often low-end markets, where things tend to be lower-priced. The plenitude of markets here may also be a factor. I was pleasantly surprised to find that good bargains can be found in urban markets (such as the place St-Sernin market in Toulouse), as well as in more off-the-beaten-track spots.

Prices are not uniformly low, however. In the Allées J. Guesde market in Toulouse, for example, prices (like the quality of the goods) are high, and I also found prices moderately high at other places (such as the Perpignan market and, to a lesser extent, the market in Béziers).

As in Provence, you can bargain fairly freely (within reason), without risk of offending the vendors. If they think that your offer is too low, they will simply tell you and you can adjust it accordingly. My own bargaining success has been mixed, but I have never had an unpleasant experience here on that score.

GETTING AROUND: HOW TO TRAVEL/WHERE TO GO

In this region, traveling to the markets by train is often feasible, although not always convenient. In Montpellier, the town itself is handy by train but the market is not. Having a car is quite advantageous; it will permit you to fit in a few markets on the same day, as you may well want to do. Many of the markets are quite close to each other by autoroute and can be reached far more quickly by car than by train.

If you don't have a lot of time, the best thing to do is to plan your visit around either Montpellier or Toulouse. If you use Montpellier as your base, you can, for example, see the markets in Lunel, Palavas-les-Flots, Montpellier, Sète, Marseillan-Plage, Nîmes (and perhaps Castries and Béziers, if it's the right weekend), all in three days, from Saturday to Monday. If you plan to go to Toulouse, be sure to arrange your itinerary so that you are there during the monthly Allées J. Guesde market.

Market Close-Ups

I have selected six market towns to feature in this chapter—Béziers, Lunel, Montpellier, Perpignan, Sète, and Toulouse. These towns are geographically diverse, and their flea markets are also generally the most significant in the region.

BÉZIERS (first Saturday of the month)

> No. of Vendors: 60 to 70
> Price/Quality Range: ✦✦ – ✦✦✦
> Scenic Value: ✦✦ – ✦✦✦
> Amenities Nearby: ✦✦ – ✦✦✦

> Featured Items: Ceramics, glassware, silver, jewelry, rustic items.

WHEN, WHERE, HOW: Béziers has a regular monthly flea market, all day on the first Saturday of the month, from 7:30 A.M. to 6 P.M., along the Allées P. Riquet, in the center of town. Parking is available along the Allées or on neighboring streets.

If arriving by train, the market is just a few minutes' walk northwest of the station. From the north side of the boulevard de Verdun, head through the Plateau des Poètes park; at the northwest corner you will find yourself at the end of the Allées.

Tourist Office: 04-67-49-24-19

UNLIKE MONTPELLIER, ITS much larger (and more beautiful) neighbor to the east, Béziers probably does not attract a lot of tourists, despite its distinction as the place where the legendary Resistance leader, Jean Moulin, was born. This is also where several thousand people were massacred in the early 13th century, in the suppression of the Cathars, an event that remains real, as well, for the people of this region.

Béziers is also considered the center of the region's wine industry. Given the turbulence in that industry over the years, and the resentment of some toward the French government, the town has also been a center of the Occitan movement. (Although adherents once sought greater regional autonomy, this movement has apparently generally moderated its goals in recent years.)

One of the good things about Béziers' relative lack of popularity among tourists is that it has retained the atmosphere of an unsullied provincial town; it may not be exciting or breathtaking, but it is real. It is also a lot more interesting and appealing than the short trip in from the autoroute would suggest. Unlike the unsightly and sprawling exurban periphery, the center is pleasant, with large plane trees providing welcome shade from the seemingly omnipresent sun. The main sight of the town is the medieval cathédrale St-Nazaire. However, the center of present-day Béziers, and perhaps the most pleasant spot for strolling and hanging out, is the Allées P. Riquet, where several restaurants and cafés are set right in the *place*, elevated on large wooden platforms and topped by giant tents.

THE MARKET

The Allées P. Riquet is also the site of Béziers' monthly flea market, held here all day on the first Saturday of the month. This is not a large market, but it is relaxed and easygoing, and you also stand a fair chance of finding something interesting at a reasonable price.

Between 60 and 70 vendors set out their wares under the shade of the plane trees in the Allées, either displayed on tables or simply spread out on the ground. You will find a moderate variety of items for sale—small decorative objects, such as ceramics, glassware, silver, and jewelry, and some rustic items, such as agricultural implements from the surrounding region. There is little in the way of furniture here, although I did see a metal café table with four wood-slatted chairs in good condition, selling for 500 francs, much less than the inflated price tag at many flea markets for this hot item.

The prices are not rock-bottom, but not especially high either; I would describe them as moderate to fairly high, with some exceptions. I found a really attractive art deco table crumb pan here for 30 francs, which I thought was fair. My efforts to bargain were rebuffed in a matter-of-fact manner by the vendor, who simply asserted that the price was appropriate, and I had to concur (she did agree, however, to throw in two ceramic Epiphany *fèves*). I noticed that vendors are generally reluctant to lower their prices by much, so that your success in negotiating may be somewhat limited.

While pleasant and potentially fruitful, the Béziers flea market is not a significant one. I would recommend checking it out if you are in the vicinity on the first Saturday of the month. However, unlike the Toulouse and Montpellier markets, for example, I would not base travel plans upon specially including it.

OTHER THINGS TO DO

Once you have finished seeing the market, sit down at one of the cafés and restaurants lining the Allées. An attractive and especially tastefully decorated spot is the Café de la Comédie, at the edge of the market. The lively restaurants in the Allées offer a variety of light snacks, including pizza and tapas.

On Friday mornings, about 15 *brocante* vendors come to sell their wares in the place du Temple general market, if you happen to be here on that day.

LUNEL (Saturday morning)

> No. of Vendors: 150 to 200
> Price/Quality Range: ✱ – ✱✱
> Scenic Value: ✱✱
> Amenities Nearby: ✱ – ✱✱

> Featured items: Kitchenware, tools, linens, secondhand clothes, rustic items (including Camargue collectibles), fishing gear

WHEN, WHERE, HOW: Lunel has a flea market every Saturday morning, from 5:30 A.M. to 12:30 P.M., in the center of town by the place des Arènes. If arriving by car, there is a parking lot by the market itself with plenty of space.

> Tourist Office: 04-67-71-01-37

TO THE FRENCH, the flat and marshy Rhône delta region known as the Camargue has symbolized a kind of adventurous and romantic frontier land, inhabited by black bulls, white horses, and cowboys. While the Camargue has changed much over the years, bulls, horses, and herdsmen (called *gar-*

diens) are still to be found here, albeit in much diminished numbers. As you tour about, you can also still see some of the traditional *cabanes* (with roofs topped with bull horns to protect against evil spirits) in which the *gardiens* lived.

Though beyond the Camargue's boundaries, the town of Lunel—which lies just south of the Canal du Bas Rhône–Languedoc and about 20 kilometers north of the 13th-century walled town of Aigues-Mortes—feels connected to that region. Its environs are similarly flat and kind of marshy, and the town has that dusty and sleepy frontierlike feel. Not possessed of particularly notable sights, Lunel is the kind of place most tourist guides would fail to mention. It does, however, have quite an interesting weekly junk market, held on Saturday mornings in the center of town at the place des Arènes.

THE MARKET

The Lunel flea market is low-end, noticeably easygoing, and low-key. Vendors chat among themselves and with passersby and seem to enjoy themselves as much as do the browsers. Things get rolling very early here (I am told around 5:30 A.M.), and while the setting is not a particularly beautiful one, and the facilities are somewhat rudimentary, it's not bad either.

This is definitely not one of those markets where the collectibles have been carefully sifted out, shined up, and attractively displayed. As is often the case in this region, you will have to do some serious digging if you hope to find a little gem among the secondhand clothes, used toys, bits of kitchen crockery, and piles of tools, generally spilled out onto blankets on the ground or stuffed into wooden crates. But, while you will have to expend some energy searching, this is one of the likelier places for your efforts to be rewarded if you are a collector of rustic objects of rural life or old everyday French household items. Those who collect things related to horseback riding, fishing, or traditional Camargue clothing may also find a little treasure here. (I was jealous when the woman next to me snapped up a really nice traditional black felt hat, complete with red ribbon, for 15 francs.)

The 150 to 200 people selling at this market seem generally to be casual vendors trying to unload their own household belongings. You may, however, encounter a few with more high-end collectibles, nicely shined and well presented (which they also hope to sell at markedly higher prices). While not rock-bottom, prices in this market are generally quite low, and vendors seem prepared to drop them fairly significantly to make a sale. I bought some beautiful silver-plated serving pieces here for 20 francs (the whole box was only going for 50 francs, but I was starting to have weight and space concerns). I also purchased—from one of the few high-end vendors—a lovely covered mustard pot (from Dijon, not Languedoc, needless to say) for 100 francs. (I saw similar ones later, in both Dijon and Belfort, for over 200 francs.)

A stopover for an hour or so at the Lunel market, while touring this region, would appeal to collectors with less rarefied tastes, and possibly to those visitors interested in a little (nonglamorous) local flavor. If, however, your interests lie in more high-end decorative objects, or more scenic spots, this is likely not the destination for you. I personally really like the Lunel market and would certainly include it in my weekly haunts if I happened to be staying in this area.

OTHER THINGS TO DO

Another large Saturday flea market is in Palavas-les-Flots, about 30 kilometers southwest of Lunel (see Montpellier, "Other Things to Do," below). I find it somewhat less interesting than the Lunel market, with less of an emphasis on regional and rustic items, but if you have time, you can get there by car in about 30 minutes.

Be sure to do a tour of both the coastal area east of Palavas-les-Flots and the Camargue. En route, visit the eerie, medieval fortress town of Aigues-Mortes. Or, for an eerie experience of a different sort, start your tour at La Grande Motte, a controversial seaside development project, on the coast between Palavas-les-Flots and Aigues-Mortes. This conglomeration of concrete buildings (and other structures) in bizarre geometric shapes and colors may well cause you to question the whole concept of futuristic architecture.

For a good introduction to the Camargue, and to traditional life in this region, visit the Musée Camarguais (and its "Camargue farm countryside" 3.5-kilometer trail), off the D570 to the southwest of Arles. (Call 04-90-97-10-82 for hours, which vary during the year.) Be sure also to see Les Saintes-Maries-de-la-Mer, the touristy but pretty town on the coast, famous for its beaches and its connection to Gypsy culture. In late May, it is a gathering place for Gypsies, who come to pay respects to their patron saint, Sarah (the African servant who is said to have arrived here from the Holy Land, in a boat with no oars or sail, along with a trio of saints named Mary—thus the name, Les Saintes-Maries-de-la-Mer).

MONTPELLIER (Sunday morning)

No. of Vendors: 500 to 600
Price/Quality Range: ✤ – ✤✤
Scenic Value: ✤
Amenities Nearby: ✤ – ✤✤

Featured Items: Kitchenware, tools, linens, garden ware, Provençal ceramics, rustic items, some furniture

WHEN, WHERE, HOW: Montpellier has a gigantic flea market on Sunday morning, from 6 A.M. to 1:30 P.M., at the Espace Mosson in La Paillade, a few kilometers to the northwest of the center of town. If arriving by car, from the center of Montpellier head west on the N109 (west of the place des Arceaux, near the promenade du Peyrou). At La Paillade, the Espace Mosson is a large paved area off the side of the road. Parking is available along the street; just follow the example of the others around you.

If you do not have a car, inquire at the tourist office to see if you can access the market by public transit.

Other Markets Discussed: Montpellier (place des Arceaux) (Saturday morning); Palavas-les-Flots (Saturday all day, morning only in summer)
Tourist Office: 04-67-22-06-16

MONTPELLIER IS AN odd mixture of a formal, elegant bourgeois city and a lively and youthful university town. (It is home, for example, to France's prestigious, and first, medical school.) The dual identity of this town is particularly evident at the gigantic marble-paved, oval-shaped place de la Comédie (called l'Oeuf, or "the egg," by the locals); site of the beautiful opera building, it is also the nucleus of Montpellier and the main meeting place for its residents, whose average age is in the mid-20s. Apparently, students make up about one-quarter of Montpellier's population.

Montpellier feels very cosmopolitan and sophisticated for a southern provincial town. For a thousand years it has been a main trading center and recently a hub of the high-tech industry, competing with such other booming towns as Grenoble and Toulouse. In the early 17th century, large parts of this Protestant center were destroyed during the Wars of Religion. Today, however, there is little sign that there has ever been any disruption in this elegant city's history.

Until a few years ago, the area at the base of the aqueduct at the western part of Montpellier's center (the place des Arceaux) was the site of a giant weekly flea market. The market's size and activity, however, ultimately demanded that it be moved to the outskirts, to the Espace Mosson in La Paillade.

THE MARKET

With estimates of between 500 and 600 vendors, the Espace Mosson market may be the largest in France, if you do not count the Puces de St-Ouen, which is really made up of several smaller markets. However, not all the stalls here are confined to selling collectibles; rather, they offer an eclectic mixture of secondhand clothing, junk, cheap new things, and a wide variety of collectibles, from low to midrange. I love this place because it is such a grab bag of things that somehow seem to coexist quite harmoniously.

The setting is not picturesque, to be sure. The market site is a gigantic paved surface, set in a fairly ugly exurban area to the northwest of the center of town. But, though not aesthetically pleasing, it is not grimy either. And, anyway, you soon forget your surroundings as you inject yourself into this hectic, and kind of festive, scene.

The smell of mint and coriander is likely the first sensation to hit you as you arrive; by the entrance there is a small North African food market. If you want to immediately check out the more high-end collectibles, head to the somewhat shaded, tree-lined area at the far side, away from the road. Here, among other things, you will find furniture, garden ware, Provençal ceramics, and a variety of quite polished and pristine rustic items.

In the remainder of the market (where it is much less shady and thus potentially brutal on a hot, sunny day), vendors sell what can only be described as junk (secondhand clothes, bits of kitchenware, and rusted hardware and tools), interspersed with generally modest and low-end, but also occasionally interesting, items. Most of the goods are piled on blankets on the ground, although some are displayed in a slightly more decorous fashion on makeshift tables. The "recently used" is mixed in indiscriminately with the old, reguiring some serious foraging, and imagination, to come up with any real treasures. This is, however, a good place to find all kinds of everyday items—old copper pots, enamelware, glassware, coffee mills, café au lait bowls, utensils, and regional ceramics. It is also a good spot to get a bargain on rustic items, garden ware, and old tools.

But get here early if you hope to make an interesting discovery. I am told that that is what the *brocante* dealers do, which comes as no surprise since this is exactly the kind of place where such finds are often made. Bargaining is active, and vendors seem generally inclined to dispose of their wares at whatever price they can get, within reason.

One word of advice: While I have personally had no problems, a good precaution at this crowded market is to carry only a small amount of cash in your pocket, leaving your purse, valuables, and your camera at your hotel. Not only will this be safer, but it will allow you more freedom to browse without worry and to bargain more effectively. (This is not a scenic spot for photos anyway, and people here may well be resistant to being photographed.)

A pleasant surprise for me (and my children) was the discovery of several food trucks here, selling all kinds of ethnic specialties—Chinese, Vietnamese, Middle Eastern—at reasonable prices. A wide selection of French fare is also available—*andouillettes, magret de canard, merguez* and *chipolatas* sausages, and the ubiquitous *frites.* As far as market food goes, this is right up there with the best of them. Some of the food trucks have tables and chairs set up beside them, so that you can sit down and enjoy a snack or lunch in the middle of your perambulations.

OTHER THINGS TO DO

Once you have seen the flea market, head back into the center of Montpellier to the place de la Comédie, a congenial spot for some serious people-watching. Although the steady stream of street performers may eventually get on your nerves, you will enjoy lounging at one of the cafés. If it's the first Sunday of the month, you might also want to visit the all-day flea market in nearby Castries, not far to the northeast of Montpellier (along the N110, after it branches off from the N113). Sète (about 30 kilometers southwest of Montpellier) also has a large flea market on Sunday mornings (see Sète, below), while there is a smaller, but still substantial, all-day (morning-only in summer) Sunday market in Marseillan-Plage, just west of Sète.

If you happen to be in Montpellier on Saturday, a small specialty market takes place in the morning at the place des Arceaux, just under the aqueduct. You will find about 20 vendors selling books, stamps, phone cards, and other small items, but not general collectibles. Also here is a high-quality food market where you can pick up some excellent bread and cheese (and lots of other things) for a picnic lunch.

A large Saturday junk market (in addition to the one in Lunel, see above) is also held in Palavas-les-Flots, about 30 minutes by car south of Montpellier (mornings only in summer, all day the rest of the year, but come early to be safe). Palavas-les-Flots is a kind of faded-looking seaside town, surrounded by the flat, marshy terrain that abuts the Mediterranean in this region. Between

150 and 200 vendors sell all kinds of odds and ends in a large parking lot in the middle of town. While much of what you will see is truly junk, and uninteresting junk to boot, you will occasionally come across some real collectibles at quite reasonable prices (for finds, of course, try to arrive early).

A conversation I had at Palavas reminded me why I love coming to markets like this. As I stood beside another browser, admiring an old pale yellow wall-mounted coffee mill, he told me how, as a young boy, his job was to grind the coffee beans for the family and that, like other French boys of that era, he wore short pants. Grinding in shorts, he said, was painful, and the day the wall-mounted grinder arrived was one of the biggest memories of his childhood. I could not help but share in the obvious pleasure he experienced in recalling this image.

PERPIGNAN (Saturday)

No. of Vendors: 30 to 40
Price/Quality Range: ✸✸ – ✸✸✸
Scenic Value: ✸✸
Amenities Nearby: ✸ – ✸✸

Featured Items: Ceramics, linens (including Catalan linens), silver, jewelry, small decorative objects

WHEN, WHERE, HOW: Perpignan has a weekly flea market, all day Saturday, from 8 A.M. to 6 P.M., at the promenade des Platanes, at the north end of town. If arriving by car, follow signs to the center, and then to the Palais des Congrès or the Office de Tourisme, which are located right by the market. Parking is available in the lot nearby, and you will have no difficulty finding a spot.

If arriving by train, the promenade des Platanes is about a 30-minute hike northeast of the train station. Follow the avenue Général de Gaulle to the place de la Catalogne, continue northeast along the boulevard Clemenceau, and then cross the canal, jogging a bit farther north to the promenade des Platanes. The market is at the far end near the Palais des Congrès.

There is also a *marché aux puces* on Sunday mornings at the avenue du Palais des Expositions; however, only the Saturday collectibles market is described below.

Tourist Office: 04-68-66-30-30

THE PROXIMITY TO Spain is very evident in this old city located not far west of the Mediterranean and north of the Spanish border. Not only are many of the locals of Spanish origin, much of the architecture and the landscape is reminiscent of that country. Indeed, for centuries Perpignan and its surrounding area, Roussillon, alternated between French and Spanish control until it became part of France permanently in the middle of the 17th century. The Palais des Rois de Majorque, in the south end of town, serves as the most significant reminder of the medieval rule of the kings of Majorca here. You will also often see the brightly colored Catalan flag as you tour around.

Perpignan has grown enormously during this century; apparently, its population is now about three times what it was at the beginning of the First World War. While perhaps not a uniformly beautiful city, it has some really nice areas, particularly the pedestrian district around the place de la Loge.

THE MARKET

The all-day Saturday market in Perpignan is not large. Between 30 and 40 vendors gather at the far end of the promenade des Platanes by the Palais des Congrès, usually setting up tables but also sometimes displaying their wares on the ground. The ambience is sleepy, as this is not a busy or lively market, but its low-key quality is kind of relaxing. The vendors are generally approachable and friendly; I had a long conversation with one woman about men, children, and grandchildren and the relative merits of each (guess which group prevailed).

You will find a somewhat limited range and variety of collectibles at this market—linens, jewelry, ceramics, books, polished rustic items, and high-end kitchenware at prices that, while not terribly high, are certainly not low either. I was particularly interested in the linens (which were not expensive), especially the colorful Catalan table napkins and place mats, in bright red, green, yellow, and blue. The woman selling them was extremely helpful and cordial, and not particularly concerned about whether I was actually going to buy anything (I did, of course).

While somewhat willing to bargain, the vendors are quite knowledgeable about the price range of their wares and are not likely to agree to a significant reduction to make a sale. Given that this is neither a large market nor one where you are likely to find a real bargain, I would not go out of my way to see it. It does, however, merit a short visit if you are in the vicinity on a Saturday.

OTHER THINGS TO DO

You will need less than a hour to see this small market, and when done, head back into the pedestrian area by the place de la Loge for a café or restaurant, as the amenities available right by the market are quite limited. If you are here on a Sunday morning, try out the more low-end flea market held at the avenue du Palais des Expositions, just across the river Têt (via the Pont Joffre) from the promenade des Platanes.

SÈTE (Sunday morning)

No. of Vendors: up to 280
Price/Quality Range: ✦ – ✦✦
Scenic Value: ✦✦
Amenities Nearby: ✦✦

Featured Items: Kitchenware, tools, books, records, secondhand clothes, linens, small decorative items

WHEN, WHERE, HOW: Sète has a weekly flea market, every Sunday morning, from around 7 A.M. to 1 P.M., in the place de la République in the northwest part of town.

If arriving by car, follow signs to the center, crossing to the west of the Canal de Sète, which runs north from the sea. If you cross at the Pont de la Civette, follow the rue Général de Gaulle west (it becomes the avenue M. Dormoy). At the end, by the Jardin du Château d'Eau, jog to the right (north) and then west on the rue du Maire Aussenac. Turn right (north) on the rue de la Révolution, which leads into the place de la République, the site of the market. You should be able to find parking on the street by the place.

If taking the train, the market is within easy walking distance southwest of the station. Cross the canal west of the station, at the Pont Sadi Carnot. Turn south (left) on the Quai de Bosc, go right at the rue du 4 Septembre, and then, west of the rue Rouget, follow the rue Daniel west to the place de la République.

Tourist Office: 04-67-74-71-71

LIKE MANY PLACES in this region, Sète, about 30 kilometers southwest of Montpellier, has that nice feel of a real and unself-conscious town. This is a place where ordinary people live and work—a busy port and fishing town, as the many boats you will see by the coast and along the canal will attest. While tourists do come here, especially during the *joutes nautiques* in the summer (a traditional sport whose objective is to push people in a competing boat into the water), Sète, perhaps thankfully, is not a really big tourist town.

Despite Sète's quite appealing setting, right on the Mediterranean with the slopes of Mont St-Clair behind, the town itself is not overwhelmingly beautiful. It is, however, a far nicer place than the drive in from the autoroute would suggest. It has a dreamy, faded feel, especially along the canal, where pale pastel-colored buildings contrast with the brightly painted fishing boats. And, on a sunny weekend afternoon, when hordes of people stroll along its pedestrian streets, sit at outdoor cafés, or dine outside at its many canal-side restaurants, it's a congenial place to be.

THE MARKET

Sète has a large weekly flea market, every Sunday morning at the place de la République in the northwest part of town. The *place* is not particularly attractive, surrounded as it is by rather mundane, not very old buildings, but if you look around from time to time, you can catch glimpses of the water below.

The *place* can accommodate up to 280 vendors, and I am told that that is how many there usually are, except when the weather is bad. Around 6:30 A.M., cars and trucks begin to arrive, at first in a small trickle and then in a steady stream. Some vendors make their way on foot, pushing carts piled with boxes or loaded down with bags in each arm. You are best advised not to arrive really early, unless you are a keen bargain hunter, since some vendors are still trailing in after seven-thirty. Much lively discussion ensues (and occasionally some altercations) as newcomers position themselves in the spaces they have been assigned. People chat and bargain as they unpack their wares, usually simply arranging them on blankets on the ground or, in the case of the more high-end collectibles, setting up tables to display them more attractively.

This is more a junk, than a collectibles, market but not a rock-bottom one. While you will see the usual piles of secondhand clothes, old toys, and mismatched dishware, you will also find more conventional collectibles such as coffee mills, enamel pots, linens, and old books. Not a lot is to be found here in the way of fine decorative objects or furniture.

Not surprisingly, prices are quite reasonable, and vendors are prepared to bargain and keen to sell. As with other markets of this sort, arriving ahead of the crowds and digging around may net you something interesting at a good price, if your interests lie in rustic or everyday items. Even if not, you may enjoy a visit to this market, which is down-home but not grungy and has a cheerful ambience. If you have children with you, there is even a play area in the corner of the *place*.

OTHER THINGS TO DO

Little in the way of congenial cafés or restaurants is to be found around this *place*. Head instead to the pedestrian area a few blocks to the southeast, once you've finished at the market. For a meal, try one of the restaurants along the canal, which serve all kinds of seafood and fish (try the local mussels and oysters). While I can't especially recommend any of the places that I have been to, you are likely to get a good, and not expensive, meal along here (most restaurants offer a three-course, set-price meal for around 75 francs).

If you have not already seen it, the gigantic Sunday-morning flea market at the Espace Mosson just northwest of the center of Montpellier is a must (see Montpellier, above). It's not far away by autoroute for those with a car, and if you leave Sète by ten-thirty or so, you can do both markets on the same morning, since the Montpellier market does not wind down until around 1 P.M. Also, just a few kilometers southwest of Sète on the N112, Marseillan-Plage has an all-day Sunday flea market (morning-only in summer).

TOULOUSE (first Friday, Saturday, and Sunday of month)
(Saturday and Sunday mornings)

ALLÉES J. GUESDE
No. of Vendors: 140
Price/Quality Range: ✦✦✦ – ✦✦✦✦
Scenic Value: ✦✦ – ✦✦✦
Amenities Nearby: ✦✦ – ✦✦✦

Featured Items: Furniture, porcelain, books, silver, militaria, linens, toys, art deco, advertising items

PLACE ST-SERNIN
No. of Vendors: 80
Price/Quality Range: ✦ – ✦✦
Scenic Value: ✦✦ – ✦✦✦
Amenities Nearby: ✦✦ – ✦✦✦

Featured Items: Kitchenware, glassware, linens, books, records, hardware, tools, toys, secondhand clothes

WHEN, WHERE, HOW: There are two regular flea markets in Toulouse. One is held on the first Friday, Saturday, and Sunday of the month, from 7 A.M. to 7 P.M. (9 A.M. to 7 P.M. on Sunday), at the Allées J. Guesde. The other takes place every Saturday and Sunday morning, from 8 A.M. to 1 P.M. (8:30 A.M. to 1 P.M. on Sunday), at the place St-Sernin. Both markets are located in the center of Toulouse. The Allées J. Guesde runs southwest from the Grand Rond in the south end of town, while the place St-Sernin is in the northern end of the city, to the west of the boulevard de Strasbourg.

If arriving by car, finding parking in Toulouse is never easy, but is particularly difficult near the place St-Sernin (both the pedestrian and one-way streets in this part of
town further complicate this problem). If you are staying in the center of Toulouse, your
best bet is to leave the car at your hotel and travel to both of these markets by foot.

If arriving by train, it is about a 15-minute walk from the station to the place St-
Sernin. Cross the Canal du Midi, head southwest along the rue de Bayard to the
boulevard de Strasbourg, then take a short jog right (northwest), on the boulevard de
Strasbourg, to the rue Bellegarde, which leads west into the place St-Sernin. You can
also take the metro from the station, getting off at the place du Capitole and walking,
from the north end of the *place*, along the rue du Taur, which leads into the place
St-Sernin.

The Allées J. Guesde market is farther from the train station, but still within walking distance. Cross the Canal du Midi farther south by the Allées Jean Jaurès, follow
the Allées Jean Jaurès until you reach boulevard Lazare Carnot (the southern extension of boulevard de Strasbourg), and follow it south (it later becomes the Allées J.
Verdier) to the Grand Rond. Veer to the southwest (the right) and you will come upon
the Allées J. Guesde. You can also take the metro to the Jean Jaurès stop, and then,
at the boulevard de Strasbourg nearby, take bus line #1 south.

Tourist Office: 05-61-11-02-22

TOULOUSE, THE OLD capital of Languedoc, is one of the few cities in France,
other than Paris, in which I could imagine living. It is vibrant and lively, and
with good reason. This is a high-tech center, for both the aeronautics and
electronics industries; Airbus aircraft, for example, are assembled here.
Toulouse is also youthful; students are said to make up almost one-sixth of
the city's population.

The cosmopolitan credentials of this place are long established. Toulouse
was subject to Roman, Gaulish, Christian, Visigothic, and Frankish influences, all prior to the ninth century, when it became the center of the rule,
until the 13th century, of the powerful counts of Toulouse (whose sophisticated court included the mythic troubadours).

One of the most arresting features of Toulouse is the rust-pink color of its
buildings' brickwork (giving the city its nickname, the Ville Rose). Also contributing to the city's appeal are the large number of pedestrian streets, the
splendid and imposing place du Capitole, and the pastoral setting of the
Garonne River, which forms the western boundary of the city's inner core. My
daughter once remarked, quite appropriately I think, that Toulouse is somewhat reminiscent of Boston; in addition to certain physical likenesses, it has
a similar civilized and urbane quality.

Several beautiful old buildings are in the center of town. Some were built centuries ago for the merchants who prospered from the production of blue dyes, until the arrival of indigo dyes from India in the second half of the 16th century. Several significant religious edifices also dominate the landscape— Les Jacobins, for example, housing the remains of St. Thomas Aquinas, and the Basilique St-Sernin (begun in the 11th century), named after the third-century evangelist of the same name.

ALLÉES J. GUESDE MARKET

A large and high-end *brocante* market takes place in Toulouse on the first Friday, Saturday, and Sunday of the month, all day (the date is determined based on when the first Friday falls, even if it happens to be the second Saturday or Sunday). The site of the market is the middle area of the tree-lined Allées J. Guesde, which runs off the Grand Rond in the south end of town. The setting is a (very welcome) green and lush one. At the edges of the market, and along its sides, are the Grand Rond and the Jardin Royal, as well as the Jardin des Plantes, a beautiful park with little play areas for children (something far too rare in France).

Here you can find just about every kind of collectible, at stalls that are appealingly arranged and sheltered by large umbrellas or large sheets of canvas. You will see lots of furniture, sometimes assembled like little living-room or dining-room sets, art deco, porcelain, silver, jewelry, linens, well-polished rustic ware, large copper pots, books, paintings, advertising items, sporting gear, high-end kitchenware, garden ware, toys, etc. Really unusual items can be found here—I recall seeing (all in the same visit) a stuffed penguin, an antique commode (potty-chair), a miniature kitchen cabinet with tiny pots (and even tinier café au lait bowls), a dentist's chair, and a wooden leg. Collectibles from the surrounding area are also to be found—for example, winter sports gear from the Pyrénées, religious souvenirs from Lourdes, and linens from the Béarn region. You will also likely encounter English antiques and collectibles, which is not surprising given the historical presence of the British in this area (for example, in Pau to the southwest).

While the variety of the wares is enormous, the price range is much more narrow. This is a market where, not surprisingly, high price tags have generally been fixed to the carefully selected and beautifully displayed collectibles. Even more rustic items or less exotic kitchenware, for example, may be as much as triple the price of similar items at low-end flea markets, such as the place St-Sernin (see below). The advantage here, however, is that, since things are presented in their most polished and pristine form (and beautifully arranged to boot), you are not called upon to exercise much imagination in deciding if they are appealing (as you often are in more nitty-gritty markets). You also don't have to spend a lot of time looking for them.

My enthusiasm about this market is somewhat tempered by the experience I had with a couple of the vendors. Though given permission by one (albeit reluctantly) to take a photo of his wares, I was immediately approached by another who asked, not entirely jokingly, if I was with *les impots,* that is, the tax department. In the face of this somewhat prickly behavior, I decided to switch to jotting down some notes, but was then questioned about what I was writing by a couple of other vendors in the next row. By now exasperated, I asked somewhat tersely if they thought that informing prospective visitors about the market was a good idea; they quickly backed off, but the experience left a bit of a sour taste in my mouth.

Notwithstanding the above, I would strongly recommend planning your visit to Toulouse to coincide with the Allées J. Guesde market. Even if your budget does not permit you to purchase much here, you will enjoy checking out the wide range of interesting and high-quality collectibles in these quite congenial surroundings. The café scene right by the market is sparse; however, at the end, near the Grand Rond, a little spot has tables and chairs where you can sit down with a drink before heading back to the center. You will also find washrooms in the garden across the street.

PLACE ST-SERNIN MARKET

In the place St-Sernin, surrounding the *basilique* of the same name, a much more lively and down-to-earth Toulouse flea market takes place, on Saturday and Sunday mornings. (Saturday is apparently bigger, in terms of *brocante,* than Sunday; the market also starts a little earlier on Saturday.) This is a fairly basic, low-end market. If you arrive via the pedestrian rue du Taur, you will know when you are almost here by the advance guard of casual vendors who have set out their (often sad-looking) wares on newspapers on the sidewalk. (The most bizarre sight I've ever witnessed here was a woman selling a pail of dead fish.)

As you first arrive at the dense and crowded place St-Sernin, you will think that you have been led astray. Stalls of cheap new goods and second-hand clothes seem to monopolize the space. There is also some food—breads and olives of all kinds and, beginning first thing in the morning, sausages cooking over grills. However, as you orient yourself and explore further, you will find that there is indeed a collectibles market here, composed of about 80 vendors, who set up their wares on tables or on the ground, in a close circle around the extraordinary *basilique,* a wonderful sight to be able to gaze at as you circle the market.

The raucous atmosphere here allows for alternatingly intense and amusing negotiations, with disputes quickly giving way to jokes and laughter. All kinds of people frequent this market; religious sisters in their habits mingle with women in traditional Middle Eastern dress, young students, and the odd tourist, rummaging through the linens or secondhand clothes or examining bits of dishware. The space is not large, and if you come late in the morning, the crowds can sometimes be a bit overwhelming.

The things for sale span a wide spectrum, but are generally in what may be considered the low to moderate range. For example, you will not find much in the way of fine decorative objects or furniture. I was pleasantly surprised to discover some of the 1940s and 1950s kitchenware that I collect, hidden amongst piles of odds and ends. You often have to ferret out the treasures, but if you are a collector of everyday items as I am, the good news is that your efforts stand a reasonable chance of being rewarded. You will unearth some interesting bits of ceramics, glassware, hardware, linens, old utensils, agricultural implements, and tools. You will also find some of the more classic collectibles—advertising items, books, postcards, *telecartes*, records, and toys.

Prices are generally quite reasonable and, in some cases, as low as in many of the "down and dirty" markets elsewhere in France. The last time I was here I bought two 1940s jadeite-colored cups (the man promised to bring the saucers the following week), a little translucent white glass bowl, and four green and yellow ramekins—all for ten francs. Bargaining is active; one gets the sense that some of the vendors are keen to unload their goods at whatever price they can get, within reason. If you know what you are looking for, or if you simply keep your eyes open and trust your tastes, you are likely to unearth an interesting find here.

OTHER THINGS TO DO

After you have finished seeing the Allées J. Guesde or the place St-Sernin market, head back to the pedestrian areas surrounding the place du Capitole for a coffee or light snack. Some spots by the place St-Sernin cater to the more low-budget and student crowd, but if that's not what you are looking for, it's hard to beat the place du Capitole's grand cafés. Try the Grand Café Florida (at 12 place du Capitole), with its zinc counter in dark wood and its painted mirrors, or the equally splendid Belle Époque café, Bibent (at 5 place du Capitole), with its high, molded ceilings and big chandeliers. These are prime spots in Toulouse for some serious people-watching (and for relaxing following the rigors of your market experience).

As you walk along the rue du Taur from the place St-Sernin, you may want to stop in at Michel Belin (closed Sunday) for some chocolates, or at Régals, famous for its Toulousian specialty of candied violets (at 9 and 25 rue du Taur, respectively).

For a reasonably priced, regionally based meal (with a big emphasis on duck), try le Bon Vivre (05-61-23-07-17), in the place Wilson, east of the place du Capitole. The service here is especially friendly, and eating outside in this lovely little square is pleasant.

Another place that the locals highly recommend, particularly for its fish and seafood, is Chez Émile (05-61-21-05-56), in the place St-Georges, not far from the place du Capitole. The time we tried to go here, no tables were left and we had to content ourselves with the pizza restaurant next door, which was pretty good. The biggest highlight was getting to sit outside in this quiet *place,* watching the children play hide-and-seek among the trees while their parents ate (something that definitely could not be done in most other parts of this busy city).

Southwest of Toulouse, the town of Muret now has a very large Sunday-morning flea market you might want to visit if you are heading west out of town that day. (See the next chapter on Southwest France.)

Sarlat

Brive-la-
Gaillarde

Dordogne

Bordeaux

Andernos

Bergerac

Garonne

Marmande

Biarritz

Bayonne

Anglet

Cahors

St-Jean-
de-Luz

A62

Ciboure

Dax

Montauban

A64

Mont-de-Marsan

St-Pierre-du-Mont

Toulouse

N17

Muret

Pau

Soumoulou

Mirepoix

Ahetze

Tarbes

Hendaye

A61

**Cambo-
les-Bains**

S P A I N

A N D O R R A

N10

The Flea Markets of Southwest France

Monday *PAU (place du Foirail) [25 vendors]
(9 A.M. to 12 P.M. and 2:30 P.M. to 6 P.M.)

Tuesday BIDART (Petit Fronton) [10 to 15 vendors]
(July and August, but check first)
(8 A.M. to 4 P.M.)

BRIVE-LA-GAILLARDE (rues Gallinat and Faro) [10 vendors]
(first and third Tuesday of month)
(8 A.M. to 5 P.M.)

Wednesday *CAMBO-LES-BAINS (Parc St-Joseph from May to October, center
other times) [15 to 30 vendors, depending on the season]
(March to December)
(9 A.M. to 6 P.M.)

MONT-DE-MARSAN (pl. St-Roch) [20 to 30 vendors]
(first Wednesday of month)
(8 A.M. to 6 P.M.)

Thursday DAX (pl. Camille Bouvet) [40 to 45 vendors] (first Thursday of
month) (8 A.M. to 6 P.M.)

TARBES (pl. Ste-Therese) [20 vendors]
(8 A.M. to noon)

Friday *BAYONNE (pl. de l'Arsenal) [50 to 60 vendors]
(7 A.M. to noon)

Saturday AIRE-SUR-L'ADOUR (Halles Couvertes) [10 vendors]
(second Saturday of month)
(8 A.M. to 6 P.M.)

ANDERNOS (Bassin d'Arachon) (pl. de l'Étoile) [20 to 50 vendors]
(first Saturday of month, from April to September)
(7 A.M. to 6 P.M.)

AUCH (Hall Verdier) [17 vendors] (second Saturday of month)
(8 A.M. to 6 P.M.)

GUÉTHARY (fronton) [25 vendors]
(June to September)
(7:30 A.M. to 2 P.M.)

LIBOURNE (pl. de la Mairie) [15 vendors]
(second Saturday of month)
(8 A.M. to 12:30 P.M.)

MIREPOIX (under les Halles) [20 to 30 vendors]
(second Saturday of month from April to September)
(8 A.M. to 5 P.M.)

MONTAUBAN (pl. Lalaque) [up to 15 vendors]
(8 A.M. to 1 P.M.)

MONTAUBAN (pl. Lalaque) [15 to 30 vendors]
(last Saturday of month from September to June)
(7 A.M. to 6 P.M.)

*PAU (pl. du Foirail) [25 vendors]
(9 A.M. to 12:30 P.M. and 2:30 P.M. to 6 P.M.)

ST-PIERRE-DU-MONT (center) [15 to 30 vendors]
(third Saturday of month)
(8 A.M. to 6 P.M.)

ST-YBARS (center) [10 vendors] (first Saturday of month)
(8 A.M. to 4 P.M.)

TARBES (Halle Mercadieu) [30 vendors] (first Saturday of month)
(8 A.M. to 5 P.M.)

Sunday *AHETZE (center) [150 vendors] (third Sunday of month)
(6 A.M. to 6 P.M.)

ANGLET (pl. des Cinq Cantons) [25 to 50 vendors]
(second Sunday of month)
(7 A.M. to 6 P.M.)

BARBOTAN-LES-THERMES (pedestrian street) [20 vendors]
(second Sunday of month from April to October)
(8 A.M. to 6 P.M.)

BERGERAC (pl. Dr. Cayla) [45 vendors] (first Sunday of month)
(8 A.M. to 12:30 P.M.)

*BORDEAUX (pl. St-Michel) [100 to 120 vendors]
(6 A.M. to 1 P.M.)

BORDEAUX-TALENCE (Parking du c. cial. Intermarché, 235 Route
de Toulouse) [90 to 100 vendors]
(7 A.M. to 6 P.M.)

BRIVE-LA-GAILLARDE (pl. de Lattre de Tassigny) [20 vendors]
(third Sunday of month)
(8 A.M. to 5 P.M.)

*CIBOURE (St-Jean-de-Luz) (Quartier de l'Union) [50 to 75 vendors]
(first Sunday of month)
(8 A.M. to 6 P.M.)

GOURDON (pl. de la Poste) [10 to 12 vendors]
(third Sunday of month from September to June)
(8 A.M. to 5 P.M.)

HENDAYE (Port de Sokoburu) [25 to 35 vendors]
(fourth Sunday of month)
(8 A.M. to 6 P.M.)

LABASTIDE D'ARMAGNAC (pl. Royale) [up to 12 vendors]
(fourth Sunday of month)
(9 A.M. to 6 P.M.)

MARMANDE (covered market) [30 vendors]
(second Sunday of month)
(7:30 A.M. to 6 P.M.)

MERCUÈS (Salle des Fêtes) [15 to 20 vendors]
(third Sunday of month from September to May)
(7 A.M. to 7 P.M.)

MIRAMONT-DE-GUYENNE (pl. de la Mairie) [15 vendors]
(third Sunday of month)
(9 A.M. to 6 P.M.)

MURET (Parking Lycée Pierre d'Aragon) [250 vendors]
(8 A.M. to 1 P.M.)

PAMIERS (center) [80 vendors]
(8 A.M. to noon)

*PAU (pl. du Foirail) [25 vendors]
(10 A.M. to 12:30 P.M.)

SARLAT (av. Gambetta) [20 to 40 vendors] (last Sunday of month)
(9 A.M. to 5 P.M.)

SOUMOULOU (Hall d'Ossau) [70 vendors] (first Sunday of month)
(8 A.M. to 5:30 P.M.)

Regional Overview

GETTING ORIENTED: ABOUT THE REGION

Southwest France, in this book, is the roughly box-shaped corner of the country bordered by the Atlantic on the west, the Spanish frontier on the south, just shy of Toulouse on the east (although continuing farther east to the south), and just above Bordeaux and Brive-la-Gaillarde at the two northern points. This encompasses a number of different areas—Bordeaux and the flat coastal area, historically known as Gascony, to its south and southeast; the Dordogne and Lot regions, lining the valleys of the Dordogne and Lot Rivers; the Pays Basque—the coastal strip from just north of Bayonne to the Spanish border, and extending into the western Pyrénées; and finally, the central part of the Pyrénées, surrounding the towns of Pau, Tarbes, and Lourdes.

Each of these regions has its own distinct look—the flat, sandy stretches of the coast south of Bordeaux; the rolling, château-dotted countryside of the lush Dordogne; the colorful fishing ports and brilliantly green inland villages of the Basque region; and the vistas of the mountainous peaks of the central Pyrénées.

There is also a huge diversity in the history (and the people) in this corner of France. For thousands of years, many think, the Basques (whose origins remain unknown) have resided in the southwesternmost part of this region.

Their unique language, Euskera, was apparently already spoken well over three thousand years ago. Centuries ago, the central Pyrénées comprised two feudal counties—Béarn and Bigorre—which managed to maintain autonomy from the French state until the late 16th and early 17th centuries. Many people, for example, still identify themselves as Béarnais, as well as French.

Gascony, the historical name for the area between the Pays Basque (and the foothills of the Pyrénées farther east) and Bordeaux, has its own romantic past. This was the stomping ground of the infamous musketeers of the 17th century. During the Middle Ages, Gascony—like Bordeaux—was part of the province of Aquitaine and was fought over by the French and the English during their three-century-long conflict. And the Dordogne region's military-looking châteaux and *bastides* are testimony to its own turbulent role during this struggle, as a dividing point between the two forces. Later, in the 16th century, it was a battleground between Catholics and Protestants during the Wars of Religion.

Despite their diversity, the different components of Southwest France also enjoy certain common features. With a few exceptions (such as Bordeaux), this is not a very urban region. It is mostly composed of towns and villages, and the few places that can be described as cities are not very populous. This is also generally a region still fairly wedded to its traditional way of life, somewhat removed from the forces of the late 20th century, so noticeable in other parts of France.

The parts of this diverse region share a generally green and lush landscape, and (except in the mountains) a usually mild, if often wet, climate. Nature manifests itself strongly in the life of the people here, whether by the sea or in the mountains. Consequently, perhaps, these are generally down-to-earth, straightforward folks, not noted for being chic or trendy; there is little chance of mistaking this coast for the Côte d'Azur, for example. Appropriately, the cuisine throughout this region is also hearty and robust—for example, the *confit de canard* (duck preserved in goose fat), foie gras, and cassoulet (a rich casserole of beans, sausages, duck, pork, and lamb) of the Dordogne and Gascony.

I love this part of France, partly because it is such a green and robust place—a real antidote to the dryness of Languedoc-Roussillon or Provence, and to the sometimes overwhelmingly ornate and rarefied Côte d'Azur. You feel revitalized by a brisk and blustery walk along the coast or a drive through the rolling countryside of the Dordogne or the Pays Basque. The sense of space and fresh air here is somewhat reminiscent of the English or Scottish countryside, or even of North America. And yet, the great thing is, you are in France.

MARKET RHYTHMS: WHEN THEY'RE HELD/WHEN TO GO

A fair number of flea markets are in this corner of France, although, given its size, perhaps not as many as in the neighboring regions of Languedoc-Roussillon and, farther east, Provence and the Côte d'Azur. Also, a significant number of the markets here are held only once a month, so you must plan your visit to coincide with them.

As in many parts of France, most of the flea markets here are held on weekends only, which is not surprising given the region's workaday nature. Exceptions include the Wednesday market in Cambo-les-Bains and the Friday-morning market in Bayonne, both in the Pays Basque. Also not surprisingly, most of the markets in this region are small to moderate in size, like the communities in which they are held. A few, however, are fairly large, such as those in Bordeaux and Ahetze, both with over 100 vendors, and the recently established market in Muret, southwest of Toulouse, which is quite substantial.

A large proportion of the markets are all day, but important exceptions include Bordeaux, Bergerac, Muret, and Bayonne, which are morning only. And as is always the case, your best bet for finding bargains is to arrive early. However, since your chances of finding a great deal here are generally not huge (less than in Languedoc-Roussillon, Provence, and Paris, for example), arriving early is not as compelling an idea as it might be elsewhere.

The late spring, early summer, and early fall are the best time of year to visit. The height of the summer is also the height of the tourist season, and in the Dordogne, for example, it can be hot and muggy then. If winter is the only time you can come, it is unfortunate but not disastrous. Along the Basque coast, at least, the weather is often quite mild then. Bayonne, for instance, has an average daily maximum temperature of 10°C. (50°F.) in January, and 15.4°C. (59.7°F.) in November.

MARKET FLAVORS: HOW THEY LOOK/HOW THEY FEEL

While difficult to generalize, the ambience of the markets of this region tends to be easygoing and low-key. While not brilliantly colorful and festive, these markets do have inviting qualities. The collectibles, and a hefty dose of local flavor, are the real highlights. Like the region itself, these markets are straightforward and down-to-earth, geared to browsing and buying. They also feel very much in tune with their surroundings and their regional heritage, which is why they will often appeal to collectors and general tourists alike. The Ahetze market, for example, takes place in a typical red-and-white-colored Basque village, in front of the village *fronton*, the high concrete wall against which the traditional Basque game of *pelota* is played. (There are many variants of *pelota;* it is not unlike squash, but faster, and the players sometimes use a bat or a *chistera,* or scooped basket, attached to their arms.)

In tune with their straightforward nature, these markets are often not prime spots for café-lounging and crowd-watching. What is so appealing, on the other hand, is that the experience feels real; you are participating in a regular, local activity.

THE COLLECTIBLES: WHAT YOU'LL FIND/WHAT TO LOOK FOR

The strong emphasis on regional collectibles in these markets means you will see lots of rustic items of all kinds, reflecting the region's rural nature. In the Pays Basque and Béarn, you will also find fine old linens, sometimes decorated with a navy (or occasionally red) stripe against a white background. Linens of a more recent vintage, in the typical Basque colors of red and green, are also to be found.

In the Pays Basque, you will come across items decorated with the Basque cross (from jewelry to old tiles). Keep a lookout for the ceramics so typical of this region, and of Béarn, in stark geometric patterns in burgundy and navy against a white background. Religious artifacts from Lourdes are also often spotted in these markets, thanks to the rampant tourism in that town over the years.

Generally, you will not see a lot of fine decorative items or many collectibles from outside France. However, sometimes you will spot things from nearby Spain, and occasionally items from Britain.

BUYING: PRICE LEVELS/BARGAINING OPPORTUNITIES

Although you might expect to find good bargains in this part of France because it's rural, people here are both conscious of the value of their regional heritage and quite savvy about the value of collectibles generally. As a result, you will discover that prices are generally not low, particularly for regional collectibles.

Also, while vendors here bargain somewhat, they often seem to expect to get close to their asking price, perhaps because, in setting it, they haven't left much room for the theatrics of major negotiating. Also, they will sometimes state the price in such decisive tones that you will feel little inclination to try to bargain. The consolation is that, though not generally low, prices are not exceptionally high either. You will likely see the purchases you make as no great bargain, but worth it nonetheless—and they will be treasured mementos of this great corner of France.

GETTING AROUND: HOW TO TRAVEL/WHERE TO GO

Having a car here is a real advantage, both for visiting the flea markets and exploring the region. Trains are not always frequent or convenient for all of the markets. Apparently, no bus or train serves the Ahetze market, the largest in the region. Also, some of the markets are small and only warrant a short stopover as you tour around, something easily accomplished by car but not by train. Driving is pretty unstressful here (except in and around Bordeaux) and parking quite easy. When in Bordeaux, be extremely careful not to leave any belongings in your car when you park. Several years ago, our car was broken into after only a few minutes when we left a small bag on the backseat.

Given that a number of these flea markets are monthly only, you should plan your trip carefully to make sure that you don't miss the ones you particularly want to see. I highly recommend scheduling your visit to coincide with the Ahetze market, on the third Sunday of the month. It will appeal to both collectors and general visitors as an authentic Basque experience. If you can't make it to Ahetze, other towns along this coast have smaller markets on the other Sundays of the month. Bayonne is also very worthwhile, both for its market and the town itself. I strongly suggest making St-Jean-de-Luz (on the coast south of Bayonne) your base in this part of the region. This quaint, yet very real and lively, seaside town is, far and away, my favorite spot in this corner of the country. (See Ciboure [St-Jean-de-Luz], below.)

If you are centered farther north, be sure to make it to Bordeaux's Sunday-morning market. I was pleasantly surprised by both the size and variety of this one. Between 100 and 120 vendors set up in the center of town, selling an eclectic mix of items at all price levels. Farther east, in the Dordogne, both Bergerac and Sarlat are interesting towns. Bergerac is, however, larger and more workaday (and its market bigger) than Sarlat, which is pretty and touristy, especially in the summer. Friends who have frequented the Bergerac market over several years have found many good bargains, particularly on collectibles from other regions.

Market Close-Ups

Six markets are featured in this chapter—Ahetze, Bayonne, Bordeaux, Cambo-les-Bains, Ciboure (St-Jean-de-Luz), and Pau. They are diverse both geographically and in terms of market schedules.

AHETZE (third Sunday of the month)

No. of Vendors: 150
Price/Quality Range: ✢ – ✢✢✢
Scenic Value: ✢✢ – ✢✢✢
Amenities Nearby: ✢✢

Featured Items: Tools, farm implements, hardware, kitchenware, toys, Basque tiles, furniture, secondhand clothing

WHEN, WHERE, HOW: Ahetze's flea market is held on the third Sunday of the month, from 6 A.M. to 6 P.M., in the center of this tiny village just east of the coast between St-Jean-de-Luz and Biarritz. Parking can be found along the side of the road; just follow the example of the other cars you will see. If you don't have a car and you are staying in St-Jean-de-Luz, for example, you may have to take a taxi; there is no train and apparently no bus service from St-Jean-de-Luz.

Tourist Office: 05-59-26-03-16 (St-Jean-de-Luz)

AHETZE IS ONE of those truly unspoiled places that you occasionally come upon in France—a small, pristine village, in perfect harmony with its surroundings and its regional heritage. Visitors have long since targeted other spots—such as Ainhoa, Ascain, and Espelette—as the picturesque rural destinations in this region to flock to, thus leaving less well-known places such as Ahetze largely undisturbed. Perhaps, ironically, because it is neither as beautiful nor as remote as other villages in this region, Ahetze has retained its natural, untarnished character.

As everywhere in this region, the buildings in this tiny village are decorated in the Basque manner, with whitewashed walls and red roofs and trim (or an occasional dark green). And as is also typical in this part of France, the main feature in the center of town is the *fronton*—in dark rose and decorated with the Basque cross and a kind of stonework motif—where the Basque sport of pelota is played.

THE MARKET

I was thrilled to discover the monthly flea market in Ahetze. It is a bargain hunter's, and collector's, dream—a market where, along with others, ordinary folks from around the region come to unload the junk and treasures they have amassed.

With my family in tow, I arrived here around dawn, as the early-morning mist was just beginning to lift. We had had to stop intermittently en route from St-Jean-de-Luz, where we were staying, so that one of my children could vomit out of the car window. No doubt his future years will be scarred by his having been dragged here in this condition, but I was not to be deterred. I had for days been anticipating coming to this market, having heard that this was not only the largest (with around 150 vendors) in the area, but also the best for good bargains and regional collectibles. Get there early, I was told; dealers begin appearing before dawn, armed with their flashlights.

As we pulled up, trucks and cars loaded down with their wares were still arriving, vying for the few remaining spots to set up in the chaos already unfolding. Some vendors and early patrons were lining up for coffee and baguettes, served in front of the town's *trinquet* (the indoor court for playing *pelota*). Eager purchasers stood by the new arrivals as their wares were being unloaded, reaching out to get first grab at such things as old copper pots and farm implements.

Vendors set up shop in the space in front of, and beside, the *trinquet* and in the *place* behind, between the village church and the *fronton*. (To get to the *place* from the *trinquet*, follow the little path along the side, bordered by whitewashed stone walls.) Many vendors simply set out their goods on the ground or in large cartons, while others pile their wares onto makeshift tables. The atmosphere is laid-back and cheerful; you get the sense that, for some, the market is a convenient meeting place as much as anything else.

You will find just about everything here, junk as well as collectibles—farm implements, tools, old clothes and linens (albeit not likely high-quality Basque linens unless you are lucky), old wooden toys, ceramics (including the regional dishes from Béarn, in geometric patterns in burgundy and navy blue on a white background), large copper pots, kitchenware of all kinds, milk jugs, Basque tiles, and furniture.

Prices are generally fairly reasonable here, although the more highly sought collectibles may well not be cheap. Bargaining does take place, although I got the impression that vendors are generally unwilling to lower prices significantly. I bought six old, striped wooden *quilles*, or pins, and balls —appropriately, in the Basque colors—for 50 francs. I initially tried to bargain the price lower, but the vendor maintained that it was totally reasonable and I had to agree.

The Ahetze monthly flea market is one of my favorite rural markets in France. If you are a bargain hunter, interested in collecting rustic items from this region, or even if you just want to experience a real local scene, I would strongly advise planning your trip around getting to this market. Even if I were living in Bordeaux, about 200 kilometers away, I would make sure to get here every month.

OTHER THINGS TO DO

Once you have seen the market, you should visit some of the wonderful little villages and towns not far from Ahetze—Ainhoa, Espelette (see Cambo-les-Bains, "Other Things to Do," below), Cambo-les-Bains (see below), St-Jean-Pied-du-Port, etc. If you hanker after a more urban experience, my all-time favorite town in this region is St-Jean-de-Luz, about a 25-minute drive away. St-Jean-de-Luz has everything—a wonderful shoreline and beach, a quaint old quarter with good shops, a real fishing-town feel, and a great food market. If you haven't already made St-Jean-de-Luz the base of your operations in the Pays Basque, be sure to leave plenty of time to explore it. See Ciboure (St-Jean-de-Luz), below.

BAYONNE (Friday morning)

No. of Vendors: 50 to 60
Price/Quality Range: ✦✦ – ✦✦✦
Scenic Value: ✦ – ✦✦
Amenities Nearby: ✦✦ – ✦✦✦

Featured Items: Regional ceramics, farm implements, Basque linens, copper pots, kitchenware, chocolate molds, religious items

WHEN, WHERE, HOW: Bayonne has a flea market every Friday morning, from 7 A.M. to noon, at the place de l'Arsenal in Petit Bayonne (on the east side of the Nive River), in the southern end of town. Parking can be found on the street by the place de l'Arsenal.

If arriving by train, the market is about a 15-minute walk from the station. Cross the Adour River at the St-Esprit bridge and continue south, along the east side of the Nive, turning left onto the rue Cordeliers, which leads into the place de l'Arsenal.

Tourist Office: 05-59-46-01-46

BAYONNE, THE DE facto capital of the Pays Basque, is an underrated town, probably in part because of its proximity to the much more touristy Biarritz, only a few kilometers away. Though it is not, perhaps, among the most beautiful cities in France, Bayonne has definite charms and is also a low-key, and relaxed place. While at the northern edge of the Pays Basque, Bayonne is clearly Basque in its appearance. The trademark colors of red (and sometimes green) on white decorate the half-timbered buildings lining the Nive River, which divides the town in two—Grand Bayonne, the larger central part on the west bank, and Petit Bayonne on the east.

Just a few kilometers inland from the Atlantic coast, Bayonne is situated where the Adour River meets up with the Nive. It is an old city, whose roots date back to the Roman Empire. Under English control for a few centuries during the Middle Ages, it was reclaimed by the French near the end of the Hundred Years' War. Its history was also marked by an influx of sephardic Jews at the beginning of the 16th century, who came here to escape persecution under the Spanish Inquisition. It is said that the chocolate-making industry, for which Bayonne is so renowned, owes much to the technical know-how the Sephardim contributed. (The town is also, apparently, the place where cocoa beans were first introduced into France.)

Bayonne is known as well for another epicurean delight; its smoked ham, *jambon de Bayonne,* is legendary throughout France. Of a less savory nature, however, is the town's prominent role, in the 18th century, in the armaments industry; it is also credited with having provided the bayonet its name.

THE MARKET

Bayonne's Friday-morning flea market, which takes place by the place de l'Arsenal in Petit Bayonne, is not picturesque. It is held in front of, and inside, an uninviting-looking building that appears to have once been a garage. My first reaction was disappointment, but this was soon dispelled in a discussion I fell into with a vendor and a local collector. The conversation was one you can maybe only have in a place like France, where the long-distant past, the recent past, and the present seem to naturally and unself-consciously coexist. The collector talked about lighters made by soldiers in the trenches during the First World War (his collecting passion), then somehow skipped to the reign of King Henry IV, the monarch born in Béarn who came to the throne in 1589 and was, we were told, a great and compassionate leader. Then our collector friend immediately switched gears to more current and mundane matters—the flea markets not to be missed in the Pays Basque. I was hooked.

With between 50 and 60 vendors, Bayonne's flea market is not big. However, given the paucity of large markets in this part of France, it is actually quite a significant one. It is also quite a good place for finding collectibles of the Pyrénées region, including the Pays Basque. You will see regional ceramics here, with geometric lines of burgundy and navy on white (popular in both Béarn and the Pays Basque). Basque and Béarn linens of all kinds are also to be found, in fine cotton (or sometimes linen or linen and cotton), and sometimes decorated with the characteristic navy blue (or occasionally red) stripe.

You will also likely find lots of farm implements and tools, old tiles decorated with the Basque cross, wooden shoes, chocolate molds, and large copper pots, used, I was told, for making *boudin,* a sausage made from pigs' intestines.

Here, I bought an old metal container from Lourdes, for holding *eau bénie,* or holy water. With its markings *1858–1958, souvenir du centenaire,* it celebrated a century since a 14-year-old girl from Lourdes, named Bernadette, claimed to have had numerous visions of the Virgin Mary. Bernadette is also said to have discovered (by following the Virgin Mary's instructions) a spring whose waters are asserted, by some, to have healing powers. A few million people visit Lourdes each year—in hopes of some miracle in their lives, as a form of devotion, or simply to witness the scene, which is very moving despite all the souvenir shops in town. Many fill containers (like the one I bought) with the so-called holy water from the spring, to take home with them.

Prices at the Bayonne market struck me as somewhat high, but there are exceptions. My little container from Lourdes was, I thought, quite reasonable at 50 francs. (This view was later reinforced when I found a much more battered duplicate at the Puces de St-Ouen in Paris for 150 francs.) A little celluloid doll, in Basque costume, was also a reasonable buy at 30 francs. While better bargains can perhaps be found at other markets in the area (such as Ciboure and Ahetze, for example), if you see something here that you covet—particularly if it is a regional collectible—your best bet is to go for it since you may not spot it elsewhere.

OTHER THINGS TO DO

Once you have visited Bayonne's flea market, be sure to spend some time looking around the city. Grand Bayonne is the most beautiful part, with its narrow pedestrian streets clustered around the huge old cathédrale Ste-Marie, which seems always to be towering in front of you, no matter which way you are headed. Stop in at two celebrated chocolate shops in town—Casenave and Daranatz—located close together at 19 and 15 rue Port Neuf. At Casenave, you can sit down and be served one of their renowned hot chocolates. Daranatz is a real feast for the senses—the window display is dazzling and the chocolates are equally wonderful.

For more ample sustenance, a great restaurant is François Miura (05-59-59-49-89), in Petit Bayonne, at 24 rue Marengo, just a few streets north of the flea market. This refined-looking restaurant serves equally elegant food at a reasonable price (when we were here, there was a 110-franc, three-course dinner menu), and the service is also very courteous. François Miura is open for lunch as well as dinner, so think about coming right after visiting the market. The meal I had here was one of the best (in its price range) that I have had in France.

Prior to its closure several years ago for renovations, the Musée Basque (also on the rue Marengo in Petit Bayonne) was renowned for its displays depicting traditional Basque life. When you arrive, ask at the tourist office whether this museum has yet reopened, as it should be well worth a visit.

BORDEAUX (Sunday morning)

No. of Vendors: 100 to 120
Price/Quality Range: ✦✦ – ✦✦✦
Scenic Value: ✦✦ – ✦✦✦
Amenities Nearby: ✦✦ – ✦✦✦

Featured Items: Furniture, ceramics, glassware, silver, jewelry, books, lamps, clocks, vases, art deco, and some Spanish, North African, and southwestern French items

WHEN, WHERE, HOW: Bordeaux has a large flea market every Sunday morning, from around 6 A.M. to 1 P.M. The market takes place in the center of town, in the place Meynard and the place Canteloup (popularly known as the place St-Michel) in front of the St-Michel church.

If arriving by car, head for the center of Bordeaux. The market is just west of the Garonne River, a short distance south of the Pont de Pierre and the place de Bir-Hakeim. While some parking is available near the *place,* your best bet is to park along the cours Victor Hugo and walk from there.

If arriving by train, the market is about a 15-to-20-minute walk from the station. Follow the cours de la Marne northwest from the station, turning right on the rue Leyteire and then right again on the rue des Cordeliers, which leads into the *place.* If you want to take public transit, take the #1 bus from the station and ask the driver for the basilique St-Michel.

Tourist Office: 05-56-00-66-00

I HAD ONLY been to Bordeaux once, before I came back to see its flea market. My first visit had been marred when, ten minutes after our arrival, someone tried to break into our car, destroying one of its locks. Because of this, my expectations of the place were quite low as I contemplated a return.

I was quite surprised then to find that, while it has its rough edges and dingy parts, Bordeaux is also a lively, impressive, and prosperous place, at least in its core. Bordeaux's history is long; once the capital of a Roman province, it was under English control for around three hundred years during the Middle Ages, when it prospered by exporting huge quantities of wine, much of it to England. At the end of the Hundred Years' War, Bordeaux reverted to France. The city's historical center, however, dates from the 18th century, when Bordeaux was a wealthy port, profiting from trade with the colonies.

The place Gambetta and the place de la Comédie, two main spots in Bordeaux, attest to the city's bourgeois elegance (although, apparently, the garden of the place Gambetta witnessed the grisly beheading of a few hundred people during the French Revolution). Today you will find several pleasant, narrow pedestrian streets in the Quartier St-Pierre, southeast of here, lined with appealing shops and restaurants. Be sure also to see the graceful Pont de Pierre, which crosses the Garonne River in the southeast end of town.

THE MARKET

Bordeaux's Sunday-morning flea market is a significant and interesting one for collectors with all kinds of tastes and interests, not to mention budgets. Starting early in the morning, between 100 and 120 vendors (somewhat fewer at the height of the summer, due to neighboring special *brocante* fairs) set up their wares in the place Meynard and the place Canteloup (commonly referred to as the place St-Michel), in front of the huge and imposing St-Michel church, and its adjacent tower. This is clearly a well-established flea market; the vendors seem remarkably undeterred by such things as inclement weather, so that even in a steady drizzle you will find them here, some barely bothering to protect their wares from the rain.

The setting is quite welcoming, though the narrow streets leading into the market feel a bit desolate and scruffy. The large square, dotted with tall, wrought-iron lampposts, is surrounded by solid-looking stone buildings, many decorated with flowers in the windows. This quarter has many *brocante* and antique stores, and several of them are also open during the Sunday-morning market. Most notable is the three-story Passage Saint-Michel, occupied by several dealers.

This is an eclectic market, where you will find old hardware and tools, in piles on the ground, next to nicely displayed art deco figurines and clocks or large armoires. The clientele is as diverse as the merchandise—you will see bourgeois Bordelais families, their primly dressed and carefully coiffed children in tow, next to men in elegant and colorful traditional Middle Eastern attire. Bargain hunters come early, along with dealers hoping to find something they can later resell at several times the price. It's casual and low-key, with vendors friendly and open in a way not always found in this region.

Here, you will see roughly equal amounts of furniture, rustic and everyday ware, and fine decorative objects—porcelain, regional dishes from Béarn in geometric patterns of navy and burgundy on white, 1940s and 1950s dishware, glassware, kitchen collectibles of all kinds (enamel coffeepots, coffee mills, copperware), jewelry, silver, books, hardware and tools, lamps and clocks, dolls, vases, art deco, leather chairs, tables, etc. Some Spanish, North African, and southwestern French influences can be felt here and there, and you may also spot the occasional item from England and even the United States. (I found some 1950s American Fire King pieces here, which the French call, generically, *opaline*).

Prices run the gamut, from a few francs for Béarn plates or 1940s and 1950s dishware to several hundred francs for old clocks and lamps. (I jealously watched a woman buying an attractive porcelain coffeepot, complete with creamer and sugar bowl, for 50 francs.) Bargaining is generally welcomed and good-natured. Try to arrive early if you hope to find a deal, since your chances of doing so are quite good. Given the hugely eclectic nature of the wares here, the kind of treasure you are likely to discover is highly uncertain, which makes the prospect especially appealing.

OTHER THINGS TO DO

Once you've finished at the market, check out the neighboring antique and *brocante* stores, especially the Passage Saint-Michel, its three stories jammed with antiques of all kinds. Inside is an attractive restaurant, the Brasserie du Passage. An inviting café—clearly a haunt of the dealers in the area—is on the *place* itself. I had an enjoyable and reasonably priced dinner nearby at la Taverne St-Pierre (05-56-48-22-19) at 13 rue des Bahutiers. This friendly, and crowded, little restaurant specializes in grilled meats, cooked over a large, open grill in the corner. The building also has an interesting history; it was apparently the home, in the mid-19th century, of a prominent women's and workers' rights advocate, Flora Tristan-Morcoso, who, it is said, was also the grandmother of the painter Paul Gauguin.

If you have a car, an all-day Sunday flea market takes place on the outskirts of Bordeaux, in the parking lot of the Intermarché shopping center in Bordeaux-Talence.

CAMBO-LES-BAINS (Wednesday, from March to December)

No. of Vendors: 15 to 30, depending on the season
Price/Quality Range: ✦✦✦
Scenic Value: ✦✦ – ✦✦✦
Amenities Nearby: ✦✦ – ✦✦✦

Featured Items: Porcelain, linens, books, postcards, small decorative objects

WHEN, WHERE, HOW: Cambo-les-Bains has an all-day (9 A.M. to 6 P.M.) flea market on Wednesdays, from March to December. From May to October, it is held at the edge of the Parc St-Joseph. Whatever direction you arrive from, follow signs to the Office de Tourisme, which is right next to the park. At other times, the market is held in the center of town.

If you are arriving by train, the station is across the Nive River from the main part of town, but the distance is walkable. Cross the river at the Pont de la Gare, head up into the main part of town, then continue a few blocks south to the park.

Tourist Office: 05-59-29-90-77

CAMBO-LES-BAINS is a pretty, albeit somewhat square, town in the heart of the Pays Basque. Noted for its treatment of people with tuberculosis and respiratory problems, perhaps its most celebrated patient was Edmond Rostand, the author of *Cyrano de Bergerac*, who came at the beginning of the 20th century and stayed for almost two decades. (His residence, the Villa Arnaga, is open to the public and is located a few kilometers outside town.)

As you drive around the periphery of the town, you can catch gimpses of some extremely posh treatment facilities. We met one respiratory sufferer here, an extremely refined elderly gentleman, who had come for treatment many years before from northern France and had remained ever since.

While Cambo-les-Bains is probably not a place you will want to spend a lot of time in, it is an actual town, unlike many places in this area, and a good stopover point on your tour of this region. Sitting outside overlooking the lower town (Bas Cambo) and gazing out at the wooded, rolling, green hills beyond has a definite restorative effect, whatever the state of your lungs.

THE MARKET

Cambo-les-Bains has quite a small flea market, which takes place all day on Wednesdays from March to December (if your visit is for early March or late December, call the tourist office to make sure that the market will be on).

Depending on the weather, and the time of year, between 15 and 30 vendors set up their wares at the edge of the Parc St-Joseph near the tourist office (from May to October) or in the town center (during the other periods).

Not surprisingly, given the market's modest size, you will find a limited variety of things. Generally, the merchandise is of a moderately high quality, with an emphasis on china and small decorative objects. You will also find fine linens (I did not see much in the way of Basque linens, however), books, and postcards. Prices are fairly high and the potential for serious bargaining may be somewhat limited.

OTHER THINGS TO DO

If you are looking for an inexpensive place to sit outside and have lunch, try the Hôtel Bellevue's restaurant (05-59-93-75-75), in the center of town overlooking Bas Cambo. We had an enjoyable meal here, out on the patio under the shade of a large canvas, while chatting with the extremely interesting man at the next table about everything from Roman history to nuclear disarmament. Here, an entrée and plat du jour, or plat du jour and dessert, was only 55 francs. The view makes the experience well worth it.

An even better idea, if you are willing and able to go a bit farther afield (about seven kilometers), is the Hôtel Euzkadi (05-59-93-91-88) in nearby Espelette (a town famous for its peppers). This beautiful vine-covered hotel, cheerfully decorated with long strands of red peppers, serves an extraordinarily hearty lunch in its large dining room with beamed ceilings and armoires filled with Basque linens. Spend a few minutes before lunch at Espelette's small, locally based food market (held on Wednesday mornings), across the parking lot from the hotel.

CIBOURE (ST-JEAN-DE-LUZ) (first Sunday of the month)

No. of Vendors: 50 to 75
Price/Quality Range: ✤ – ✤✤
Scenic Value: ✤ – ✤✤
Amenities Nearby: ✤ – ✤✤

Featured Items: Linens, kitchenware, tools, rustic items, secondhand clothes

WHEN, WHERE, HOW: There is a monthly flea market in Ciboure (just to the south of St-Jean-de-Luz, on the other side of the port), all day on the first Sunday of the month, from around 8 A.M. to 6 P.M. From Ciboure's port, follow the road along the coast—the boulevard Pierre Benoit—to the northwest of the village. The market is about two kilometers from the center, in the Quartier de l'Union; you should see signs for it posted as you go. If you have no car, it is a bit of a trek on foot from the train station in St-Jean-de-Luz to the market; while it's walkable, you might choose instead to take a taxi.

Tourist Office: 05-59-26-03-16 (St-Jean-de-Luz)

THOUGH AN INCREASINGLY popular vacation destination, St-Jean-de-Luz (along with its quieter and much less touristy neighbor to the south, Ciboure) has managed to retain its wonderful quality of a real and vibrant fishing town (albeit that the whales and cod of centuries ago have long since been replaced by tuna, sardines, and anchovies). The town's large, crescent-shaped shoreline and sandy beach make it a very appealing seaside resort. A fine walk along the coast is from the harbor to the rocky lookout at the town's northeastern edge. The long beaches just beyond Ciboure are spectacular, as well.

The old center of St-Jean-de-Luz is extremely charming—picturesque in a way that manages to be real, not fake. Needless to say, the typical Basque colors of red, white, and green predominate. This place has a long history; over a thousand years ago, it was already a significant whaling port. This town's most memorable event, perhaps, occurred in 1660, when Louis XIV married Maria Teresa, the daughter of the king of Spain, here in the oak-galleried St-Jean-Baptiste church on the rue Gambetta. As is often told, after the ceremony, the door used by the couple to leave was permanently closed off. The buildings in which they each stayed during the preparations for their elaborate wedding remain as prominent tourist sites in town.

You could happily spend days here, strolling about reveling in the fresh, sometimes bracing Atlantic air and eating *soupe de poisson,* Basque chicken, *piperade* (a Basque dish of scrambled eggs, peppers, onions, and tomatoes), and gâteau Basque at one of the town's many inviting, and often quite reasonably priced, restaurants. Interesting, and short, excursions in the surrounding area abound. St-Jean-de-Luz is well located for both drives around the French Basque countryside and forays into the Spanish Basque region just across the border. (The city of San Sebastian is only about thirty minutes away by car.)

THE MARKET

Unfortunately, St-Jean-de-Luz itself has no regular flea market, but Ciboure next door does, in the Quartier de l'Union, about two kilometers northwest of the village center. Compared to the picturesque environs, the setting of the market is a little disappointing. The site appears to be a kind of modern (at least by Pays Basque standards) housing development, although the traditional Basque architectural style and colors have largely been respected.

The ambience is, however, good—low-key and easygoing. This is not a busy market; vendors while away the time chatting together, sharing lunch, or taking a break at the little restaurant nearby. The laid-back scene must certainly contribute to the willingness of these vendors to converse with browsers and talk about their wares. One man I asked about the price of a little toy gendarme (French police officer) ended up giving it to me, after learning that I was a Canadian, as a memento of my trip. When I then picked up a little sailor figure, he offered it to me as well, and I decided that I had better stop asking.

This flea market has a truly local flavor; you get the impression that people from the surrounding region come here to sell things that they had at home. In this down-home scene you are, however, unlikely to find well-polished, high-end collectibles. The emphasis is on everyday items—old and less old—and while much is clearly uninteresting, there are some exceptions. Look out for linens from the region. I bought a Basque tablecloth, and a set of matching napkins, in red and green stripes on white (and embroidered in red with the letter *H*); while not terribly old, they were very attractive. You will also see kitchenware of all kinds, tools, ceramics, and some rustic items.

Prices are generally quite reasonable, particularly for things without an obvious regional cachet. I could not turn down a set of ten Depression-era plates for 20 francs (which I later left in a hotel room because I just did not have room for them in my luggage. Oh, the woes of a *chineur!*). You don't see a lot of heavy bargaining here. As elsewhere in this corner of the country, you get the feeling that the prices set pretty much reflect the vendor's idea of what things should go for.

I would recommend visiting this market if you happen to be in the vicinity on this day and if your tastes lie in everyday items, rather than fine collectibles. You might find something pleasing for only a few francs, and if you come early, you might actually make a real find. For some reason, the Ciboure market is not well-known, even though it is not new. To make sure it's going to be on, call the tourist office ahead of time, and persist if the person you are talking to has never heard of it.

OTHER THINGS TO DO

For a truly regional, flavorful, and inexpensive meal in St-Jean-de-Luz, try Le Tourasse (05-59-51-14-25) on the rue Tourasse in the center of town. A good two-course lunch—starter and main course (try the *poulet sauce basquaise*) or main course and dessert (they make their own gâteau Basque and it is very creamy)—can be had here for around 55 francs.

A fun bar, with a great view, is Le Brouillarta, right along the water by the Hôtel de la Plage (a good, moderately priced place to stay, with rooms overlooking the ocean). This bar's dark woodwork and yellow walls decorated with paintings provide a cheerful backdrop even if the day is rainy and blustery. Also, be sure to visit St-Jean-de-Luz's food market, on Tuesday and Friday mornings, not far from the tourist office. A picnic lunch of *jambon de Bayonne,* some *brebis* (a Pyrénées sheep's milk cheese), and gâteau Basque from Arrastia's stall is hard to beat.

The pedestrian area in the center of town houses many stores selling items for which this region is known—fine Basque linens (at Jean-Vier, but there are also many other shops), the Basque walking stick called the *makila,* and jewelry decorated with the Basque cross. Food lovers will want to try the macaroons at the Maison Adam, or the wonderful caramels at Pariès, both on the rue Gambetta.

PAU (Monday, Saturday, and Sunday morning)

No. of Vendors: 25
Price/Quality Range: ⚜⚜ – ⚜⚜⚜
Scenic Value: ⚜ – ⚜⚜
Amenities Nearby: ⚜ – ⚜⚜

Featured Items: Regional linens, furniture, silver, china, glassware, coins, militaria

WHEN, WHERE, HOW: Pau has a market on Saturday (9 A.M. to 12:30 P.M. and 2:30 P.M. to 6 P.M.), Sunday (10 A.M. to 12:30 P.M.), and Monday (9 A.M. to 12 P.M. and 2:30 P.M. to 6 P.M.), at the place du Foirail in the north end of town. If arriving by car from the autoroute, follow signs to the center and then to the "marché biologique/marché à la brocante." The place du Foirail is just southwest of the intersection of the rue Carnot and the boulevard d'Alsace-Lorraine.

If arriving by train, the station is at the south end of town by the Gave de Pau. The distance to the market from here is walkable, but if you want to take public transit, take the funicular to the boulevard des Pyrénées, walk the short distance northeast to the place Georges Clemenceau, then take either the #3, #4, or #6 bus, which all go near the place du Foirail. (Ask the driver where to get off.) If walking, from the place Clemenceau, head northwest on the rue Serviez and turn right on the rue Carnot; the place du Foirail is about five blocks up, on your left.

Tourist Office: 05-59-27-27-08

WHILE NOT A big stop on the tourist circuit, Pau is an important place in the political system of this region, as it has long been. Centuries ago it was the capital of Béarn (as well as the birthplace of the much revered King Henry 1V), while today it is the capital of the Pyrénées-Atlantiques department. In the mid-19th century, it was a popular place among the English. Some military officers, here years earlier with Wellington, later settled in this town with their families, and Pau was also touted as a healthy haven for turberculosis sufferers. (At one point, it is said, almost a sixth of Pau's population was British.)

Although located a little off the beaten track for general tourists to France, Pau serves as a gateway to a tour of the Pyrénées and as a good base for a visit to the town of Lourdes, about 40 kilometers to the southeast. From this attractive little city you can see some of the peaks of the Pyrénées on a clear day.

THE MARKET

All day (albeit with long lunch breaks) on Saturday and Monday, and on Sunday morning, Pau has a small collectibles market. This is not the usual kind of flea market, as the site is a market building where the vendors have reserved stalls. I am including it, however, partly because of the paucity of flea markets in this corner of the region, and also because of its frequency.

Several of the 25 or so stalls here are set up like little living or dining rooms. A number of the vendors specialize in furniture, and fine decorative items such as china, silver, and glassware, which enliven the scene. You will also find stalls featuring coins, books, and militaria.

However, I spent most of my time at the stand specializing in linens (and also crammed with all sorts of other things). This is a good place for traditional linens, which are becoming increasingly difficult to find, from Béarn and the Pays Pasque. Here, you will see sheets, tablecloths, dish towels, place mats, and all sorts of other items, in cotton, linen, and *métis* (cotton and linen). I bought an old and beautiful large piece of fabric (kind of an all-purpose cloth or towel), in white with the classic blue stripe, which I was told was hand-loomed in Béarn. I paid the asking price, 40 francs, without trying to bargain (a reduction would probably have been given for buying more than one item). I also had a pleasant conversation with the two female vendors, who kindly complimented me on my French. Sadly, though, they thought that I had said that Canada was a *vilain* (evil) country, rather than a *bilingue* (bilingual) one, as I had intended. So much for international communications.

Unless you are interested in purchasing some regional linens, you should not go out of your way to see this market. In addition to its being small, the prices are not low. The linens are, however, a big attraction, and if that is your interest, a short detour off the highway, if you are in the vicinity, is a good idea.

OTHER THINGS TO DO

Whatever your religious views, or your opinions about miracle cures, you must be sure to visit Lourdes while you are in the area. Tourism has been exploited to the hilt here (Lourdes is said to have the second-highest number of hotel rooms in France, after Paris), and the place is inundated with tacky souvenir spots. Nonetheless, the shrine marking the spot where the young Bernadette was supposed to have had visions of the Virgin Mary, almost a century and a half ago, is very moving. Crowds of people gather daily at this grotto sanctuary (where old crutches dangle from the entrance), with their sick and disabled relatives, hoping for some kind of miracle. It's a sad spectacle, to be sure, but an extraordinarily human scene as well.

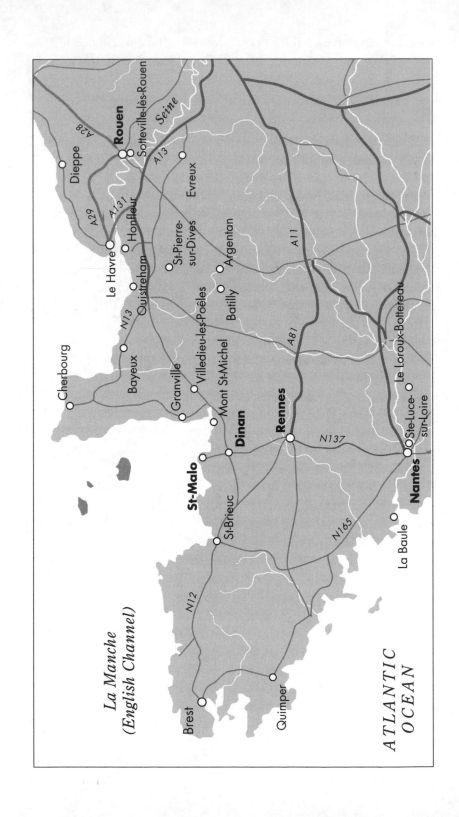

The Flea
Markets of
Brittany and
Normandy

Tuesday *ST-MALO (Quai Solidor) [20 to 25 vendors] (from late June to
beginning of September)
(8 A.M. to 6 P.M.)

Wednesday *DINAN (pl. St-Sauveur) [30 vendors] (from third Wednesday in
June to third Wednesday in September)
(7 A.M. to 7 P.M., but some vendors leave by noon)

Thursday *RENNES (boul. de la Liberté) [30 to 40 vendors]
(8 A.M. to 4 P.M., but many vendors leave by 2 P.M.)

*ROUEN (pl. des Emmurées) [60 vendors]
(8 A.M. to 6 P.M., but most vendors leave by noon)

STE-MARIE-SUR-MER (near Pornic) (place du Marché) [30 vendors]
(July and August)
(8 A.M. to 1 P.M.)

Saturday BREST (Halles St-Louis) [35 to 40 vendors]
(second Saturday of month)
(7:30 A.M. to 6 P.M.)

CHERBOURG (pl. des Moulins) [20 vendors]
(first Saturday of month)
(8 A.M. to noon)

EVREUX (Halles expos.) [30 vendors]
(first Saturday of month from September to June)
(8 A.M. to 6 P.M.)

*NANTES (pl. Viarme) [60 to 100 vendors]
(7:30 A.M. to noon)

*ROUEN (pl. St-Marc) [40 vendors]
(8 A.M. to 6:30 P.M., but most vendors leave by noon)

Sunday BATILLY (near Argentan) (Marché St-Roch) [10 to 15 vendors]
(last Sunday of month from March to October)
(9 A.M. to 6 P.M.)

LA BAULE (Bois des Aulnes) [40 vendors] (July and August)
(9 A.M. to 1 P.M.)

GRANVILLE (rue E. Lefranc) [20 to 30 vendors]
(9 A.M. to 6 P.M.) ($)

HONFLEUR (pl. St-Léonard) [35 to 40 vendors]
(second Sunday of month)
(8 A.M. to 6 P.M.)

LE LOROUX-BOTTEREAU (in front of Palais de Congrès)
[30 to 50 vendors] (second Sunday of month)
(9 A.M. to 1 P.M.)

OUISTREHAM (Grange aux Dimes) [20 to 30 vendors]
(second Sunday of month)
(7 A.M. to 7 P.M.)

*ROUEN (pl. St-Marc) [40 vendors]
(8 A.M. to 1:30 P.M.)

STE-LUCE-SUR-LOIRE (pl. C. de Gaulle) [80 to 90 vendors]
(first Sunday of month except August)
(7 A.M. to noon)

ST-PIERRE-SUR-DIVES (under les Halles) [35 vendors]
(first Sunday of month)
(9 A.M. to 6 P.M.)

SOTTEVILLE-LÈS-ROUEN (pl. de l'Hôtel de Ville) [20 vendors]
(second and fourth Sunday of month, but check ahead)
(9 A.M. to 1 P.M.)

VERTOU (marché Merlet) [50 to 80 vendors]
(last Sunday of month)
(6 A.M. to 2 P.M.)

Regional Overview

GETTING ORIENTED: ABOUT THE REGION

For those who dream of rocky seaside vistas and rolling green fields, Brittany and Normandy are the regions of France to visit. In this area, the countryside and the small towns and villages hold the greatest appeal, rather than the large centers.

This corner of France has a long history. Brittany was occupied by the Gauls and the Romans, before the Celts settled here many centuries ago (bringing their religious fervor and their language). An independent duchy from the 9th century, Brittany did not join France until the 16th century and even as a French province retained a strong independent identity.

Normandy has long been a battleground between competing forces. Prior to the arrival of the Norsemen from Scandinavia (from whom its name derives), it had already been the subject of numerous other struggles and occupations, involving the Celts, the Romans, and the Franks. United with France at the beginning of the 13th century, Normandy then endured the long French-English conflict, the Wars of Religion, and most recently the ravages of World War II.

Apart from their extraordinary countryside and coastline, Brittany and Normandy offer many sites of interest to the visitor—among them, the fairy-tale-like abbey of Mont-St-Michel, rising from the sea; the medieval Bayeux tapestry, depicting the Norman conquest; the spots symbolizing the martyr-dom of Joan of Arc, burned at the stake in Rouen's place du Vieux-Marché; and the D-day beaches of the Battle of Normandy, where so much devastation and loss of life occurred.

These regions have recently enjoyed enormous popularity as summer tourist spots. Brittany is now apparently the second most desirable summer vacation destination in France, after the Côte d'Azur. They are both wonder-fully relaxing places to visit, where driving around the countryside in search of fresh butter, cream, calvados, and Camembert cheese, or good seafood restaurants in rocky seaside towns, can easily fill the days.

I once spent a week with my family in an old stone house in the country-side not too far from Mont-St-Michel. I loved walking along country roads looking at cows and trudging along the cliff-backed beaches in the light driz-zle. One day, our landlord, a local farmer, brought us to see his "lifelong pas-sion," a little museum he had created, based on his personal collections of both every kind of agricultural implement and mementos of World War II. The day we were leaving, he arrived with a book on the history of Normandy and a bottle of his calvados. We were definitively hooked on the place.

MARKET RHYTHMS: WHEN THEY'RE HELD/WHEN TO GO

This is not a part of France with big flea markets; the largest, in Nantes, has at most around 100 vendors. The majority are in the 30-to-35-vendor range, which means that you will likely be slotting visits to the flea markets into your other travel plans. Below are some factors to consider in doing so.

Several of the flea markets in this region are year-round. However, some (located in prime tourist destinations) are held only during the summer, or from late June to early or mid-September—St-Malo, Dinan, and La Baule, for example. (While a couple of others do not take place in August, or in either July or August, these are generally in less significant spots, from a tourist perspective.)

The summer is also the best season for visiting. Mild temperatures are, naturally, considered desirable here, to best enjoy the coast and the beaches. For this, of course, July and August are the prime months; the average daily maximum temperatures then in Brittany are 25.1° and 24.2°C. (77° and 75.6°F.), respectively, while in Normandy they are 21.6° and 22°C. (70.9° and 71.6°F.). However, not surprisingly, this is also the peak tourist season, and these regions—especially Brittany—are inundated with tourists then, both French and others.

If warm beach weather is not as big a concern for you, both June and September can be quite nice—average daily temperatures during these months are 22.7° and 21.2°C. (72.9° and 70.2°F.) in Brittany, and 20° and 18.2°C. (68° and 64.8°F.) in Normandy. (Brittany is generally a little warmer than Normandy.) Visiting at other times of the year is more risky. October, for example, is apparently Normandy's rainiest month, and Brittany also gets a lot of rain during the fall. And not only is the weather problematic in the late fall, winter, and early spring, many of the places that cater to tourists are closed for periods of the off-season.

Taking all factors together—weather, crowds, flea markets—the best time to come is late June and early September, or July and August if you want warmer weather and you don't mind the crowds. (Even so, try to make it either early July or late August, since these are likely to be the least crowded intervals during this two-month period.)

The best time of day to visit these markets is probably late morning, when they tend to be liveliest. Even some of the markets billed as all-day affairs start to wind down by noon or soon after. There is usually little incentive to arrive early, since the potential for finding great bargains is limited. Instead, relax and fit the markets in with your plans for the day. (However, in a few cases, coming early might net you a good find—the Nantes and Rouen markets, for example.)

MARKET FLAVORS: HOW THEY LOOK/HOW THEY FEEL

The markets in this region are quite varied in their appearance (although less so in their range). While some are held in quite beautiful settings—St-Malo and Dinan, for example—others are located in more mundane spots, of little scenic or tourist value—such as the Nantes and Rennes markets.

While the atmosphere at these markets is somewhat a reflection of their varying aesthetic appeal, as a general rule they are not particularly festive or lively. Their ambience tends, rather, to be somewhat reserved and low-key, perhaps in keeping with the general tone of this part of the country. These are, however, relaxing and pleasant places for browsing for an hour or so, as part of your discovery of the region.

THE COLLECTIBLES: WHAT YOU'LL FIND/WHAT TO LOOK FOR

Although their flea markets are modest-sized, Brittany and Normandy are regions rich in collectibles. The most well-known (certainly to North Americans) is the colorful, naive faience ware from Quimper. While Quimper ware can be found at markets throughout France—and often at prices comparable to those you will see here—the advantage of coming here is that you will find many examples of it, of a wide variety.

Other regional items of interest to look out for in these markets are copperware, including that from the big Normandy copper-making town of Villedieu-les-Poêles, lacework and lace-making implements, milk jugs, cider pitchers, butter molds, religious figures, LU biscuit tins (from Nantes), traditional clothing and accessories, functional ceramics, Breton dolls, marine and nautical items (paintings, ship instruments and accessories, books, prints and postcards, and decorative items made from shells), and agricultural tools.

BUYING: PRICE LEVELS/BARGAINING OPPORTUNITIES

Generally speaking, I have not found many good deals on collectibles in this region. One reason may be the scarcity of low-end junk markets; another is probably the tourist focus of some of these markets. Also, and perhaps surprising to some, you are not likely to find great bargains for regional collectibles, whose cachet and value is well appreciated by vendors.

As for bargaining, while you will usually succeed in getting prices reduced by the standard 10 to 15 percent, the potential for much greater reductions is not huge. Vendors will often quote you a price and then, either immediately or soon afterward, name a lower figure that they would be willing to accept. My experience has been that the chances of doing much better than that are not great.

GETTING AROUND: HOW TO TRAVEL/WHERE TO GO

While train service in Brittany and Normandy is surprisingly extensive, having a car here is not only convenient but desirable, since it will allow you to see, at your leisure, all of the little communites for which this part of the country is so renowned. Driving here is also less crowded and hazardous than in many parts of the country (especially outside the peak tourist season). Consider picking up the car once you get to the region (by train)—for example, in Rennes or Rouen. That way you can avoid the hassle and stress of getting out of the Paris area.

As for where to go, no major or must-see markets are in this region. Some, however, are certainly worth including in your travel plans, being either fairly large or located in particularly appealing settings or towns—the markets in Rouen, Nantes, St-Malo, and Dinan, for example.

If you can, plan your visit to the northeast part of Brittany so that you are in St-Malo on Tuesday, Dinan on Wednesday, and Rennes on Thursday (so as to see all their markets). Those interested in Quimper ware should also try to make sure to include a visit to this town while in the region. As for Normandy, in addition to Rouen's markets, try to plan your visit to coincide with the second Sunday of the month, so that you can see both the Honfleur and Ouistreham flea markets. (Honfleur is an especially appealing seaside town.)

Market Close-Ups

The flea markets of five towns are featured below—Dinan, Nantes, Rennes, Rouen, and St-Malo. Together, they provide a variety of market experiences, on several days of the week.

DINAN (Wednesday, from the third Wednesday in June to the third Wednesday in September)

No. of Vendors: 30
Price/Quality Range: ✦✦✦

Scenic Value: ✦✦ – ✦✦✦
Amenities Nearby: ✦✦ – ✦✦✦

Featured Items: Quimper ware, nautical items, copperware, religious figures, Breton dolls, wooden shoes, books, prints, china, clocks, enamelware, rustic items generally

WHEN, WHERE, HOW: The Dinan flea market takes place on Wednesdays, from the third Wednesday in June to the third Wednesday in September. This is an all-day market, from 7 A.M. to 7 P.M., but several vendors leave around noon. It is held in the place St-Sauveur, in the old part of town within the ramparts.

If arriving by train, the market is about a 10-to-12-minute walk from the station. Head east on the rue Carnot to the place Général Leclerc and then south (right) on the rue Thiers to the place Duclos-Pinot, where you will enter the old quarter. Follow the Grande Rue to the place des Cordeliers, jog a bit to your right to the place des Merciers and then left on rue de l'Apport, turning right on rue de la Larderie, which leads into the place St-Sauveur.

If arriving by car, try to find parking in one of the lots along the rue Thiers or around the place Général Leclerc.

Tourist Office: 02-96-39-75-40

ALTHOUGH BRITTANY IS most famous for its coastal attractions, the country-side is also appealing, and Dinan is widely considered one of the region's most picturesque inland towns. Surrounded by ramparts dating from the 13th century, its well-preserved old quarter boasts many beautiful half-timbered buildings lining the narrow streets. From the east end of the ramparts, by the Jardin Anglais, you can see the Rance River below, which flows by the town, framed by rolling fields. A pleasant (albeit short) path alongside the ramparts —the promenade de la Duchesse Anne—takes you, ultimately, to the town's château.

This is a popular tourist town, seemingly especially among the English. However, it is a discreet form of tourism that manages not to mar Dinan's appeal. The town's small population of around 12,000 also makes this an easy place for a short stopover on your tour of the region.

THE MARKET

The place St-Sauveur, located in the heart of Dinan's old quarter, has long served as a marketplace. A covered meat market existed here before the mid-18th century. Dinan's weekly flea market is now held here all day (though several vendors leave around noon) on Wednesday, from the third Wednesday in June to the third Wednesday in September.

Although not large, the *place* is edged by some fine 17th- and 18th-century buildings and dominated at the far end by the église St-Sauveur. About 30 vendors set up their wares in this tree-lined spot—mostly arranged on tables, although a few vendors, offering more rustic items, display their goods on the ground. This is a fairly high-end market, with both regional items—decorative and rustic—and general collectibles. From Brittany, apart from Quimper ware, you will see religious figures, Breton dolls, paintings and prints of Breton subjects, nautical items of various kinds, and agricultural implements.

One gets the impression that this market is largely aimed at tourists, a view reinforced by its short, summer-based schedule. The reserved manner of the vendors, however, gives no suggestion of any inclination to pursue that clientele actively; vendors do not go out of their way to volunteer information, although they do answer politely enough if you ask questions. (A number of the vendors also sell at other markets in the region, no doubt attempting to capitalize on the relatively short prime tourist season.)

Prices are moderate to fairly high. The regional cachet of things is well appreciated by vendors, and prices reflect that. This is not a place to get a great deal on a pair of wooden shoes or a ship's model, for example. Ironically, your best bet for unearthing any kind of find here may well be collectibles from outside the region, whose value may not be completely appreciated. As for bargaining, I noticed vendors often taking the initiative, offering a some-what lower price when the prospective purchaser hesitated.

This market makes for a pleasant, and short, stopover for both general tourists and collectors. Although I would not recommend that you go far out of your way to see it, I would suggest planning your trip to this part of Brittany so that it falls on a Wednesday. While you may not find a lot here that you want to purchase, combining a round of the flea market with your visit to this picturesque town is a good idea.

OTHER THINGS TO DO

For an inexpensive and light lunch, served in a classic half-timbered building, try the Crêperie Connetable, at 1 rue de l'Apport (02-96-39-02-52), just around the corner from the market. This place, which serves up fine *galettes* and crepes (as well as other things), accompanied by the trademark *bolée* (bowlful) of cider, also provides friendly and efficient service—all in all, a quite satisfactory experience.

Dinan's flea market is wedged in between two others not far away—the

Tuesday market in St-Malo and the Thursday market in Rennes (see both, below). Despite some overlap in the vendors at these markets, I would recommend that you plan your visit to Brittany so that you get to see all three, if possible.

NANTES (Saturday morning)

No. of Vendors: 60 to 100
Price/Quality Range: ✦✦ – ✦✦✦
Scenic Value: ✦ – ✦✦
Amenities Nearby: ✦✦

Featured Items: Kitchenware, tools, Quimper ware, lamps, glassware, linens, jewelry, books, nautical items, furniture

WHEN, WHERE, HOW: Nantes has a flea market every Saturday morning, from around 7:30 A.M. to noon. The market is held in the place Viarme, in the northwest corner of town.

If arriving by train, the market is a few kilometers from the station. Either take a taxi or public transit (tram 1, direction Bellevue, to the Commerce stop and then, on the cours des Otages, a little to the north, bus #40, which will take you to the place Viarme).

If arriving by car, you should have little difficulty finding parking on the street nearby.

Tourist Office: 02-40-20-60-00

ALTHOUGH NANTES IS now included in another administrative region—the Pays de la Loire—it has historically been part of Brittany, and is still widely considered a Brittany town. Indeed, this is the site of the Château des Ducs de Bretagne, built in the 15th century by the rulers of the once-independent duchy of Brittany.

Thanks to its strategic position on the Loire River, not far from the sea, Nantes prospered greatly in the 18th century from shipping and colonial trade, including, sadly, the slave trade. Today, it is a significant city, with a poulation of over a quarter million people. Nothwithstanding the modern apartment buildings and industrial-looking sites outside its center, the core of Nantes is quite appealing, with impressive squares and lots of interesting little streets and shops. One of the most remarkable sites is the Passage de Pommeraye, a 19th-century precursor of the modern shopping mall (although on a much finer scale). Built on two levels, it is elaborately decorated with stone statues and covered by a glass ceiling.

THE MARKET

While not huge—with up to 100 vendors—the Nantes flea market is significant for this region. (The number of vendors here actually sometimes dips to around 60, especially during the summer high tourist season, when some sellers are temporarily lured away by special *brocante* fairs in the region.)

The market takes place every Saturday morning, in the place Viarme, in the far northwest corner of town. More like a parking lot than a public square, the place Viarme is not particularly appealing. The buildings that surround it are modern, at least by French standards, and not of any great interest.

This is, however, quite a good market from the point of view of collectors, if not general tourists. It offers a wide range of goods to appeal both to those interested in modest, everyday collectibles and those looking for finer decorative objects. One side effect, perhaps, of this market's lack of quaintness is its down-home quality; many vendors simply lay their wares out on the ground, piled in crates or poured onto blankets, while others, with finer-quality items, set up displays on tables.

You will find a hodgepodge of things here—kitchen crockery, enamelware, copperware, porcelain canister sets, tools, fixtures, old bed warmers, Quimper ware, ships' models, fishing gear, watering cans, glassware, jewelry, books, linens, and some furniture. One of the weirdest things I have ever seen at a flea market I spotted here—a fully dressed, life-size dummy, apparently used to train horses to become accustomed to riders.

Prices are all over the map at this market, in keeping with the wide diversity of the wares. I bought a lovely old Brittany sugar tin for 50 francs (the vendor first asked 70 francs) and a polka-dotted pitcher for 30 francs. As is typical of this region, the Quimper ware is not cheap, but there is a fair selection to choose from. Rustic items, while also not low-priced, are generally less expensive than in the more tourist-based markets of St-Malo and Dinan, for example.

OTHER THINGS TO DO

Once you've finished scouring the collectibles, head immediately for the center of town. While you will find a couple of places right by the market for a coffee, far more congenial spots are elsewhere. Perhaps the most beautifully and lavishly decorated café/brasserie that I have been to in France is in Nantes—La Cigale, in the place Graslin (02-51-84-94-94). Built at the end of the 19th century, this spot is a visual feast. Tiled images of whimsical cicadas (*cigale* is "cicada" in English) decorate the walls, sharing the lime-light with other tiled geometric designs and painted murals of romantic scenes. The colors are brilliant—a perfect match for the elaborate moldings and beveled mirrors. Come for lunch (the lunch menu is not expensive), or at least for a late-morning coffee; the café au lait is one of the best I have had in France.

For some wonderful chocolates, try Gauthier Debotté, an elegant mid-19th-century shop around the corner from the tourist office, at 9 rue de la Fosse. Be sure to sample the *mascarons* (chocolates with a praline filling), one of their specialties.

RENNES (Thursday)

No. of Vendors: 30 to 40
Price/Quality Range: ✦✦✦
Scenic Value: ✦✦
Amenities Nearby: ✦✦ – ✦✦✦

Featured Items: Quimper ware, nautical items, religious statues, kitchenware, books, postcards, linens, glassware, ceramics, some furniture

WHEN, WHERE, HOW: Rennes' flea market takes place on Thursday, from 8 A.M. to 4 P.M. (although many vendors pack up by 2 P.M.). It is held in the center of town, at the corner of the boulevard de la Liberté and the rue Jules Simon, alongside the food-market hall.

If arriving by train, the market is about a 10-minute walk from the station. As you exit, follow the avenue Jean-Janvier north and then turn left on the boulevard de la Liberté. The market is a couple of blocks to the west. If arriving by car, you should be able to find parking on neighboring streets.

Tourist Office: 02-99-79-01-98

RENNES IS OFTEN described as not typically Breton in appearance, although it has been Brittany's capital since the region joined France in the first half of the 16th century. Perhaps its non-Breton look has to do with the fact that much of the city burned down in a big fire in 1720 and had to be rebuilt; only a few of the quaint old streets with their half-timbered buildings remain.

Rennes is not considered a major tourist attraction, but it's actually quite a pleasant little city (which, thanks to the TGV, can now be reached by train

from Paris in around two hours). A workaday town, its population is significant, with around 200,000 people. Two splendid features—in addition to the
old quarter around the place Ste-Anne—are the place de la Mairie and the
Palais de Justice (which managed to survive the early-18th-century fire).

THE MARKET

Rennes' flea market, while not a great one, is certainly worth a visit if you are
in the vicinity on a Thursday. Between 30 and 40 vendors set up on the sidewalk along the periphery of the modern food-market hall, in the southern part
of town. Although the setting is not very appealing, this market has fairly
high-end wares, with prices to match. A fair range of collectibles is to be
found here—fine decorative objects (porcelain, glassware, art deco, lamps,
figurines); some rustic items (wooden shoes, tools, wooden implements); and
regional goods (a fair selection of Quimper ware, as well as religious statues,
old Brittany souvenirs, and nautical items such as ship models, paintings of
maritime subjects, and ship instruments and accessories).

This is not a busy market, nor is its ambience particularly congenial; not
only is the setting somewhat mundane, but the atmosphere is not animated or
lively. Vendors also tend to stand back and wait for you to approach them,
instead of volunteering information or assistance. (I recognized a few of them
from other markets in the vicinity; as noted in Dinan, above, doing the market circuit seems to be a common practice during the summer in this region.)

This market is, however, certainly worth at least a quick look, particularly
if you are interested in collectibles from this region, or items with a nautical
theme. While the Quimper ware is not cheap, some of the examples I saw
here (a fish-shaped dish and a piggy bank, for instance) were somewhat
unusual, if not, perhaps, particularly old. This market, however, would not
greatly appeal to general tourists, given its small scale and rather prosaic
setting.

OTHER THINGS TO DO

For a café or restaurant after seeing the market, head north to the old part of
town, around the place Ste-Anne. Particularly promising for this purpose are
the rues St-Michel and Penhoët. Another street to check out on this score is
the rue St-Georges, southeast of the Palais de Justice. To buy food for a picnic lunch, look no further than the food-market building itself and neighboring stores. I was quite impressed with both the bread and pastries (especially
the buttery regional specialty, called *kouign-amann*) at M. Laigre, at 28 rue
de Nemours (just west of the market), where the kind woman serving us
offered to heat our portion up, claiming that it tastes better that way.

Collectors of Quimper, and others interested in the history of this famous ceramic style, will want to be sure to visit the town of Quimper itself while in the area. I took the train here from Rennes, a journey of only a few hours. The town is quite charming (although, sadly, lacking a regular flea market), with a small medieval quarter. To find two of its main attractions—the HB-Henriot Faïenceries and the Musée de la Faïence—follow the south side of the Odet River (which is crisscrossed at regular intervals by little pedestrian bridges, decorated with flowers), southwest of the old quarter.

Faience ware has been made in Quimper for over three centuries, first begun by a man from Provence, Jean-Baptiste Bousquet (whose name supplied the B in HB-Henriot). Since 1984, the HB-Henriot Faïenceries, on the rue Haute, which has been carrying on this tradition, has been owned by an American couple. Interesting tours of the *faïencerie* are offered from March to October (call 02-98-90-09-36, for hours and information), and the store next door offers a wide selection of Quimper ware for you to buy. (Prices are not cheap, but you will understand why after you have toured the facilities.) The nearby Musée de la Faïence, at 14 rue Jean-Baptiste Bousquet, is also quite interesting, with some extraordinarily detailed and fine examples of earlier Quimper ceramics. (Open from mid-April to the end of October, Monday to Saturday, 10 A.M. to 6 P.M. Phone: 02-98-90-12-72.)

ROUEN (Thursday)
(Saturday and Sunday morning)

PLACE DES EMMURÉES
No. of Vendors: 60
Price/Quality Range: ✦✦ – ✦✦✦
Scenic Value: ✦ – ✦✦
Amenities Nearby: ✦✦

Featured Items: Linens, coffee mills, enamelware, champagne capsules, tools, books, records, phone cards, spice canisters, advertising items, copperware, irons

PLACE ST-MARC
No. of Vendors: 40
Price/Quality Range: ✦✦ – ✦✦✦
Scenic Value: ✦✦ – ✦✦✦
Amenities Nearby: ✦✦✦

Featured Items: Copperware, linens, records, books, kitchenware, glassware, china, butter and cream makers, figurines, postcards, some furniture

WHEN, WHERE, HOW: Rouen has two weekly flea markets. One is held all day Thursday, from 8 A.M. to 6 P.M. (although most vendors leave by noon), in the place des Emmurées, in the Rive Gauche, on the south side of the Seine. The other takes place in the place St-Marc, in the Rive Droite (on the eastern edge of the old quarter), on Saturday (theoretically, all day from 8 A.M. to 6:30 P.M., but almost all vendors pack up around noon) and Sunday mornings (from 8 A.M. to 1:30 P.M.).

If arriving by train, the place des Emmurées market is not within easy walking distance of the station. Take the subway south from the station, exiting at the Joffre-Mutualité stop. The market is no more than a 4-to-5-minute walk from here; as you exit, follow the cours Clemenceau east and then turn right (south) on the rue François Arago, which leads, a short block down, into the place des Emmurées. If arriving by car, parking can be found nearby.

The place St-Marc is about a 15-minute walk southeast from the train station; head south on the rue Jeanne d'Arc, turning left (east) on the rue Ganterie (which then becomes the rue de l'Hôpital). Then turn right (south) on the rue de la République, jogging east again on the rue d'Amiens and then south on the rue Armand Carrel, which leads into the place St-Marc. (You can also take bus #8 from the station, or take the subway partway, getting off at the Palais de Justice stop and walking the short distance southeast from there.) If arriving by car, a parking lot is at the south end of the place St-Marc.

Tourist Office: 02-32-08-32-40

WHEN I RECENTLY visited Rouen for the first time—to check out its flea markets—I couldn't believe that it had taken me so long to finally come here. This beautiful, historically significant city is within easy reach of Paris by TGV, the high-speed train. Chosen capital of Normandy in the tenth century, upon the creation of the duchy of Normandy, Rouen's history actually goes back much further, to the Romans and the Gauls before them. This was a powerful city, both before and after the Norman conquest, and was bitterly fought over during the long English-French conflict that culminated in the Hundred Years' War. After sustaining a lengthy siege during that struggle, Rouen fell to the English, who then ruled here for 30 years.

Probably Rouen's biggest claim to historical fame occurred during the Hundred Years' War. Joan of Arc, captured by allies of the English, the dukes of Burgundy, was tried by the Rouen ecclesiastical court on charges of witchcraft and heresy (she claimed to be inspired in her campaigns against the British by voices she heard and images she saw). In 1431, she was condemned to death and burned at the stake in Rouen's place du Vieux-Marché. A quarter-century later, however, in the same place in which she had been condemned, Joan was declared "rehabilitated" by the Church.

The story of Joan of Arc somewhat dominates the tourist agenda of Rouen, offering numerous landmarks to visit (for instance, the site where Joan was sentenced to death, the keep of the castle where she was imprisoned, and the spot where she was burned at the stake). Rouen has many other interesting sites besides those relating to Joan of Arc: the cathédrale de Notre-Dame, so immortalized by Monet; the Gros Horloge (the large clock that, since the early 16th century, has spanned a central shopping street, the rue du Gros-Horloge); and the eerie but remarkable 14th-century Aître St-Maclou, a burial site for victims of the Plague (which is encircled by timber beams carved with macabre images of bones, skulls, shovels, and crosses).

The big tourist attractions aside, just walking along Rouen's old streets lined with half-timbered, lead-windowed buildings—some with overhanging upper stories—is enjoyable. While many parts of Rouen were ravaged during World War II, some fortunate enclaves were spared.

PLACE DES EMMURÉES MARKET

The Thursday all-day flea market in the place des Emmurées is quite far removed from the medieval splendor of Rouen's center (although very accessible from it, via the city's modern subway system). Located on the Left Bank —which, sadly, lacks the charm and character of the Right—the place des Emmurées is an unremarkable little square. The flea market takes place in the ground floor of a parking lot, hardly a promising setting.

And yet, while certainly not quaint, this concrete backdrop is sort of appealing—even cosy. Perhaps it is due to the yellowish lighting, which assists the natural light in casting a bit of a warm glow on the vendors' stalls. The ambience is also relaxed and low-key, with vendors taking the time to answer questions and share information, without putting any pressure on you to buy.

Despite its somewhat inauspicious setting, this is a collectibles, not a junk, market, with a good mix of both modest and decorative items, which will appeal to a broad range of collecting tastes. Many of the 60 or so vendors here specialize in one (or a few) items, such as linens, coffee mills, enamel coffeepots, books, champagne capsules, records, coasters, phone cards, advertising items, irons, ceramics, and tools. A few offer a more eclectic (as well as more haphazardly displayed) array of wares. Regional collectibles, if not particularly featured, can be found, such as copperware, farm implements, cowbells, and Normandy linens. (I was told that linens from this region can be somewhat distinguished by their slightly yellowish, as opposed to grayish, tinge.)

Prices are not cheap, but not excessive either. The best deals might be found on something from another region of France altogether. I bought (for 50 francs) an old Alsatian ceramic baking mold, used to make that region's kugelhopf cake. (The vendor did not know what the mold was for or where it came from.) I also bought a 1950s pale jadeite-colored salt-and-pepper holder for 30 francs. (Everyday items from this era have recently started to become quite sought-after in France.)

This is a market of interest to collectors of good quality, but modest, everyday household items. Given its less than scenic setting, general tourists, on the other hand, are best advised to visit Rouen's place St-Marc market instead (see below), on Saturday and Sunday mornings.

PLACE ST-MARC MARKET

Located on Rouen's Right Bank, the place St-Marc is a large, flower-bedecked square, edged by elegant redbrick buildings. On Saturday and Sunday mornings, collectibles share the *place* with a bustling outdoor food market (which occupies the northern end). While the Saturday flea market is billed as an all-day affair, most vendors actually pack up by just after noon. Sunday is apparently quite a bit more lively and busy than Saturday.

This flea market offers a wide variety and range of collectibles. In addition to what you will find at the place des Emmurées (some vendors do both markets), here you will also see large pieces of furniture and, at the other end of the spectrum, the occasional pile of secondhand clothing and old linens. There is perhaps a somewhat greater regional focus here than at the place des Emmurées—more copperware and agricultural implements, for example, as well as such things as butter and cream makers.

Prices run the gamut, like the wares. Arriving fairly early might reward you with a good find. I would recommend this market to general visitors as well as to collectors; its setting is appealing, you can combine it with a tour of the food market, and it is conveniently located close to many of Rouen's other sights.

OTHER THINGS TO DO

Those interested in checking out antique shops or the faience of Rouen (old and new) will find many stores of interest in and around the place Barthélémy and on the rue St-Romain. You might also consider visiting Rouen's Musée de la Céramique (open from 10 A.M. to 1 P.M. and 2 P.M. to 6 P.M. Phone: 02-35-07-31-74).

For an appealing café or restaurant, check out the place du Vieux-Marché or the area around the St-Maclou church; the only problem you will encounter is choosing the quaintest-looking one. I had a hearty and reasonably priced lunch at Le P'tit Bec (02-35-07-63-33), at 182 rue Eau de Robec, close to the place St-Marc market. This cheery and lively local hangout also offers an impressive selection of especially good desserts.

ST-MALO (Tuesday, from late June to the beginning of September)

No. of Vendors: 20 to 25
Price/Quality Range: ✦✦ – ✦✦✦
Scenic Value: ✦✦✦ – ✦✦✦✦
Amenities Nearby: ✦✦ – ✦✦✦

Featured Items: Nautical items, Quimper ware, Breton dolls, religious figures, silver, glassware, books, postcards, copperware, some furniture

WHEN, WHERE, HOW: St-Malo has a flea market all day Tuesday, from around 8 A.M. to 6 P.M., from late June to the beginning of September (call to confirm actual dates). The market takes place at the Quai Solidor, a few minutes' walk southeast of the walled center of St-Malo.

If arriving by train, the market is about a 25-minute walk from the station. Head west on the avenue Louis Martin to the central tourist office. Turn left (south) along the quay just before the ramparts and continue southeast to just beyond the car-ferry terminal. From here, jog slightly westward toward the sea. Follow the walkway along the beach—the Plage des Bas Saisons—southwest, and then, at the end of the walkway, continue south (across the neck of the peninsula that juts out at the end of the beach) to the other side, where you will arrive at the Quai Solidor, site of the market.

If arriving by car, your best bet is to try to park in the lots at the south end of the ramparts and to walk the short distance from there.

Tourist Office: 02-99-56-64-48

UNTIL I SAW St-Malo, I didn't think that any other Atlantic town could match the appeal of St-Jean-de-Luz, in the Pays Basque. At first glance, this uniformly gray, walled town looks austere and somber. A short walk around its ramparts, however, will quickly make you aware of its great charms, particularly its extraordinary setting. The coastline of this seafaring town—famed for its explorers and shipbuilders—is wonderfully varied. Long, flat, sandy beaches are interrupted by lavalike rock formations, and the seascape is punctuated by rugged peninsulas and little islands.

A lot of tourists are here, especially in the summer, but St-Malo manages to rise above even that impediment. It has a festive feel, despite its stolid, gray walls; the little streets within the ramparts are filled with shops, cafés, and surprisingly casual and affordable restaurants. (Much of the town was actually rebuilt after its devastation during World War II, although you wouldn't know it when you stroll around.) For Canadians, St-Malo has a special significance. Jacques Cartier, who explored the St. Lawrence River, lived and set sail from here, and a statue along the ramparts, looking out to sea, commemorates his travels.

THE MARKET

St-Malo's flea market takes place outside the walls, at the Quai Solidor, a few minutes' walk along the coast to the south. A more serenely picturesque setting can hardly be imagined. The market faces the sheltered, crescent-shaped bay, which is dotted with little islands and colorful sailing boats. Jutting into the bay, to the west, is a tower-cum-museum, called the Tour Solidor, surrounded by a little flower garden. In contrast to the walled citadel, this is a quiet, relatively undiscovered little enclave, a bit reminiscent of a small fishing town.

The flea market, held all day Tuesday during the summer, is small, with 20 to 25 vendors who display their wares along the walkway in front of the beach. The atmosphere is relaxed—even sleepy. You can hear the cry of the seagulls and the clanging sound of the breeze on the sailboat masts as you stroll along. These qualities (so welcome to travelers weary of crowded urban scenes) compensate somewhat for this not being a busy, or lively, market.

The things you will see have a distinct marine or nautical focus—paintings of ships and seascapes, old ship parts (instruments, anchors, cords, pulleys), decorative items made from shells, and books on nautical subjects. You will also see other Brittany collectibles—Quimper ware, religious figures, dolls— as well as general collectibles such as silver, glassware, copperware, dishes, postcards, and some furniture. Prices are not low; you get the impression that vendors have been collecting things over the year, in anticipation of the tourist season, and hope for a decent return on their work.

Even if you do not buy anything here, I would recommend planning your visit to St-Malo to coincide with this market. The setting is lovely and the atmosphere relaxing—a welcome respite from the crowded tourist scene within the walls.

OTHER THINGS TO DO

After seeing the flea market, sit down for an outdoor lunch at one of the little restaurants across the street. It's hard to beat the setting, with views of both the market and the sea. The Crêperie Solidor, at 7 esplanade Menguy, offers delicious Breton *galettes* served with a wide choice of fillings. Wash it all down with some cider, which in Brittany is served in large cups.

Inside the eastern end of St-Malo's ramparts, you will also find a wide range of casual restaurants to choose from, offering all kinds of seafood (and other things) at quite reasonable prices. And in between lying on the beach and rampart-strolling, consider trying your luck at St-Malo's Casino (located right along the shore, just east of the walls).

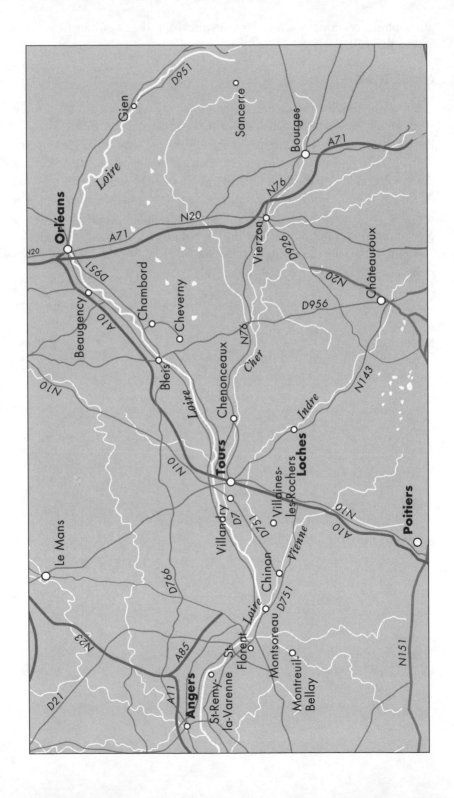

The Flea
Markets of
the Loire Valley

Wednesday   *TOURS (pl. de la Victoire) [30 to 40 vendors]
(8 A.M. to 5 P.M., but almost all vendors leave by 1 P.M.)

Friday   LE MANS (pl. du Jet d'Eau) [10 vendors]
(8 A.M. to 12:30 P.M.)

*POITIERS (pl. Charles de Gaulle) [30 vendors]
(8 A.M. to 6 P.M., but several vendors leave by 1 P.M.)

TOURS (rue de Bordeaux) [25 vendors]
(first and third Friday of month)
(8 A.M. to 6 P.M.)

Saturday   *ANGERS (pl. Louis Imbach) [40 vendors]
(8 A.M. to noon)

*LOCHES (pl. de Verdun) [25 to 30 vendors]
(first Saturday of month)
(8 A.M. to 6 P.M.)

*ORLÉANS (boul. A. Martin) [100 to 110 vendors]
(8 A.M. to 5 P.M., but almost all vendors leave by 12:30 P.M.)

*TOURS (pl. de la Victoire) [30 to 40 vendors]
(8 A.M. to 5 P.M., but almost all vendors leave by 1 P.M.)

Sunday   BEAUGENCY (pl. du Martroy) [20 to 30 vendors]
(first Sunday of month from April to November)
(7:30 A.M. to 6 P.M.)

BLOIS (Mail St-Jean) [35 to 40 vendors] (second Sunday of month)
(7 A.M. to 7 P.M.)

CHÂTEAUROUX (Quartier des Marins) [300 vendors]
(first Sunday of month from October to July)
(7 A.M. to 1 P.M.)

CHINON (Parking Dr. Mattrait) [50 vendors]
(third Sunday of month)
(7 A.M. to 7 P.M.)

MONTREUIL-BELLAY (pl. des Ormeaux) [30 to 40 vendors]
(fourth Sunday of month)
(8 A.M. to 7 P.M.)

MONTSOREAU (Quai de la Loire) [60 vendors]
(second Sunday of month)
(9 A.M. to 6 P.M.)

ST-FLORENT (pl. Mairie) [30 vendors]
(first Sunday of month from April to December)
(7 A.M. to 7 P.M.)

ST-RÉMY-LA-VARENNE (pl. de l'Église) [15 to 25 vendors]
(third Sunday of month)
(9 A.M. to 6 P.M.) ($)

SANCERRE (Nouvelle Place) [50 to 60 vendors]
(third Sunday of month from November to April, but check)
(8 A.M. to 6 P.M.)

*TOURS (boul. Béranger) [150 vendors] (fourth Sunday of month)
(7 A.M. to 7 P.M.)

VIERZON (pl. de l'Ancienne Mairie des Forges) [40 vendors]
(last Sunday of month)
(8 A.M. to noon, but may go later)

Regional Overview

GETTING ORIENTED: ABOUT THE REGION

The Loire valley is, in some ways, the most magical region of France; its many graceful châteaux evoke the fairy tales of our youth. At first glance, however, you might wonder what the advance billing was all about; the landscape seems neither dramatic nor unique, and many of the towns, while attractive, are not especially picturesque when compared to other places, such as in Alsace or the Alps, for example.

But the Loire region soon gets to you as you spend a few days here, traveling through its pastoral countryside or sitting by the river among the willows. And everything becomes more enhanced as you explore this area's many fabulous châteaux—with names like Chambord, Chenonceau, Cheverny, Azay-le-Rideau, Ussé—where romance and intrigue seem to permeate the walls. You need several days here to take it all in; packing in too many sites in a short time is just too overwhelming. But if you combine visits to the châteaux with garden tours, then throw in a few urban hits—not to mention, of course, a healthy dose of flea markets to maintain equilibrium—your experience of this region will be memorable.

This is a land of rivers—in addition to the Loire (the longest river in France), there are the Cher, the Indre, the Vienne, the Layon, the Sarthe, the Maine, etc. This is also a place of rolling fields devoted to serious agriculture —asparagus, strawberries, beans, apples, pears, potatoes, etc.—not to mention wine. Forests also abound here, something you see too little of in France.

In this book, the Loire valley encompasses that part of the Loire River from east of Sancerre, in the east, to around Angers in the west. It also includes the area from near Châteauroux, in the south, to a little above Orléans and Le Mans in the north, and just beyond Angers on the west. While not generally considered part of this region, I have included Poitiers in this chapter. It is about the same distance south of the Loire as Châteauroux, and only 100 kilometers from Tours.

It is remarkable that such a mythical place could be so close to such a giant metropolis as Paris. With the advent of the high-speed train, you can be in Orléans or Tours in an hour or so. Yet once you are here, Paris can seem light-years away. Instead, your world becomes peopled with the likes of Richard the Lionhearted, Charles VII, Catherine de Médicis, Diane de Poitiers, Joan of Arc, and even Leonardo da Vinci, who spent the last years of his life near Tours, at Amboise.

MARKET RHYTHMS: WHEN THEY'RE HELD/WHEN TO GO

This is not an especially prolific part of France for flea markets—less plentiful than the Côte d'Azur, Provence, and Languedoc-Roussillon, for example, although comparable to nearby Brittany and Normandy (particularly if you take into account the area involved). At least half of the markets take place on Sundays, and then only once a month, although a few are held during the week (which I have highlighted in this chapter).

Though not a lot of markets are in this region, some are substantial in size. For example, the Châteauroux market, the largest in the region by far, has 300 vendors, while Tours' boulevard Béranger market has around 150, and Orléans' boulevard A. Martin market has at least 100 vendors. (The Châteauroux market's somewhat restricted schedule—the first Sunday morning of the month, from October to July only—means that, for many tourists, this is not an accessible market. For this reason, I have not featured it separately in the individual markets highlighted, although it is described below in some detail under Loches, "Other Things to Do.")

The markets here are mostly year-round; however, while not cold, the region does not have a particularly mild climate in winter. (The average daily maximum temperature during December, January, and February, for example, is between 7° and 9°C. [44.6° and 48.2°F.], compared to a range from 11° to 14°C. [51.8° to 57.2°F.] in Provence, Languedoc-Roussillon, and the Côte d'Azur.) Accordingly, the best time to come here is in the late spring, summer, and early fall. (In the early spring it can be nice, but sometimes still quite cool; I have been here in early April, for example, when, although it was sunny, the wind was bitterly cold.) Avoid the height of the summer if you want to avoid crowds, although the average daily maximum temperatures then are not especially high (around 25°C.—77°F.—in July and August).

As for the time of day to arrive, as always morning is best, but especially here, where some markets, billed as all-day affairs, actually virtually empty out by noon or 1 P.M. (Tours' place de la Victoire, Orléans' boulevard A. Martin, and to a lesser extent, Poitiers' place Charles de Gaulle, markets, for example). Avoid disappointment by planning to arrive at your destination well before noon. A few of the markets are limited to morning only—Angers and Châteauroux, for example.

MARKET FLAVORS: HOW THEY LOOK/HOW THEY FEEL

While not particularly festive, the flea markets in this region are pleasant and easygoing, in keeping with the pastoral and gentle setting of this corner of France. The focus here is on the collectibles, as opposed to spectacles or entertainment. In other words, these are good markets for strolling along looking for finds, rather than for market-side café-sitting and people-watching.

Many of the markets in this region (particularly the major ones) are located in town centers—such as in Orléans, Tours, Angers, Poitiers, and Châteauroux. While their sites are certainly not unattractive—the parking lot of a *place,* or along the middle of a wide boulevard—they are not especially picturesque either. However, these markets feel integrated with their urban surroundings and are a popular attraction with the locals. You are likely to encounter lots of parents out for a stroll with their children, or couples wandering along browsing together. The ambience is low-key and relaxed.

THE COLLECTIBLES: WHAT YOU'LL FIND/WHAT TO LOOK FOR

This corner of France is not particularly noted for its regional collectibles, and that impression is somewhat reinforced in the flea markets, where you will find things from all over the country, just as you do in Paris.

That said, however, a number of collectibles do typify, or are identified with, this region. For example, you will see a lot of dishware from Gien, and you may also come across the functional ceramics—in a golden glaze decorated with blotches of darker brown—that apparently come from the Sarthe department (the area around Le Mans).

Large wooden trunks are often to be spotted in these markets (they are apparently typical of this region), as well as baskets. Basketry has a long history in this region; for example, baskets have been made in the town of Villaines-les-Rochers, to the southwest of Tours, since the 16th century. (The town's basketry cooperative has been in existence for almost 150 years.)

Tapestries and fine fabrics can also be found in this region, as well as lace and lace-making materials (which, I am told, come from the area southeast of the Loire). Garden ware and agricultural implements also abound. A number of times, I have even spotted some reasonably priced glass garden *cloches,* or bells (usually so hard to find and expensive). Finally, as in other wine-producing regions, you will see wine-making implements here, of different kinds.

BUYING: PRICE LEVELS/BARGAINING OPPORTUNITIES

The flea markets in the Loire valley tend to be of moderate to fairly high quality (in harmony with the pretty refined nature of this region), and prices generally reflect that. However, while not a region for nitty-gritty markets, you can usually find a number of vendors offering more down-home, everyday, and rustic wares, at quite good prices. In fact, my experience is that you can get some great deals that way, although it is hit-and-miss. Reasonably good markets for bargain hunters include Orléans, Angers, and Châteauroux.

Bargaining occurs here, as elsewhere in France (though the tone and manner are perhaps more formal and reserved than in the south, for example). However, while you will usually succeed in reducing the asking price somewhat, you are unlikely to get vendors to agree to a substantial reduction, particularly in the more high-end markets.

GETTING AROUND: HOW TO TRAVEL/WHERE TO GO

You can get to the major flea markets in this region quite easily by train. Train service to Orléans, Tours, Angers, Poitiers, and Châteauroux, for example, is generally frequent and convenient (and fast, if you are traveling by TGV, the high-speed train system, which you can often do from Paris). As well, once you arrive, it is usually only a few minutes' walk to the market from the station. Slower trains, and buses operated by the SNCF—France's rail system— also provide pretty frequent service to many of the smaller localities, such as Loches.

However, if, like most people, you intend to include visits to several of the châteaux and gardens in the vicinity, you are certainly best advised to rent a car; it will also allow you to explore the countryside at will. Consider picking up your car once you arrive in the region by train—in Tours, for example— thereby avoiding the hassle of driving out of Paris.

I would recommend using Tours as your base, given its central location and its access to both the flea markets in the area and to the châteaux and other attractions. If at all possible, plan your visit to coincide with Tours' boulevard Béranger market on the last Sunday of the month. If you are also here on Saturday—and you're really energetic—you could see, in addition to Tours' place de la Victoire market, either the Orléans or Angers markets. Collectors in this area on the first weekend of the month, from October to July, should definitely plan to get to Châteauroux's large Sunday-morning flea market. With an estimated 300 vendors, it is one of the largest in France, offering a wide variety of wares, in all levels and price ranges. (On the first Saturday of the month, all year, Loches, to the northwest of Châteauroux, has a much smaller market.)

Market Close-Ups

Five flea market towns are featured in this chapter—Angers, Loches, Orléans, Poitiers, and Tours. Geographically diverse, they span both the eastern and western Loire and the area to the south. They are also diverse in market schedules—with markets on Wednesday, Friday, Saturday, and Sunday.

ANGERS (Saturday morning)

No. of Vendors: 40
Price/Quality Range: ** – ***
Scenic Value: **
Amenities Nearby: ** – ***

Featured Items: Kitchenware, garden items, tools, hardware, advertising items, furniture, books, ceramics, linens, accessories, copperware

WHEN, WHERE, HOW: Angers has a flea market every Saturday morning, from 8 A.M. to noon, in the place Louis Imbach in the middle of town. If arriving by car, head for the center; the market is just west of the place Mendès France, which is at the intersection of two main streets—the boulevard Carnot (the eastern continuation of the boulevard Avrault) and the boulevard Bessonneau (the northern continuation of the boulevard Foch). Look for parking nearby, which could be difficult as a large general market is held in this area on Saturday mornings.

If arriving by train, it is an easy 15-minute walk to the market from the station. From the exit, head northeast (right) along the rue Denis Dapin, which jogs a little to the northwest (as the rue du Haras), then becomes, successively, the boulevard Foch and the boulevard Bessonneau. At the place Mendès France, take the rue Guitton to the left (west), which leads into the place Louis Imbach.

Tourist Office: 02-41-23-51-11

BEFORE I CAME to see its market, I had never been to Angers and had heard little about it. My first impression was favorable; this lively, attractive city has a population similar to that of Tours, and somewhat larger than Orléans. The city is a harmonious mix of old—its heyday was in the early Middle Ages, under the counts of Anjou—and new. While Angers boasts some historical sites of real interest, it also has its fair share of busy pedestrian streets and modern buildings.

The most imposing sight in Angers is its large medieval château overlooking the Maine River (which flows into the Loire). Its onetime moat is now populated by deer. The château houses the renowned 14th-century Tapestry of the Apocalypse. (A 20th-century tapestry series, called Le Chant du Monde—apparently created as a kind of reply to the Apocalypse—is located across the river, in the Musée Jean Lurçat et de la Tapisserie Contemporaine.) Also of interest are the cathédrale St-Maurice (its walls lined with tapestries) and the intricately carved Maison Adam nearby.

THE MARKET

The place Louis Imbach, site of Angers' Saturday-morning flea market, is certainly no match for these far more splendid settings, but it's not terrible either. It also has the advantage of linking up with Angers' large and appealing general market, which takes place at the same time. With around 40 vendors, this is a reasonable-sized flea market of some interest to a fairly wide range of collectors, given its mix of goods—both decorative and rustic—and price ranges. A number of vendors set out their wares on the ground (particularly in the western end of the *place*), while others (offering more interesting and valuable collectibles) display their merchandise on tables.

My immediate reaction to this market was positive; a good sign was the way in which low-end wares were mixed in with high-end, hinting at potential finds. Here you will find all sorts of everyday objects from decades past —kitchenware of different kinds, ceramics (including the golden casseroles and cooking pots, with splashes of darker brown, apparently from the nearby Sarthe department), forged tools, hardware, linens, garden ware and farming equipment, copperware, cast-iron ware, and a fair amount of furniture. I noticed here, as I also did in Orléans, some large, green-tinged glass garden *cloches,* or domes (if only they weren't so difficult to transport!), selling for about half of what I had seen them for in Paris. One of the vendors who had a couple on display was kind and accommodating, even rearranging them on his table so that I could take photographs.

Prices run the gamut here. You can find a few things in the ten-franc range (I got a nice old Brittany tin for 10 francs and just missed a 10-franc set of old fire bellows), while fine decorative objects and furniture will be selling at many multiples of that. In this market you could make a bit of a find, and it is, therefore, worth arriving early, perhaps even well before 8 A.M. when it really gets going.

OTHER THINGS TO DO

Once you have scoured the flea market, take a stroll through Angers' general market. Fresh vegetables are offered next to brilliantly colorful bunches of flowers, in reds, pinks, purples, and yellows. On a sunny day (or even a cloudy one) your spirits will be buoyed by the experience, if the flea market hasn't already done that for you. Afterward, head for one of the cafés or restaurants in Angers' central *place,* the place du Ralliement. For a little dessert, try one of the beautiful pastries at Le Trianon, at 7 rue Lenepveu, a main walking and shopping street nearby.

If you are traveling east from Angers, consider also visiting the Saturday-morning (and also Wednesday-morning) flea market in Tours at the place de la Victoire (see Tours, below). Loches, about 45 kilometers southeast of Tours, also has a modest-sized market all day on the first Saturday of the month (see Loches, below). And if you are heading west, Nantes has a fairly substantial flea market every Saturday morning, which is well worth visiting, especially for bargain hunters (see the previous chapter, on the flea markets of Brittany and Normandy).

LOCHES (first Saturday of the month)

No. of Vendors: 25 to 30
Price Quality/Range: ★★ – ★★★
Scenic Value: ★★
Amenities Nearby: ★★

Featured Items: Ceramics, glassware, books, linens, tools, militaria, copper-ware, postcards, rustic items generally

WHEN, WHERE, HOW: The town of Loches has a flea market all day on the first Saturday of the month, from 8 A.M. to 6 P.M., in the place de Verdun in the center of town. If arriving by car, the market is on the northern edge of town, and you should have no difficulty finding parking right here. If arriving by train (or by an SNCF-operated bus), the market is less than a ten-minute walk from the station; as you exit, head west, crossing the Indre River, and continue west on the rue de la République, turning right at the place au Blé, on the rue Descartes, which leads into the place de Verdun.

Other Markets Discussed: Châteauroux (first Sunday morning of the month, from October to July)
Tourist Office: 02-47-59-07-98

LOCHES IS A small town (of under 7,000 people), located along the western edge of the Indre River, about 45 kilometers southeast of Tours. It's a quiet, but appealing, little place. Its claim to fame is its walled citadel, consid-ered one of the most interesting in the region. Here, you will see the Logis Royal—where Joan of Arc visited Charles VII (whose mistress also once lived here), after the victory against the English in Orléans—and the dun-geon, where Nazi collaborators were apparently imprisoned during the Second World War.

THE MARKET

The monthly Loches flea market is about as sleepy as the town itself. It takes place in the rather cavernous place de Verdun—which dwarfs this small market of around 25 to 30 vendors——dominated at the far end by the beautiful Palais de Justice.

At this market, you will find a hodgepodge of things, both rustic and decorative—dishware, pots, glassware, books, postcards, tools, linens, copperware, and militaria. Prices are fairly high, with some exceptions, and you get the sense that not a lot of buying takes place here. This is one of those markets where you can't help asking yourself whether somewhat lower prices might not improve both sales and the liveliness of the market. I bought some linens here that were actually quite a good deal—mint green, crocheted window liners, at 10 francs each—but I didn't see many other interesting-looking bargains.

This is not a market to go out of the way to visit, but if you happen to be in the vicinity on this day, it is certainly worth a quick look. Its low-key nature might well be a welcome change from the much more bustling ambience in nearby Tours, for example.

OTHER THINGS TO DO

If you are here on the first weekend of the month, from October to July, the modest-sized, workaday city of Châteauroux, about 75 kilometers southeast of Loches, has a very large flea market on Sunday morning, with about 300 vendors. This market takes place on the avenue des Marins and nearby streets, in the northwest corner of town. It is only about a 15-minute walk to the market from the train station, and if you are arriving by car, you can find parking in a lot nearby.

While the site of the Châteauroux market is not particularly appealing or scenic, it does take place in a low-key area of mixed residential and commercial buildings. Lots of cafés and restaurants are to be found along the market for a break while you are browsing. In addition to the 300 or so stands selling collectibles and used goods, some vendors offer crafts and food. The ambience is quite animated; you might be entertained by a jazz ensemble, or even a marching band, as you amble along.

At this market you will find a wide range of collectibles—rustic, everyday, and decorative—as well as secondhand items. Mixed in with the Quimper, fine porcelain, jewelry, glassware, and furniture, children may be selling their used toys and CDs. Prices run the gamut, just like the wares. While generally the real collectibles are moderately priced, rather than cheap, you could make an interesting discovery here and find a good deal.

ORLÉANS (Saturday morning)

No. of Vendors: 100 to 110
Price/Quality Range: ✦✦ – ✦✦✦
Scenic Value: ✦✦ – ✦✦✦
Amenities Nearby: ✦✦ – ✦✦✦

Featured Items: Dishware (including from Limoges and Gien), baskets, militaria, wooden chests, garden ware, tools, hardware, toys, fashion accessories, furniture, secondhand clothes

WHEN, WHERE, HOW: Orléans has a flea market on Saturday mornings, from 8 A.M. to 12:30 P.M. (while officially all day until 5 P.M., almost all vendors leave by 12:30), along the boulevard A. Martin in the northeast part of town.

If arriving by car, the market is a few blocks north of the cathédrale Ste-Croix and runs southeast off the place Gambetta. Meter parking can be found along the street in the area around the market.

If you arrive by train, the market is no more than a five-minute walk southeast from the station. As you exit, head south on the avenue de Paris and then turn left onto the boulevard de Verdun, which becomes the boulevard A. Martin just east of the place Albert 1er. The market starts right here.

Tourist Office: 02-38-53-05-95

HAVING HEARD ORLÉANS described as a kind of bedroom community of Paris (especially now, with France's high-speed train, the TGV), I was not expecting much when I came here to visit. I was pleasantly surprised by this little city of over 100,000 people, located about 130 kilometers south of Paris. It is a relaxed, and easily navigable, place; the center is compact and has a number of pedestrian streets lined with small shops, cafés, and restaurants, which make for pleasant strolling.

Orléans exudes a feeling of prosperity, modernity, and well-being, which is not surprising given its proximity to Paris. Set on the northern hump of the Loire River, Orléans is also considered the gateway to the towns of the Loire valley, although it is quite different from them in both appearance and ambience. Its great claim to fame is its connection to Joan of Arc, who is credited with having liberated the city from a siege by the English in 1429. Everywhere you will see signs of her presence here, but especially in the enormous cathédrale Ste-Croix, where she is said to have celebrated her victory. The cathedral is located just off the rue Jeanne d'Arc—at the end of which, in the place du Général de Gaulle, is the Maison de Jeanne d'Arc—

and near the place du Martroi, dominated by a large statue of Joan of Arc on horseback.

THE MARKET

I was even more pleasantly surprised by Orléans' Saturday flea market, which takes place in the morning along the boulevard A. Martin, just north of the cathedral. Given the city's bourgeois image and its proximity to Paris, I expected a high-end and expensive market—one with fine antiques beautifully displayed, but offering little for more eclectic and rustic tastes. Instead I discovered a lively, bustling market, with all kinds of things at all price ranges. As I arrived here early in the morning, blithely leaving my spouse and children to fend for themselves, I experienced that great rush of excitement and anticipation you sometimes get when you know you have happened upon the kind of market that is just right for you. Other concerns, such as spouses and children, temporarily diminish in importance.

The market consists of two long rows running along both sides of the center of the boulevard. While not many amenities are in the immediate vicinity, the spot itself is pleasant, shaded by large trees. About two-thirds of the vendors display their wares on tables, while the remaining third pile their offerings in boxes or on blankets on the ground. The atmosphere is relaxed and low-key; while busy, the market is not excessively crowded, and the pace is leisurely. Vendors sit together over a drink, joking with browsers standing by. You get the feeling that this is a regular haunt for people in the region.

What I really like about this market is the incredible hodgepodge of things, from swords and mannequins to old glass garden bells. While a fair percentage of the wares are moderately high-end, you will see all sorts of more modest odds and ends, squeezed in between the better-quality collectibles. Dishware from Gien and Limoges, old baskets, wooden chests, militaria, tools, farm implements, furniture, clothing accessories, toys, linens, and secondhand clothes are to be found at this eclectic market. I would be sure to come every week if I lived nearby, because you could find just about anything here. (I remember one vendor selling a pile of old chef's hats.)

Prices are also generally fairly reasonable, particularly for rustic items. I bought a lovely, colorful embroidered pillow for 30 francs; I didn't even try to bargain, since the price was eminently fair, but I'm sure I could have. You will see lots of enthusiastic, but good-humored, negotiating here. If you are hoping to get a real bargain, try to arrive early, well before 8 A.M. Be aware that a number of vendors will begin to leave by noon, while others will stay until 12:30 or 1 P.M.

OTHER THINGS TO DO

If, after scouring the market, you feel like a light and inexpensive lunch, head a few blocks south to the pedestrian rue de Bourgogne, which has a number of little restaurants of different kinds. I liked the Crêperie Breton; not only is its interior decorated with interesting collectibles, but you will get true Brittany crepes and *galettes*. Wash them down with the traditional complement of cider, before you move on to explore some of Orléans' sights.

If you are heading west from here, you will want to check out the Saturday-morning flea market in Tours' place de la Victoire (see Tours, below). Angers also has a Saturday-morning flea market at the place Louis Imbach (see Angers, above).

If you are heading southeast, and you like French dishware, I strongly recommend a stopover in nearby Gien, where you can visit not only the Faïencerie de Gien's store, which has a large discount-shopping section, but also the museum nearby.

POITIERS (Friday morning)

No. of Vendors: 30
Price/Quality Range: ✦✦ – ✦✦✦
Scenic Value: ✦✦ – ✦✦✦
Amenities Nearby: ✦✦ – ✦✦✦

Featured Items: Rustic items, baskets, tools, books, wooden trunks, farm and fishing implements, ceramics

WHEN, WHERE, HOW: Poitiers has a flea market on Friday in the place Charles de Gaulle in the center of town. While theoretically all day, from 8 A.M. to 6 P.M., a number of vendors leave by 1 P.M.; as a result, I have described this as a morning market.

If arriving by car, head for the center and you will have little difficulty in finding the market, which is right in the middle of town near the Notre-Dame-la-Grande church and the Palais de Justice. Meter parking can be found (with patience) on the streets to the east of the market.

If arriving by train, the market is about a 15-minute walk northeast from the station. Take the boulevard Solferino (northeast off the boulevard de Pont-Achard), which then continues southeast as the rue Boncenne. Just before the Palais de Justice, jog a little north and turn right (east) onto the rue de la Regratterie, which leads into the place Charles de Gaulle.

Tourist Office: 05-49-41-21-24

A SERENE AND relaxed town in a region of giant fields of sunflowers, Poitiers is just a little too far off the beaten track to be a major tourist destination. And yet, from Tours via the A10 autoroute, you can be here in less than an hour. For this reason, and despite the fact that it falls a little outside the generally accepted boundaries of the Loire valley (in Poitou-Charentes), I have included Poitiers in this chapter.

In Poitiers, you feel that you are seeing a real piece of France—unself-conscious and unembellished. Located on a hill, the town center is edged by two rivers—the Clain and the Boivre. The large modern buildings you see if you arrive from the north give no inkling of the charming, and also ancient, nature of this small city of just under 80,000 people. Poitiers has a distinguished history—for example, its baptistère St-Jean dates from the fourth century, while other sites in town, such as the interior of the Palais de Justice, recall Poitiers' status centuries later as a base of the rulers of Aquitaine. By the place Charles de Gaulles stands the church of Notre-Dame-la-Grande, which dates back to the 12th century, with its extraordinarily detailed exterior carvings. Today, Poitiers is a pleasant city to stroll in, in part because of the large area of its center dominated by pedestrian streets lined with lots of little cafés and restaurants.

THE MARKET

Like the town itself, Poitiers' Friday flea market, held in the place Charles de Gaulle in front of the Notre-Dame-la-Grande church, is tranquil and laid-back. The market is moderate in size, with about 30 vendors, a number of whom simply lay out their wares in crates on the ground. Interspersed amongst the vendors are a couple of trucks selling snacks and drinks; you can get kabobs, sausages, and Turkish coffee served in glasses. The atmosphere is restful, especially on a nice day when the sun shines brightly down on the *place*.

For some reason, this feels a bit like a farmers' market, perhaps because of the pronounced rustic emphasis in the kinds of things you will find here—wooden shoes, earthenware jugs, baskets, old farm implements, wooden wheels, large wooden chests, tools, and fishing gear. (The Atlantic coast is not far west of here.) I especially noticed these strange, rakelike spears used for fishing. More decorative items, such as glassware and porcelain, can also be found. I was tempted by a pillowlike leather pouch, used for making lace (from the region east of Poitiers, I was told). Attached to it was a work-in-progress, with thin strands of thread weighted down by over a dozen long and shapely wooden spools.

While the market has a bit of a rural feel, there is nothing "countrylike" in its prices; they are generally fairly high, even for the more rustic items. Despite their apparent lackadaisical nature, vendors seem generally aware of the value of what they are selling. Even so, enough variety is here that you do have a chance to make a bit of a find, particularly in the case of collectibles from outside the region, whose significance and value may not be fully appreciated.

OTHER THINGS TO DO

Once you've finished at the market, sit down for a drink at one of the cafés by the place Charles de Gaulle or the nearby place du Maréchal Leclerc. There are a wide variety of restaurants to choose from here and in surrounding streets—try particularly the rue Carnot.

TOURS (Wednesday and Saturday morning)
(fourth Sunday of the month)

PLACE DE LA VICTOIRE
     No. of Vendors: 30 to 40
     Price/Quality Range: ✤✤ – ✤✤✤
     Scenic Value: ✤✤
     Amenities Nearby: ✤✤✤

     Featured Items: Baskets, fabrics, linens, glassware, rustic items, books

BOULEVARD BÉRANGER
     No. of Vendors: 150
     Price/Quality Range: ✤✤✤ – ✤✤✤✤
     Scenic Value: ✤✤ – ✤✤✤
     Amenities Nearby: ✤✤ – ✤✤✤

     Featured Items: Porcelain, silver, glassware, jewelry, fine linens and lace, copper, lamps, clocks, cameras, books, high-end kitchenware, postcards, records, and pens

WHEN, WHERE, HOW: Tours has two regular flea markets—one is held every Wednesday and Saturday, from 8 A.M. to 1 P.M. (this is theoretically an all-day market, to 5 P.M., but almost all vendors are gone by 1 P.M.), at the place de la Victoire; the other is on the fourth Sunday of the month, from 7 A.M. to 7 P.M., along the boulevard Béranger. Both markets are located in the center of town.
     If arriving by car, the place de la Victoire is on the western edge of the old quarter, along the rue de la Victoire, which heads south from the Loire River. Look for park-

ing on nearby streets to the west, or in the lot in the place Rouget de l'Îsle to the south. The boulevard Béranger, several blocks farther south, is an east-west street, just west of the central place Jean Jaurès, site of Tours' City Hall.

If arriving by train, the boulevard Béranger market is at most a five-minute walk from the station. From the exit, head north through the place du Général Leclerc to the boulevard Heurteloup, then turn left (west), following the boulevard to the place Jean Jaurès, after which it becomes the boulevard Béranger. The market starts here, on the west side of the *place*. The place de la Victoire market is about a twenty-minute walk northwest of the station. From the place Jean Jaurès, follow the boulevard Béranger west and turn right (north) on the rue Chanoineau, which leads into the place Gaston Pailhou. Adjoining this *place* at the northwest corner is the place Rouget de l'Îsle. At its northwest end, take the rue de la Victoire north. Halfway up the block you will see the place de la Victoire on your right.

Tourist Office: 08-36-35-35-39

TOURS, THE CENTRAL town of the Loire valley, feels like a city in transition. Its imposing, elegant stone buildings project a stodgy, and conservative image, but its crowded streets, busy cafés, and fashionable stores give the impression of a youthful, and even trendy, place. Tours' apparent rejuvenation is no doubt due in part to the TGV, France's high-speed train, which gets you to Paris in about an hour, even though it is over 230 kilometers away.

I have spent several days here, using Tours primarily as a base for visiting the many châteaux and gardens nearby. The city suffered a lot of damage from bombings during the Second World War, and as a result many modern buildings are scattered among historical ones. This is perhaps why I find this place a bit impenetrable, and too large-scaled, even though it is not a really big city (about 130,000 people). The old quarter is, however, enormously appealing, with its many irregular-shaped and swollen-looking half-timbered buildings dating from the 12th to the 15th centuries. Its narrow pedestrian streets are filled with shops, cafés, and all kinds of ethnic restaurants.

PLACE DE LA VICTOIRE MARKET

Tours is somewhat unusual in having a twice-weekly flea market, on Wednesday and Saturday mornings, in the place de la Victoire. Although located on the edge of the picturesque old quarter, this is not a beautiful *place*, surrounded as it is by a number of uninteresting, modern buildings. (Perhaps this was one of the casualties of World War II.)

The market is not large, with between 30 and 40 vendors, but is certainly worth including as part of your visit to this region. You will see both fine decorative items—beautiful old fabrics, linens, porcelain, and glassware—and rustic items, such as old baskets, tools, farm equipment, etc. Prices are not low; indeed, I found them to be generally higher than at Orléans and Angers, especially for the more rustic items.

While interesting, this is not a market that warrants altering your plans to get to see. If you can, try to plan your trip to Tours to coincide with the last weekend of the month; that way, you can see both this market, on Saturday, and the much larger monthly boulevard Béranger market, on the Sunday (see below).

BOULEVARD BÉRANGER MARKET

Tours' boulevard Béranger flea market ranks up there as one of the best in France. It is both big (with around 150 vendors) and eclectic. The market takes place all day on the fourth Sunday of the month, along the shady, tree-lined center of the boulevard, close to the Palais de Justice and the Hôtel de Ville.

Here, you will observe a good deal more browsing than actual buying. This market is a popular destination for families out for an afternoon walk after Sunday lunch or for groups of elderly couples on an outing. As you walk along, one preoccupation is avoiding running into a stroller or colliding with a group of women who have stopped to gossip.

The things you will find are generally quite high-end. Most of the vendors display their well-polished and pristine wares on makeshift tables, often topped with parasols. A small minority pile their things on the ground; these vendors, needless to say, will be the ones selling more modest, lower-priced items.

A wide variety of collectibles is to be found—ceramics from all over (including Gien, Limoges, and Quimper), glassware, jewelry, fine linens and lace, accessories of all kinds, copper, lamps, clocks, cameras, high-end kitchen collectibles, books, etc. Some vendors specialize in small collectibles —postcards, pens, records, key chains, watches. There is some furniture, but it represents a small percentage of the things for sale here.

Not surprisingly, prices are not low, although some decent deals can be found. Attempts to bargain are not usually rebuffed, and negotiations are generally conducted in the kind of polite, refined manner one would expect of this city. My friend paid 70 francs for a lovely Quimper dish marked at 90 francs, and also purchased for 35 francs a Villeroy and Bosch pitcher marked at 45 francs. I found a couple of ridiculously good bargains from one of the vendors selling odds and ends piled on the ground—a ceramic foie gras terrine for 3 francs (you almost never see them for less than 20 francs) and a

Depression-ware plate, also for 3 francs. While these prices are certainly not typical of this market, they demonstrate some notable exceptions.

I would highly recommend this market to collectors of all kinds, as well as to general visitors looking for a diversion from the rigors of châteaux touring. Like the Orléans market, this market can be visited as part of a day trip from Paris. Not only is it about an hour by TGV (you have to switch to a little commuter train just outside of town to make it into the city's station), from the station it is but a five-minute walk to the market itself.

OTHER THINGS TO DO

Once you have visited the flea market, head for the old quarter, in the labyrinth of streets around the place Plumereau, for a drink. There is no more congenial spot in Tours than this. The streets and squares are filled, especially in the late afternoon, with people (a lot of them young) catching the sun and whiling away the hours. If you are craving a non-French culinary experience, this is where you will find a restaurant to satisfy your urges. My children, who were brought up with the idea that *restaurant* means Chinese food, were happy to try out a few of the places here.

If two flea markets in Tours are not enough for you, a third, smaller flea market (with around 25 vendors) is also held on the first and third Friday of the month, on the rue de Bordeaux.

The area around Tours has many great sights, as you will no doubt already know from other guidebooks. I highly recommend that you visit at least the following three châteaux—Chenonceau, Cheverny, and Chambord (all within an hour's drive of Tours). In the case of the Loire châteaux, the old adage "Once you've seen one, you've seen them all" definitely does not apply. Each of these châteaux is extraordinary in its own way—Chenonceau because of its beautiful proportions, its decor, and its magical location on (literally) the Cher River; Cheverny because of its elegant classical style and its wonderfully decorated walls and ceilings (especially in the dining room, depicting the story of Don Quixote); and Chambord for its spectacular size and setting (in a gigantic wooded park), and its eclectic architectural style. I brought my rather jaded teenage children here; while absolutely oblivious to such things as the great cathedrals of France, they were (much to my surprise) thrilled with our visit to the châteaux, even clamoring to see more.

Another place that I highly recommend, and my children also loved (oddly enough), is the gardens of the château at Villandry, about a 30-minute drive southwest of Tours. Dating from the 16th century, the gardens—with their plants, flowers, and shrubs carefully arranged based on different colors, sizes, and shapes—create wonderful geometric designs and patterns. You don't have to love gardening to like it here; I am not a garden person, and I found the overall effect splendid (as did my spouse, who mostly likes to read books in the parking lot while we do the sight-seeing).

If you have time, head for the little village of Villaines-les-Rochers (another 30-minute drive south from Villandry, past Azay-le-Rideau and its impressive château). A number of the townspeople belong to the local basketry cooperative. You will not only find a wide assortment of baskets to purchase, but you can also watch the basket-making in action.

The Flea Markets of Paris

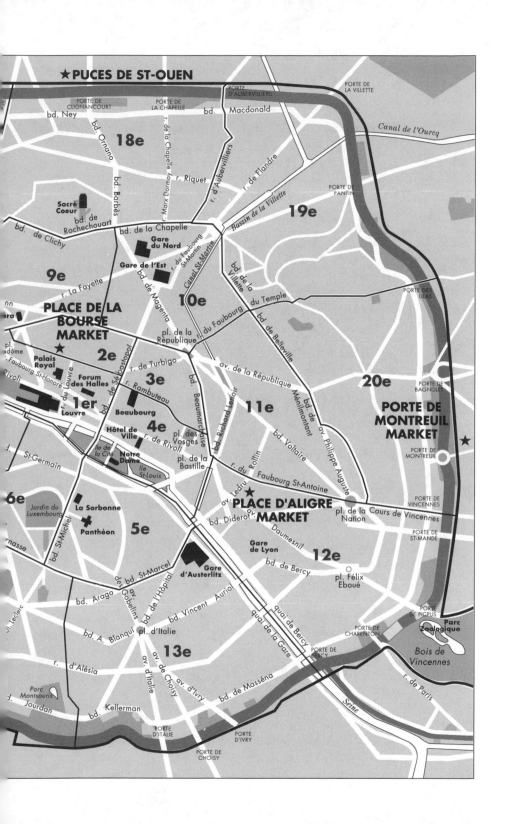

Monday   *PORTE DE MONTREUIL (20th arrond.) [100 vendors]
(7 A.M. to 5 P.M.)

*PUCES DE ST-OUEN (Porte de Clignancourt) [about 1,000 vendors] (11 A.M. to 6 P.M.)

Tuesday   *PLACE D'ALIGRE (12th arrond.) [25 vendors]
(9 A.M. to 12:30 P.M.)

Wednesday   *PLACE D'ALIGRE (12th arrond.) [25 vendors]
(9 A.M. to 12:30 P.M.)

Thursday   *PLACE D'ALIGRE (12th arrond.) [25 vendors]
(9 A.M. to 12:30 P.M.)

Friday   *PLACE D'ALIGRE (12th arrond.) [25 vendors]
(9 A.M. to 12:30 P.M.)

*PLACE DE LA BOURSE (2nd arrond.) [40 vendors]
(last Friday and Saturday of month)
(8 A.M. to 6 P.M.)

Saturday   *PLACE D'ALIGRE (12th arrond.) [25 vendors]
(9 A.M. to 12:30 P.M.)

*PLACE DE LA BOURSE (2nd arrond.) [10 to 15 vendors]
(last Friday and Saturday of month)
(8 A.M. to 6 P.M.)

*PORTE DE MONTREUIL (20th arrond.) [150 vendors]
(7 A.M. to 5 P.M.)

*PORTE DE VANVES (14th arrond.) [200 vendors]
(7:30 A.M. to 6 P.M. [theoretically] on the avenue G. Lafenestre, but only until 1 P.M. on the avenue M. Sangnier and the avenue M. d'Ocagne)

*PUCES DE ST-OUEN (Porte de Clignancourt)
[2,000 to 3,000 vendors]
(9 or 9:30 A.M. to 6 P.M.)

Sunday   *PLACE D'ALIGRE (12th arrond.) [25 vendors]
(from 9 A.M. to 12:30 P.M.)

*PORTE DE MONTREUIL (20th arrond.) [150 vendors]
(7 A.M. to 5 P.M.)

*PORTE DE VANVES (14th arrond.) [200 vendors]
(7:30 A.M. to 6 P.M. [theoretically] on the av. G. Lafenestre, but only
until 1 P.M. on the av. M. Sangnier and the av. M. d'Ocagne)

*PUCES DE ST-OUEN (Porte de Clignancourt)
[2,000 to 3,000 vendors]
(10 A.M. or 11 A.M. to 6 P.M.)

City Overview

GETTING ORIENTED: ABOUT PARIS

Paris is a place that cannot be briefly described or introduced. For information about the city, I strongly recommend that you consult the many excellent guides available that devote themselves entirely to this subject. Instead, to provide a context for your collecting in the City of Light, here is a short description of the long history of the flea markets in this city.

HISTORY OF THE FLEA MARKETS

The flea markets of Paris have their origins in the thriving rag and junk trade of a few centuries ago. With the approval of the archbishop of Paris, flea market historians tell us, rag and junk merchants (some called *chiffonniers*) were given a limited right to sell their wares—scrap metal, rags, and bits of used items of all kinds.

Efforts in the 19th century to drive these merchants out of the center of Paris (for reasons of hygiene and, allegedly, the potential for revolutionary activity) proved unsuccessful. At night, they would gather up discarded items of every kind and description that could be recycled or transformed into something useful—scrap metal, broken glass (to remelt for windows), fat (for candles), old bones (to turn into buttons), and many different varieties of cloth (from the most rough material to the finest silk) to be used for all kinds of purposes.

In 1883, a city official named Poubelle (now the French word for "garbage can") initiated, as a health measure, the requirement that garbage receptacles in Paris be sealed, putting the livelihoods of these *chiffonniers* at risk. When they protested, the decree was softened, allowing them limited access to the bins at certain times. Meanwhile, we are told, rents in Paris had become prohibitive for many of these scrap dealers, who began to move their operations to the periphery of the city, especially around the Porte de Clignancourt. Apparently, as early as 1885, a scrap-metal market was taking place in St-Ouen, the nearby commune.

The concept of flea markets, as we know it today, evolved from these origins. The Parisian bourgeoisie, which had been busily accumulating objects at a rapid pace, began to feel the need to purge itself of possessions no longer in fashion, providing fodder for merchants. Around 1892 or 1894, market historians inform us, a small group of *chiffonniers* got together in a space between the city of Paris and the commune of St-Ouen and began offering to the curious public some of the wares they had collected. (Although some use the 1885 date, referred to above, as the beginning of flea markets in Paris, others date it from this later period in the mid-1890s.)

A huge fad was now starting to emerge. People from other parts of the city would come to St-Ouen to cast a glance at this new phenomenon. Objects of all kinds were sold at these primitive outdoor markets (where the expression *marché aux puces* began to be used). The regulations for the profession of *brocanteur*, describing the things these merchants could sell, give some inkling of the items found in the market—old furniture, linens, clothing, jewelry, books, dishes, arms, metals, scrap iron, and other merchandise *au hasard* (at random).

The St-Ouen market, we are told, was a festive affair, a place for relaxing, gambling, and playing games in the midst of the *brocante* trade. By 1908, one could get there from the center of Paris by metro in only a few minutes. Around 1920, the first permanent markets at St-Ouen were installed—first the Marché Vernaison and soon after the Marché Malik. Others followed over the next few years and decades.

Flea markets elsewhere in Paris developed in a similar fashion. The Porte de Montreuil market began when rag and junk merchants were driven from the center of the city toward the east, but really took hold in a big way after World War II. The Porte de Vanves market goes back to the period after World War I to around 1930. (This market had to move, from a small distance away, a couple of times during its history, but has been in its present location since 1965.) The place d'Aligre was apparently already the site of a clothing market before the French Revolution and generally continued in this way into this century. Indeed, it has only recently evolved into a general flea market, in which bric-a-brac and other things besides secondhand clothes and old linens are sold.

A huge injection of new energy was given to the *puces* in the late 1960s, when the hippie generation made the wearing and use of secondhand goods a kind of mantra of their age. Old objects symbolized craft and artistry, in opposition to the commercialization and anonymity of the era. Such sentiments remain as part of the appeal of flea markets of today, although some have continued to reflect such notions far better than others.

MARKET RHYTHMS: WHEN THEY'RE HELD/WHEN TO GO

The flea markets in Paris are year-round, but you should try to come at the most congenial time. In my view, that is either late spring or early fall. While the Paris winter is not cold by North American standards, it can feel bone-chillingly frigid. Also, though people wax eloquent about the luminous quality of the Paris winter sun, when the weather is cloudy or rainy, Paris feels positively bleak and somber.

Given the huge influx of tourists, the heightened air pollution, and the heat, summer is not the best time for visiting these markets. Avoid August, especially; although the flea markets carry on as usual, many shops and restaurants close during this month.

As is befitting a huge city, the flea markets in Paris are not limited to weekends—the place d'Aligre market is held every day except Monday; the place de la Bourse market takes place on the last Friday (as well as Saturday) of the month; and both the Porte de Montreuil and St-Ouen markets are held on Monday (albeit in a diminished form), as well as Saturday and Sunday. The weekend is, however, the best time to come. That is when the Porte de Vanves market—all things considered, probably my favorite market in France—takes place. Also, the other markets will be more interesting and lively then than during the weekdays (except for the Bourse market, which is much larger on Friday than Saturday).

As for the time of day to come, the place d'Aligre is a morning-only market, but it does not start early (at around 9 A.M.). The Porte de Vanves market, while one part is theoretically all day, is also mostly a morning-only market; it gets going at around 7:30 A.M., which is not particularly early either. The other markets—the place de la Bourse, the Porte de Montreuil, and the Puces de St-Ouen—are all-day affairs.

MARKET FLAVORS: HOW THEY LOOK/HOW THEY FEEL

The most notable thing about the flea markets in Paris is that they run the gamut—in their wares—from the most nitty-gritty (the Porte de Montreuil and place d'Aligre markets, for example) to the most high-quality and high-end (the Puces de St-Ouen). In terms of beauty and ambience, however, the spectrum is narrower. These are not wonderfully quaint and picturesque places for strolling along or for relaxing at a congenial market-side café. The most visually appealing markets are the Porte de Vanves and the place de la Bourse, and neither is the kind of stuff of which tourist dreams are made. Both the Porte de Montreuil and the environs of the Puces de St-Ouen are what can be described as rather grotty, while the place d'Aligre is far from being one of the finer squares in Paris.

If you accept, ahead of time, that your objective is to browse and buy, not to look for photo opportunities, you will not be disappointed. (Also, you'll soon forget all about any grime you encounter in your travels once you get back to the hotel with your finds.) These are markets for serious foragers; if those traveling with you (spouses, children, etc.) have no interest in scouring markets for finds, send them off to do something else, so that you can fully enjoy yourself without having to listen to them complain. And if you don't relish a nitty-gritty scene, avoid the Porte de Montreuil and the place d'Aligre and concentrate instead on the Porte de Vanves and the place de la Bourse (or even the St-Ouen markets, where the extraordinarily high-end nature of the wares offsets the unappealing environs).

THE COLLECTIBLES: WHAT YOU'LL FIND/WHAT TO LOOK FOR

The range in the flea markets here makes it hard to generalize about the kinds of things you will find. As is befitting such a cosmopolitan center, you can find just about anything, from just about anywhere—from outside France and from all of the different regions of France.

You will not spend your time here trying to identify collectibles unique to Paris, but you may come across a few items relating to this city—old souvenirs of such sights as the Eiffel Tower; advertising or tourism posters, or other items, featuring Paris; and mememtos of significant historical events—the liberation of Paris, the building of the Paris metro, etc.

BUYING: PRICE LEVELS/BARGAINING OPPORTUNITIES

The huge variety of things for sale in these markets is accompanied by a correspondingly wide range in prices. Prices also partly reflect the level of the market; if you find something interesting at the Porte de Montreuil or the place d'Aligre market, for example, the price will likely be much lower than at the place de la Bourse, and especially at the St-Ouen markets.

One rather odd thing I have noticed is that the prices for regional items are often lower in Paris than in the region itself. Maybe the value of regional items is not so readily evident here, where there are collectibles from everywhere, or maybe it is simply that prices are lower because there is so much to choose from. The irony is that you can sometimes find Quimper ware, for example, at a lower price in Paris than in Brittany, or Savoyard ceramics cheaper here than in the Alps. (Of course, the selection in Paris, for these items, will be more limited—and chance will play a bigger part in your overall collecting success—but if you are going to be in Paris for a while, you could amass some interesting collections of regional objects at quite reasonable prices.)

Bargaining is conducted at all of the markets in Paris, just as it is elsewhere in France. I find bargaining here quite pleasantly straightforward. Generally, not a lot of emotion is injected into it, and you can usually succeed in getting at least the usual 10 to 15 percent off the original asking price. Parisians are certainly used to tourists, and if you speak some French I think you will find that being a foreigner does not significantly hamper your bargaining success. A vendor at the Porte de Vanves recently claimed that he was accepting my offer on an Alsatian pitcher because I was his *cousine canadienne*. (Of course, I wasn't totally taken in, but it did suggest that my nationality was not an impediment.)

GETTING AROUND: HOW TO TRAVEL/WHERE TO GO

A number of the flea markets in Paris take place at the extremities of the city, by the *portes*—the Porte de Vanves in the south, the Porte de Montreuil on the east, and the Porte de Clignancourt on the north (for the Puces de St-Ouen). While they are outside the city center, the good news is that all of these markets are accessible by metro, and also within easy walking distance of the stations (especially the Porte de Vanves market). Both the place de la Bourse and place d'Aligre markets are in the center of Paris—the first is right at the metro stop, while the second is about a five-to-seven-minute walk away.

I strongly recommend that you use the metro to travel to the markets (and all around Paris, for that matter). It is convenient, not dangerous, and the best buy in town. (You can purchase a *carnet* of ten tickets for around 52 francs.) Also, despite initial appearances, it is not terribly difficult to find your way around; always bear in mind both the number of the line you want and the name of the end station in the direction you are heading.

In case you were under any illusions to the contrary, having a car in Paris is a nightmare, both to drive and to park. Also, taxis are neither cheap nor particularly timesaving. Bus routes are hard to figure out and probably to be avoided in favor of the metro.

As for the markets to visit, make sure above all else to get to the Porte de Vanves, whatever your collecting interests. Then, if you are a serious bargain hunter, also try to fit in the Porte de Montreuil and the place d'Aligre, in that order. If you like high-end antiques and collectibles (whether or not you can afford them), or if you have an interest in the flea markets as an historical phenomenon, spend some time at the St-Ouen markets; it will take you at least a full day to see them in any detail at all. The Bourse market is good for a wide range of collecting tastes and can be quickly visited in between other sites, given its central location.

A great idea for those staying in Paris at length is to take day trips to other flea markets in the surrounding regions. Now, with France's high-speed train, the TGV, distances that would have seemed prohibitive only a few years ago can be traveled in an hour or two. I recently visited a number of flea markets this way, and it was remarkably easy and pleasant. Rouen, Orléans, and Tours, for example, which all have good flea markets, can be reached in an hour or so. The markets are also either within easy walking distance from the station or only a few minutes away by public transit. (For the Tours and Orléans markets, see the chapter on the Loire valley, and for Rouen, see the chapter on Brittany and Normandy.) Other markets a little farther afield are also easily accessible by train as a day visit. (See the chapter "Practical Advice on Visiting the Flea Markets" on rail passes.)

A big advantage of day trips from Paris to other markets is that you arrive entirely unencumbered by your luggage (which quickly becomes your enemy as you travel). You can also fit in a lot of touring in a day, after visiting the flea market, returning to Paris sometime in the evening. The Paris train stations are on the metro lines, so getting there and back is pretty simple.

Market Close-Ups

Five flea markets are featured below, in alphabetical order—the place d'Aligre, the place de la Bourse, the Porte de Montreuil, the Porte de Vanves, and finally, the Puces de St-Ouen (which comprises several markets). Together, they offer the visitor to Paris an extraordinarily varied experience in their locations, schedules, kinds of collectibles, and price ranges.

PLACE D'ALIGRE (every morning except Monday)

No. of Vendors: 25
Price/Quality Range: ✦ – ✦✦
Scenic Value: ✦ – ✦✦
Amenities Nearby: ✦✦✦

Featured Items: Kitchenware, tools, books, records, secondhand clothing

WHEN, WHERE, HOW: There is a small flea market every day except Monday, from 9 A.M. to 12:30 P.M. (perhaps ending a bit later on Saturday and Sunday), at the place d'Aligre in the 12th arrondissement. If arriving by metro, take Line 8 (Balard–Créteil Préfecture) and get off at the Ledru-Rollin stop. As you exit the station, head east on the rue du Faubourg St-Antoine (which runs between the place de la Bastille and the place de la Nation); turn south on the rue Charles Baudelaire, then east (left) on the rue Théophile Roussel, which leads into the place d'Aligre. If arriving by car, try to find parking on neighboring streets.

THE PLACE D'ALIGRE was apparently already the site of a clothing market before the French Revolution, remaining so into the 20th century. With the social upheaval of the 1960s, it became a trendy place for the younger generation to find fun and unusual things with which to clothe and accessorize themselves. By the mid-1980s, the major focus of this market was still old clothing and linens, with only a couple of merchants selling bric-a-brac; these proportions have been reversed in recent years.

My first visit to the place d'Aligre market got off to an inauspicious start; I arrived on a Saturday afternoon to find that it had already ended. All that was left in the *place* were some people sweeping up the garbage from the big fruit and vegetable market that also takes place here. I decided to come back early the next day, thinking that, since this was billed as a true junk market, I might make a great find then.

Boy, was I disappointed. Again, things got off to a rocky start, as the glances of the few people I encountered at 8 A.M. along the rue du Faubourg St-Antoine made me suddenly wonder whether it was such a hot idea to be walking alone here at this hour. It was a bit of a relief to arrive at the place d'Aligre itself. By Paris standards—which are admittedly harsh—this is not a beautiful *place*, lined as it is by rather grim-looking, newish buildings. However, the big market building in the center, the Marché Beauvau (dating from the mid-19th century), is appealing.

By this time, it was around eight-fifteen, and getting here early was revealed as a bad idea—only a couple of tables of what could be described as collectibles were set up, and they did not look at all interesting. Fortunately, the food market was well under way, and some people were milling about. On further examination, it became evident that they were all men, and I slowly realized that one of them was following me about. I then spent the next several minutes attempting to dodge my persistent, but thankfully silent, admirer, finally seeking shelter in the frozen-food section of a supermarket facing the *place*. (If nothing else, this sideshow did kill some time.)

Just before 9 A.M., as I emerged from my frigid lair (no signs of my suitor about), I noticed that the activity in the *place* had suddenly picked up. A rather official-looking portly gentleman had arrived and seemed to be assigning stalls to a ragtag group of rag and junk merchants who stood politely by awaiting their turn. Then the unloading and unpacking began in earnest, and what a sight it was. The most surreal event (among many here that day) was the sight of two men pouring garbage bag after garbage bag filled with bowls, plates, pots, and glasses onto some grimy blankets spread on the ground, entirely ignoring the crashing and smashing noises that this produced, as at least one item in ten was destroyed. *"Cinq francs les deux"* (two for five francs), they called out in the most oblivious and weary fashion, as people (including me, my puritan sensibilities outraged) milled about checking out the wreckage.

Another figure, of truly magestic and mythical proportions, presided over a table of what can only be described as sheer junk, including piles of old shoes, which he would draw to the browsers' attention with a sweep of his arm. They were 40 francs a pair, although in the store they would have gone for 800 francs, easily, he proclaimed to all who would listen. I was too busy taking in his extraordinary appearance to look too closely. His large figure was draped in a seedy, but also kind of elegant, cape, topped with a long silk-like scarf that accented his flowing yellow hair. Here was a true Dickensian figure, which one rarely sees in the late 20th century—a fascinating combination of shabbiness and foppishness. Just getting to watch this spectacle made the whole market experience strangely worthwhile. Of course, it would have been more worthwhile if I had found something I remotely wanted to buy, but that feat (almost invariably so easy for me) proved impossible, and I soon headed off, back to the hotel.

Subsequent visits have somewhat altered my generally negative first impressions. This market does have a way of growing on you, in that nostalgic kind of way (although I haven't seen the man with the cape recently). But, also, my views have softened because of the treasures I have unearthed. The last time I was here, I found an old Napoleon candy tin for 20 francs, while my friend bought a Quimper bowl, in good condition, for 50 francs. The biggest find that day, however, was a large needlepoint wall-covering (in a medieval design) for 80 francs, which I then saw the next day at the Porte de Vanves for 1,200 francs. (Admittedly, mine had one corner that needed finishing, and it hadn't yet been blocked, but these were not major concerns.)

Prices here are generally quite low—this is what is sometimes described as a ten-francs-an-item market—although there are numerous exceptions, some of which are entirely inexplicable. Unless the price is clearly reasonable, bargain like everyone else; haggling is done here with that degree of mock seriousness typical of this kind of market.

The place d'Aligre market is definitely not for everyone, and even collectors of low-end everyday items and rustic objects should prepare to be disappointed. Nonetheless, you can find interesting bargains here, particularly if you come regularly. A photographer I know—who lives nearby, and whose studio is filled with all sorts of weird and wonderful objects—swears by this place; he picks up not only collectibles, but also fixtures and tools, for next to nothing. I've gotten into the habit, when I am in Paris, of making a quick trip here every morning the market is on, just to get a bit of a fix.

OTHER THINGS TO DO

If you're staying in an apartment in Paris and want to stock up on some fruit and vegetables, the place d'Aligre street market has the reputation among some as the most inexpensive in Paris. Also, right next to the market, on the rue Théophile Roussel, is a wonderful place for *pain biologique* (or organic bread) of all kinds, called Le Pain Moisan. A historic little bakery south of the market—Jacques Bazin (the sign outside says "Boulangerie Viennoise"), at 85 bis rue de Charenton—serves, among other things, great little breads filled with bits of cheese or ham.

For a light snack near the market, try Caoua (01-43-48-60-97), at 207 rue du Faubourg St-Antoine; the coffee is delicious, as are the tarts—both sweet and savory. On your way along the rue du Faubourg St-Antoine, glance in the window of À La Providence, a wonderful hardware store, its old floor-to-ceiling wooden shelves (antiques in themselves) filled with knobs and fixtures of every description.

In the other direction along the rue du Faubourg St-Antoine, toward the place de la Bastille, you can pick up great paninis at Folie's Café, while *pains au chocolat* to absolutely die for are to be had at Paul Bugat, at 5 boulevard Beaumarchais, just north of the place de la Bastille. A little farther afield, in the Marais district (the old Jewish quarter)—my favorite part of Paris—is a wonderful place for falafels (and other Middle Eastern food), called Chez Marianne, at the corner of the rue des Rosiers and the rue des Hôpitalières St-Gervais (01-42-72-18-86).

PLACE DE LA BOURSE (last Friday and Saturday of the month)

No. of Vendors: 40 on Friday, 10 to 15 on Saturday
Price/Quality Range: ✦✦ – ✦✦✦
Scenic Value: ✦✦ – ✦✦✦
Amenities Nearby: ✦✦✦

Featured Items: Militaria, books, dolls and toys, Limoges boxes, records, phone cards, 1950s and 1960s ware, kitchen collectibles, perfume samples, pens, advertising posters

WHEN, WHERE, HOW: The place de la Bourse (*bourse* means "stock exchange")—in the second arrondissement—has a flea market on the last Friday and Saturday of the month, all day from 8 A.M. to 6 P.M.

If arriving by public transit, the market is at the Bourse stop on metro Line 3 (Pont de Levallois-Bécon–Gallieni). As you emerge from the station, taking the rue Vivienne exit, you will find yourself right at the site of the market, in the *place* in front of the stock exchange building. If arriving by car, try to find parking on neighboring streets, which is difficult but not impossible.

IT IS A bit odd to put a flea market in front of a stock exhange building, but this is where this one is located, on the last Friday and Saturday of the month. The place de la Bourse, in the second arrondissement, is a kind of austere and imposing expanse of concrete, dominated in the center by the very elegant stock exchange building itself. Not surprisingly, this is not one of those typical, brilliantly colorful market scenes, with lots of people strolling along shaded rows of stalls. And given that it is located in the financial district, any real traffic this market gets is on Friday, not Saturday. Friday is the day to come, if possible, as many fewer vendors bother to return for the second day. But, even if you come on Friday, this is not a busy place; unfortunately, for the vendors at least, this market seems not to have really been discovered by people in this city.

Odd as its setting is, this is quite a good *brocante* market—a wide variety of interesting collectibles is to be found (small items, mostly); the market is fair-sized with around 40 stalls; the vendors are quite approachable; and, most surprising of all, the prices are fairly reasonable (at least, compared to what one might expect).

Most of the vendors here—who have nicely arranged displays of their wares on tables set up throughout the *place*—specialize in a few items. This market would be of special interest to people looking to augment particular collections—military items, champagne capsules, advertising posters, records, phone cards, Limoges boxes, pens, miniature perfume samples, baby rattles, café au lait bowls, or corkscrews, for example. You will also find such things as 1950s and 1960s collectibles (which have only recently started to become a hot item in France), dolls, toys, and jewelry.

Prices are not low, of course—this is in the high-end center of Paris—but they are generally in line with comparable midrange markets elsewhere. I bought an unusual 1950s opaque-glass bowl, in a light shade of jadeite (which was described as *opaline*), for 40 francs, while my friend purchased an interesting bracelet made from an old silver-plated spoon for 100 francs. We both bargained, and each of us succeeded, without any difficulty, in having the price reduced by 15 to 20 percent, which seems to be fairly typical here.

This is a market for both general visitors and collectors. Given its central location, you could drag an uninterested spouse and children here, as part of your tour of Paris, without their really noticing. The stopover will be short and the setting is by far the most pristine (but also antiseptic) of the flea markets in Paris. This is a market I would definitely come to—at least for a quick scour—monthly.

OTHER THINGS TO DO

For a good lunch right nearby, try Aux Lyonnais (01-42-96-65-04), about a two-minute walk from the market, on a tiny street called the rue St-Marc (at number 32). This old-fashioned bistro, with its reassuringly faded decor, is a popular spot with office workers and businesspeople in the vicinity, offering a hearty lunch menu for around 90 francs. (For my main course, I had cassoulet—a casserole of white beans and meats.) Another place of interest, frequented by the more trendy (and seemingly well-heeled) business crowd, is the Brasserie Le Vaudeville (01-40-20-04-62), just across the street from the flea market, at 29 rue Vivienne.

To pick up a light snack, head east to the rue Montorgueil, a market street lined with shops offering just about everything—cheeses, meats, fish, fruits and vegetables, bread and pastries. A place that has gained an almost mythical reputation, both for its decor and its pastries, is Stohrer, at 51 rue Montorgueil (first established in 1730). Stop in for a drink at La Grille Montorgueil, at number 50, a bit of an oasis away from the traffic and noise in this area. For one of those legendary café experiences, in the opposite direction from the Bourse market (near the Opéra), try the Café de la Paix (whose building has been declared a historic monument), one of Paris' most famous cafés, at 12 boulevard des Capucines.

And finally, for real peace and quiet in an unbeatable setting, walk a few minutes south from the Bourse to the Jardin du Palais Royal. You can spend a few tranquil moments in this gigantic courtyard, admiring the flowers or watching the perfectly dressed little children play in the sandbox. (My spouse used to come here for his morning run when we stayed nearby; it's a real challenge for joggers to find an even remotely congenial place to run in Paris.)

PORTE DE MONTREUIL (Saturday, Sunday, and Monday)

No. of Vendors: 150
Price/Quality Range: ✦ – ✦✦
Scenic Value: ✦
Amenities Nearby: ✦ – ✦✦

Featured Items: Linens, kitchenware, tools, hardware, secondhand clothes, books, records, ceramics, old radios and other electrical gadgets

WHEN, WHERE, HOW: The Porte de Montreuil flea market takes place all day on Saturday, Sunday, and Monday, from 7 A.M. to 5 P.M., at the east end of Paris. If arriving by metro, take Line 9 (Pont de Sèvres–Mairie de Montreuil) and get off at the Porte de Montreuil stop. As you exit, following signs for the avenue de la Porte de Montreuil *numéros impairs* (the odd numbers side), head east on the avenue de la Porte de Montreuil to the place de la Porte de Montreuil. Cross the *place* (a traffic circle just above the *boulevard périphérique*), then turn left (north) onto the avenue du Prof. André Lemierre. The flea market is interspersed throughout the large lot here and farther north parallel to the *boulevard périphérique*.

If arriving by car, exit the *boulevard périphérique* at the Porte de Montreuil. Look for a parking spot along the street, either east or west of the place de la Porte de Montreuil, and walk to the market from there.

IF YOU DON'T mind—but rather relish—a really nitty-gritty flea market experience while you are in Paris, the Porte de Montreuil market is the spot for you. This market takes place all day Saturday, Sunday, and Monday, from 7 A.M. to 5 P.M., by the Porte de Montreuil in the east end of Paris. The market site is particularly uninviting, consisting of a large paved area just east of the *boulevard périphérique* (which circles the perimeter of the city). As you emerge from the metro, you will likely begin to experience strong misgivings about having come (I always do at first). You have to cross the unsightly place de la Porte de Montreuil (above the *boulevard périphérique*) and then head through an unappealing strip of stalls selling cheap new goods—socks, suitcases, plastic kitchenware—and horrible-looking trinkets of all descriptions. Vendors are loudly hawking their wares, music may be blaring, and at times the crush of people can be disconcerting (or exhilarating, depending on your views).

But, if you persist, and as you head farther into the bowels of the market, you will soon notice—interspersed among all the new junk—vendors selling old plates, soup tureens, chipped teapots, and old advertising tins (things that can fairly be described as collectibles, rather than junk). Once you've checked out this area, continue north, and at the end of the market (alongside the *boulevard périphérique*), you will find a tumbled-down-looking alcove, under an old sign saying *Marché à la Brocante*. (For some reason, this area makes me think of Dickensian England, especially of *Oliver Twist*.) This section is devoted entirely to used items (I hesitate to use the word *collectibles* to describe a lot of them), of a fairly to seriously low-end nature—old tools, hardware, crockery, old radios, linens, etc. The wares are not pristine, and little effort has been expended on them. Indeed, the last time I was here, some of the vendors did not even bother to try to protect their wares from a sudden heavy rain shower; old phonographs, secondhand clothes, and linens all got soaked.

Nonetheless, I have been quite thrilled with some of the things I have found at this market, particularly once I had cleaned them up. The prices were also really good—for example, a beautiful café au lait bowl, old but in good condition, for 5 francs (it would have cost at least 50 francs anywhere else); large, square linen pillowcases and cotton *nid d'abeilles* (meaning "bee's nest," the term describing a waffle texture) hand towels at 10 francs each; covered ceramic foie gras terrines—with the labels still on them—for 20 to 30 francs each; etc.

Not all prices are low at the Porte de Montreuil; surprisingly, they span a fairly wide spectrum, and the rationale is often difficult to fathom. Do not hesitate to bargain, even if the price is not excessive; the vendors expect, and almost seem to enjoy, it. I remember being locked in a battle of wills recently with one really tough negotiator. When he ultimately emerged victorious, he then turned around and, good-humoredly, threw in for free something else I'd expressed an interest in. His gesture made perfect sense; he didn't care about the price, at least not nearly as much as he cared about winning the battle. And in victory he could afford to be gracious.

Despite its aesthetic and sanitary drawbacks, this is one of the best places in France to find everyday collectibles at low prices. What you need is a combination of energy—to ferret out the gems amid all the junk—and imagination, the ability to see the appeal of an object once its grime has been cleaned off. If the thought of all this work does not appeal to you, or if you prefer to see only the more pristine side of Paris (an understandable sentiment), this is definitely not the market for you. If you do come, leave your camera at the hotel and bring only a small amount of cash to keep in your pocket or in a pouch around your neck.

OTHER THINGS TO DO

Before it threatens to tarnish your overall impression of Paris, I recommend that you head back to the center once you have seen the Porte de Montreuil market. The amenities here (both food and drink) are minimal, although a couple of trucks at the end of the market selling sausages and good, but greasy, fries may help to tide you over if you are famished.

PORTE DE VANVES (Saturday and Sunday)

No. of Vendors: 200
Price/Quality Range: ✦✦ – ✦✦✦
Scenic Value: ✦✦
Amenities Nearby: ✦✦

Featured Items: Ceramics, glassware, linens, books, toys, art deco, 1940s and 1950s ware, hardware, furniture, kitchenware, paintings and prints, militaria, silver, secondhand clothes and accessories, watches, clocks

WHEN, WHERE, HOW: The Porte de Vanves flea market is held on Saturday and Sunday, in the south end of Paris. It takes place on the avenue Georges Lafenestre and the avenue Marc Sangnier (and its continuation, east of the avenue G. Lafenestre, as the avenue Maurice d'Ocagne). While the market is all day on the avenue G. Lafenestre, from 7:30 A.M. to 6 P.M. (although many vendors leave early), it is only until 1 P.M. on the other two streets. Accordingly, be sure to come in the morning.

If arriving by public transit, take the metro Line 13 (St-Denis-Basilique or Gabriel Péri [Asnières Gennevilliers]–Châtillon-Montrouge) and exit at the Porte de Vanves stop. As you leave the station (following signs for the avenue Marc Sangnier), you should find yourself on the boulevard Brune. Head west and you will immediately come upon the place de la Porte de Vanves. Turn left (south) here and the avenue Marc Sangnier is the first street south (about a two-minute walk from the station).

If arriving by car, the market is just north of the Porte de Vanves. Parking is difficult, but can be found on neighboring streets.

ALL THINGS CONSIDERED, the Porte de Vanves flea market is probably my favorite in France (not to mention my favorite, by far, in Paris). However, it is certainly not the most beautiful, being located at the far south end of Paris, near the unsightly, busy *boulevard périphérique* that circles the city. Nor is this the largest market, although, with around 200 vendors, it is substantial.

The primary appeal of the Porte de Vanves market is its huge variety of collectibles—art deco, 1940s and 1950s chrome ware, old books, records, baskets, radios, lamps and fixtures, accessories (purses, hats, gloves, canes), toy cars, paintings and prints, enamel coffeepots, ceramic canister sets, advertising signs, bistro items, café au lait bowls, silver, toy soldiers, watches and clocks, fine linens, etc. You are almost guaranteed to spot something you covet (and within your budget) every time you come. Some of my absolute favorite possessions I purchased here over the years.

This is a collectibles, not a junk, market and yet you will find just the right mix of vendors selling more inexpensive bits and pieces to satisfy those whose tastes lie in more modest everyday wares and rustic items. At the same time, collectors of such things as paintings and prints, books, ceramics, and decorative objects of all kinds will revel in the selection. This is the best market I have been to for unearthing regional collectibles from every corner of France (sometimes simply mixed in with a jumble of things)—green-glazed dishes from Vallauris in the Côte d'Azur, polka-dotted jugs from the Savoie, Béarn plates from southwest France, Alsatian pitchers, Quimper ware from Brittany, etc. As well, this is one of the best markets for finding odd objects from other countries. For example, I have bought old Christmas nutcrackers from Germany, porcelain cooking bowls from England, and 1940s and 1950s Fire King ware from the United States.

Another not insignificant feature of this market is its accessibility—a two-minute walk from the Porte de Vanves metro station. As well, to get to the heart of this market, you are not required to cross busy roads or wade through rows of stalls selling cheap new trinkets—as at St-Ouen and the Porte de Montreuil. It's also quite pleasant here. Strolling along the avenue Marc Sangnier, under the shade of the large, leafy plane trees, you have little sense of the proximity of the *boulevard périphérique*. Even on the avenue G. Lafenestre, nearly above the *boulevard,* the overwhelming density and activity of the market obscures the sound of traffic nearby.

While this is a lively, busy market, it is a manageable scene (especially if you arrive before the late morning). At times you even feel that you could be in a provincial town, rather than in a huge city. Wandering along, you may come across a woman hawking copies of *Aladin* (a monthly collectors' magazine), joking with vendors as she makes her way. Another elderly woman may pass you pushing a coffee cart, while at the corner of the avenue Marc Sangnier and the avenue Georges Lafenestre a food truck serves drinks, sandwiches, crepes, and other light snacks. Other street vendors appear from time to time—a man hawking savory tarts or another roasting chestnuts on a large drum.

The mood is noticeably cheery; vendors seem in a pretty good frame of mind here. Sales made are interspersed with easygoing banter across the row with other vendors and with passersby. While some sell a hodgepodge of things, most tend to specialize in a few items and are quite knowledgeable about their wares. Well used to foreigners, a fair number also speak some English.

You can find something in just about every price range here, from 10 francs —for old plates, pastis glasses, or old French Pyrex baking bowls—to a few thousand francs, for old paintings or large armoires. The arrangement is very democratic, with crockery piled on the ground right next to silver, porcelain, or art deco figurines. I have found some things here at surprisingly reasonable prices—as low as anywhere else in France, particularly for regional collectibles. Perhaps regional items are not as appreciated or coveted in Paris as they are in the regions themselves. For example, on recent trips, I have bought an Alsatian covered pitcher for 50 francs, old Béarn plates for 5 francs, an old Bécassine doll (a character from Brittany) for 25 francs, and a couple of small green Vallauris dishes for 10 francs.

Bargaining is quite active here, and you can usually succeed in paying about 15 to 20 percent less than the asking price. If you are a bargain hunter, or a collector looking for a great find, arriving here early could net you something wonderful at a good price. (Early, here, means by 7:30 A.M., not dawn, as in some other markets in France.) Some people think that the best time to find bargains is first thing Saturday morning, while others contend that Sunday is good because vendors are keen not to have to repack their wares and take them home.

If you only have time for one flea market in Paris, I highly recommend that you make it this one, whether you are a collector of fine decorative objects, a bargain hunter, or an aficionado of such everyday objects as café au lait bowls, coffee mills, dish towels, or enamel coffeepots. While other markets have features that may better appeal to one constituency or another, this one has the best combination of qualities to offer everyone.

OTHER THINGS TO DO

A few cafés are in the vicinity, but I recommend that you head straight back to the center of Paris once you've finished at the market.

Bargain hunters and collectors of everyday objects might consider going directly from here to the Porte de Montreuil market (see Porte de Montreuil, above). To get there, return north on metro Line 13 to Champs-Élysées–Clemenceau; switch to Line 1—in the direction of Château de Vincennes—and get off at the Nation stop. Then, take Line 9—toward Mairie de Montreuil—exiting at Porte de Montreuil. Or, for a more central market—which will take much less time—head for the place d'Aligre (see place d'Aligre, above). To get there from the Porte de Vanves, go to the Champs-Élysées–Clemenceau stop, then take Line 1—in the direction of Château de Vincennes—to Bastille. There you will switch to Line 8—toward Créteil Préfecture—getting off at the first stop, Ledru-Rollin.

PUCES DE ST-OUEN (Saturday, Sunday, and Monday)

No. of Vendors: 2,000 to 3,000 (with many fewer on Monday)
Price/Quality Range: ✦✦✦ – ✦✦✦✦
Scenic Value: ✦✦
Amenities Nearby: ✦✦ – ✦✦✦

WHEN, WHERE, HOW: The Puces de St-Ouen is the name used to describe the large number of permanent flea markets, open to the public on Saturday, Sunday, and Monday, just north of the *boulevard périphérique* between the Porte de St-Ouen and the Porte de Clignancourt. These permanent markets generally open (with a few exceptions) at around 9 or 9:30 A.M. on Saturday, between 10 and 11 A.M. on Sunday, and around 11 A.M. on Monday (although a significant percentage of vendors are closed on Monday). Before the permanent markets open, you will also find numerous casual vendors already selling on the street.

If arriving by metro, take Line 4 (Porte d'Orléans–Porte de Clignancourt) north and get off at the end of the line, at the Porte de Clignancourt stop. As you leave the station, follow signs for boulevard Ornano *numéros impairs* (odd numbers), and signs for rue Belliard and boulevard Ney. (Recently, signs indicating the way to the *marché aux puces* have also been put up to assist visitors.) Outside, head north along the avenue de la Porte de Clignancourt, which crosses the rue René Binet and then passes under the *boulevard périphérique*. The markets start here, in the area northwest of the intersections of the avenue Michelet (the northern continuation of the avenue de la Porte de Clignancourt) and the rue Jean-Henri Fabre (which is just north of, and parallel to, the *boulevard périphérique*).

If arriving by car, exit the *boulevard périphérique* at the Porte de Clignancourt and look for parking in one of the parking lots you will see in this area—for example, under the Marché Malassis or the Marché Serpette, on the rue des Rosiers (these lots are, however, usually busy and also fairly expensive).

FIRST ESTABLISHED AS permanent markets beginning in 1920—but with a history of flea market activity that goes back much further, to the late 19th century—the Puces de St-Ouen (also called the Porte de Clignancourt) markets differ somewhat from other flea markets featured in this book. As permanent—as opposed to temporary—installations, housing many small and separate stalls, they are similar to *brocante*, or antique, malls or centers.

Moreover, the high quality of the goods, and the prices, have little in common with what is often understood by the term *flea market*. Don't let the shabby surroundings, and sometimes primitive facilities, fool you. This is high-end stuff, which often passes from the hands of one professional to another, rather than to the ordinary collector. If your budget is limited, you will likely not buy anything at these markets. You might, however (with a fair amount of luck), find something of interest at the impromptu spots set up by the transitory vendors on nearby streets (an activity described as *la vente sauvage*). Arriving early in the morning, these people (called *les volants*, "the flying ones") often disappear once the permanent markets open.

Though somewhat different from other flea markets featured, I have included the St-Ouen markets in this book, given their origins, their historical importance, and their continuing appeal to visitors to Paris. Also, with 2,000 to 3,000 vendors in total, this is certainly one of the largest collectibles markets in the world.

The Puces de St-Ouen are made up of several separate markets, each with its own distinctive look and personality. Seven are featured below, in rough geographical order moving from east to west—the marchés Vernaison, Biron, Malassis, Dauphine, Serpette, Paul-Bert, and Jules-Vallès.

MARCHÉ VERNAISON (99 rue des Rosiers, 136 avenue Michelet)

The Marché Vernaison is, by far, my favorite of the St-Ouen markets (followed by the Marché Paul-Bert) and the one to see if your time is limited. It is also the first of the permanent markets, apparently established in 1920 by Romain Vernaison, an owner of some land in St-Ouen. He erected some prefabricated huts made of wood and began renting space to *brocante* dealers, and others.

Not only is the Marché Vernaison a substantial market, with around 250 vendors, it is by far the most visually pleasing and atmospheric of all the St-Ouen markets. It also, apparently, does much of its trade with nonprofessionals, unlike some other markets. While years ago it might have been thought that this market would be dwarfed by newer and fancier facilities (such as the Marché Dauphine and the Marché Malassis across the rue des Rosiers, for example), the Marché Vernaison has managed to hold its own.

Triangle-shaped and bordered by the rue des Rosiers, the rue Voltaire, and the avenue Michelet, the Marché Vernaison is a rabbit warren of alleyways filled with little shops jammed with things of every description. The shops are identified by numbered awnings, but because the alleyways are quite winding, you can easily get lost here, as I have several times. Best to forget about figuring out where you are and abandon yourself to observing all the things around you. Here, small collectibles of all kinds reign—dolls, jewelry, kitchenware, toys, books, tapestries and sewing notions, linens and lace, clocks, watches, key chains, postcards, lamps, militaria, Mickey Mouse collectibles, etc. Vernaison is an especially good market for collectors of decorative, but modest, everyday objects; one stall, for example, has its walls filled with lovely ceramic containers for holding salt and matches (*boîtes à sel* and *boîtes à allumettes*).

MARCHÉ BIRON (85 rue des Rosiers)

The Marché Biron, which opened in 1925, is one of the oldest markets of St-Ouen. It is also fairly large, stretching from the rue des Rosiers to the avenue Michelet, between the rue Biron and the rue Villa Biron. The market is in two long rows; one row, with stands on either side, is open-air, while the other, with stalls on only one side, is covered by a kind of corrugated-tin roof. On this row are to be found small shops with glass doors, decorated like actual rooms, with fine antiques.

This is a high-end market; that reputation once earned it the nickname *Faubourg St-Honoré des Puces.* You will find a lot of fine furniture, as well as bronzes, lamps, paintings, engravings, and glassware. Specialized stands sell marine items, posters, fans, Russian objects, etc.

MARCHÉ MALASSIS (142 rue des Rosiers)

This market opened at the south end of the rue des Rosiers in 1989, just two years before the Marché Dauphine next door. It is located in a modern two-story building housing about 100 vendors. At various points, a glass ceiling lets in some natural light, giving this a somewhat airy feel. It looks more like a small office building, however, than a flea market.

Here you will find high-end collectibles of all kinds—lots of furniture, bronzes, oriental art, carpets, paintings, toys, cameras, archaeological objects, etc. A lot in the basement has 200 parking spots.

MARCHÉ DAUPHINE (140 rue des Rosiers)

The Marché Dauphine is a fairly recent newcomer to the Puces de St-Ouen. It opened in 1991, next to the Marché Malassis on the rue des Rosiers, in a new two-story, redbrick building with emerald green metalwork and a glassed roof. I think it resembles a shopping mall, albeit a tastefully designed one, rather than a flea market, but its fairly open, modern look does give it a light, open feel (particularly on the second floor).

With more than 150 stands, the Marché Dauphine is a good market for people who collect small decorative objects of all kinds, and who don't mind paying a fairly high price for them. Here you will find books, paintings, prints, 1940s and 1950s kitchenware, dolls, watches, clocks, cameras, and jewelry, as well as some furniture. In the things it offers, this place is somewhat reminiscent of the Marché Vernaison, but without the atmosphere. For those whose budgets don't permit them to buy much, this is a good place to broaden their knowledge about the range of things collected in France. If you do buy something, you can apparently get a *certificat d'expertise* (a certificate of valuation) here, for around 120 francs.

MARCHÉ SERPETTE (110 rue des Rosiers)

The Marché Serpette is located right next to the Marché Paul-Bert and is bordered by the rue des Rosiers and the rue Paul-Bert. This covered market, with about 130 stands, dates from 1977. It features high-end antiques, especially furniture, and reputedly is an active market for the export trade. Some of the stalls specialize in appealing themes; for example, one is devoted to large, comfortable-looking leather chairs, while another features bistro items of all kinds.

Like many of the markets in St-Ouen, this one is a bit intimidating for the casual browser. You will see well-dressed vendors standing around drinking wine with each other or with prospective clients. In the middle of this market, I was amused to find a little lunch bar, La Petite Salle à Manger, selling—in additon to sandwiches and coffee—Iranian caviar (see "Other Things to Do," below).

MARCHÉ PAUL-BERT (96 rue des Rosiers, 18 rue Paul-Bert)

The Marché Paul-Bert was opened in 1946, although its original shacks were apparently replaced by more permanent installations in 1953 and 1954. This is a good-sized open-air market, composed of a number of little alleyways, with entrances off the rue Paul-Bert and the rue des Rosiers. The alleyways are lined with small boutiques, each numbered and often decorated with awnings over the doorways. Walking along here, looking inside the stalls, you almost get the sense of being in a tiny village.

This is, however, a high-end market, with lots of furniture, but also ceramics, bistro ware, garden ware, art deco, and kitchen collectibles. The atmosphere is pleasant (more so than at most of the St-Ouen markets), with vendors sitting outside their little stores, playing cards and chess together. One special place, especially for collectors of everyday French kitchenware, garden ware, and wine objects, is Bachelier Antiquités at Allée 1, stand 17. Here, you will find such things as Provençal ceramics, *boules*, baskets, cutting boards, corkscrews, glass garden bells, wooden frames for drying fruit, watering cans, etc. The vendor is particularly friendly and informative. If you can't afford to buy, this is a good place to get some inspiration about what you should be looking out for in your flea market travels.

MARCHÉ JULES-VALLÈS (7 rue Jules-Vallès)

This market, located on the rue Jules-Vallès, one block east of the rue Lecuyer and west of the rue des Rosiers, is quite old, first opened in 1938. In this small, U-shaped, covered market, the stalls on either side of the two rows open up like garage doors. Here you will find lots of militaria, but also religious objects, toys, lamps, advertising items, some furniture, and china. This is not a very large market.

OTHER MARKETS

Other markets in the area have not been featured here, either because they are quite small or because they are of less interest to visitors. The Marché Malik, at 53 rue Jules-Vallès, while the second-oldest St-Ouen market, is confined mostly to new and used clothing. The Marché Cambo, at 75 rue des Rosiers, was destroyed by fire in the early 1990s; now reopened, with 20 stalls on two levels, it sells high-end furniture and decorative objects. The Marché Antica, at 99 rue des Rosiers, has fewer than 15 boutiques; the Marché des Rosiers, at 3 rue Paul-Bert, is also very small, with around 10 vendors, and specializes in art nouveau and art deco; the Marché l'Usine, at 18 rue des Bons Enfants, is reserved to professionals; the Marché l'Entrepôt, at 80 rue des Rosiers, sells large items; and finally, the Marché Lecuyer-Vallès, between the rue Lecuyer and the rue Jules-Vallès, with about 45 vendors, is perhaps the most down-to-earth-looking of the St-Ouen markets.

OTHER THINGS TO DO

Visiting the St-Ouen markets can be exhausting, so before you head back to the center of Paris you may feel a serious need for a restorative drink or meal. Some spots right in the vicinity of the markets are worth investigating. The most famous place, deep in the bowels of the Marché Vernaison, is Chez Louisette (01-40-12-10-14), where it is rumored that Edith Piaf had her singing debut. You will still find Piaf-style singers entertaining the lunchtime diners (who may include a fair number of tourists). The atmosphere is raucous and fun, although, no doubt, quite removed from the Piaf days, and the food is decent, but not inexpensive.

Another popular place for a light meal, and a reasonably priced one, is Le Paul-Bert (01-40-11-90-28), at 20 rue Paul-Bert. Inside the Marché Serpette, along the main hallway, is the small La Petite Salle à Manger (01-40-12-38-91). At Malassis, a large, well-recommended, and not expensive restaurant, Le Saint-Framboise (01-40-11-27-38), is locatd on the second floor. Finally, by the Marché Biron is the somewhat crowded Le Biron (01-40-12-65-65), apparently a hangout for the vendors in this area. Other restaurants are also in the immediate vicinity of the market.

Those who don't mind foraging through a lot of junk to find a little gem might also want to check out the *ventes sauvages*—the wares of the casual vendors who come here to sell odds and ends (mostly junk) along the street. These sales take place in a number of spots in the vicinity of the permanent markets, but particularly along the rue Henri-Fabre and the rue Lecuyer.

OTHER THINGS TO DO IN PARIS

CHARITY SHOPS

If you have time and you are a bargain hunter, below are three interesting charity shops worth visiting in Paris (the first two somewhat more than the third).

LES ORPHELINS-APPRENTIS D'AUTEUIL (40 rue la Fontaine, in the 16th arrondissement, a short walk from the Jasmin stop on metro Line 9). Open Monday to Friday, 2:30 P.M. to 6 P.M., from September to mid-July, but check before you go. Phone: 01-44-14-76-79.

LE RADEAU-NEPTUNE (32 boulevard Paul-Vaillant-Couturier, in Montreuil, right near the Mairie de Montreuil metro stop). Open Tuesday to Saturday, 9 A.M. to 12:30 P.M. and 2 P.M. to 6 P.M., and Sunday from 2 P.M. to 6 P.M. Again, call ahead. Phone: 01-48-51-54-62.

L'ARMÉE DU SALUT (12 rue Cantagrel, in the 13th arrondissement, not far from the Porte d'Ivry stop on metro Line 7). Open Tuesday to Saturday, 10 A.M. to noon and 2 P.M. to 6 P.M. Phone: 01-53-61-82-00, to confirm.

OTHER RESTAURANTS AND CAFÉS

In addition to those recommended above in the section discussing individual markets, below are a few restaurants (both expensive and modest) and cafés that I really enjoyed, by arrondissement:

L'AMBROISIE (at 9 place des Vosges, in the 4th arrondissement. Phone: 01-42-78-51-45). This is an elegant, romantic Michelin three-star restaurant for those willing and able to splurge on a great meal.

L'ÉBOUILLANTÉ (at 6 rue des Barres, in the 4th arrondissement.) This is a pleasant, simple, and reasonably priced place to have a drink or a light snack, while sitting outside in the tranquil enclave near the St-Gervais church. It is also located close to the antique stores of the St-Paul quarter.

MA BOURGOGNE (at 19 place des Vosges, in the 4th arrondissement. Phone: 01-42-78-44-64). This is a classic café, on the corner of perhaps the most splendid *place* in Paris, the place des Vosges, which dates from the 15th century. You can sit outside watching the people in the *place* or inside in the warm, wood-decorated interior.

DE BOUCHE À L'OREILLE (at 15 rue des Tournelles, in the 4th arrondissement. Phone: 01-44-61-07-02). When I came here the place was closed, but it offers a great concept—a combination restaurant-*brocante* store, where you can have a meal and then buy some of the collectibles on the shelves around you.

LA LOZÈRE (at 4 rue Hautefeuille, in the 6th arrondissement. Phone: 01-43-54-26-64). This simple, tiny restaurant serves hearty food from the Lozère region in south-central France at reasonable prices.

PIERRE GAGNAIRE (at 6 rue Balzac, in the 8th arrondissement. Phone: 01-44-35-18-25). This beautiful restaurant—classic, simple, elegant—serves exciting food (and sometimes improbable, but wonderful, combinations of ingredients). It is also a Michelin three-star restaurant. Its lively and friendly proprietor formerly had a restaurant in St-Étienne, an industrial town near Lyon, and only moved to Paris a few years ago. Again, an expensive place but, if you can swing it, worth it for a special meal.

CLOWN BAR (114 rue Amelot, in the 11th arrondissement. Phone: 01-43-55-87-37). This is a great place—a café, wine bar, and restaurant, from the early 20th century, located near the big Cirque d'Hiver (Winter Circus). The decor is wonderful—beautifully colorful tiles of clowns on the wall and clown memorabilia throughout. The food is fresh, nicely prepared, and not expensive.

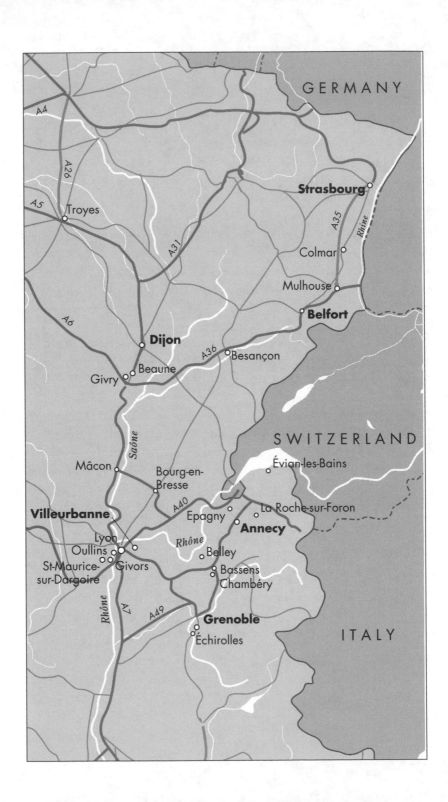

The Flea Markets of Burgundy, Franche-Comté, Alsace, and the Alps

Monday   CHAMONIX-SUD (pl. de Chamonix-Sud) [50 vendors]
(July and August)
(9 A.M. to 6 P.M.)

Wednesday *STRASBOURG (rue du Vieil Hôpital and pl. de la Grande
Boucherie) [25 vendors]
(9 A.M. to 6 P.M., but vendors start to leave after noon)

Friday   COLMAR (pl. de l'Ancienne Douane) [up to 15 vendors]
(first and third Friday of month)
(8 A.M. to 5 P.M.)

LA ROCHE-SUR-FORON (near Geneva) (Halle Grenette)
[20 to 30 vendors] (last Friday of month, from April to November)
(9 A.M. to 6 P.M.)

Saturday *ANNECY (center) [170 vendors] (last Saturday of month)
(8 A.M. to 7 P.M.)

CHAMBÉRY (pl. St-Léger) [25 vendors] (second Saturday of month)
(8 A.M. to 7 P.M.)

CHÂTENAY-EN-BRESSE (R.N. 73, Les Vignes Renard)
[30 vendors]

ÉPAGNY (Parking du Magasin Trouvailles) [35 vendors]
(first Saturday of month except February)
(8 A.M. to 6 P.M.)

ÉVIAN-LES-BAINS (pl. Charles de Gaulle) [15 vendors]
(third Saturday of month)
(8 A.M. to 7 P.M.)

GIVORS (pl. de l'Hôtel de Ville) [50 vendors]
(third Saturday of month)
(7 A.M. to noon)

*GRENOBLE (Quartier Hoche) [75 vendors]
(first Saturday of month)
(8 A.M. to 6 P.M.)

MULHOUSE (pl. de la Réunion) [15 to 20 vendors] (last Saturday
of month from March or April to September or October)
(8 A.M. to 6 P.M.)

OULLINS (rue D. Crancre, Quartier de la Saulaie) [80 vendors]
(7 A.M. to 6 P.M.)

ROGNY-LES-SEPT-ÉCLUSES (Ferme du Bourg) [10 vendors]
(first Saturday of month)
(10 A.M. to 7 P.M.)

ST-MAURICE-SUR-DARGOIRE (center) [50 vendors]
(second Saturday of month)
(7 A.M. to 6 P.M., but most vendors leave by noon)

*STRASBOURG (rue du Vieil Hôpital and pl. de la Grande
Boucherie) [40 vendors]
(9 A.M. to 6 P.M., but several vendors leave earlier)

VILLEFRANCE-SUR-SAÔNE (pl. des Marais) [20 to 30 vendors]
(second Saturday of month)
(8 A.M. to 6 P.M.)

VINAY (pl. de l'Hôtel de Ville) [15 vendors]
(third Saturday of month from April to September)
(8 A.M. to 6 P.M.)

Sunday AVALLON (62 rue de Lyon) [10 to 15 vendors]
(second Sunday of month)
(9 A.M. to 6 P.M.)

BASSENS (near Chambéry) (Parking de la Boîte à Outils)
[30 to 40 vendors]
(6 A.M. to 1 P.M.)

*BELFORT (pl. d'Armes) [170 to 220 vendors]
(first Sunday of month from March to December)
(6 A.M. to noon)

BELLEY (pl. de la Gare) [up to 40 or 50 vendors]
(7 A.M. to 1 P.M.)

BESANÇON (Parc des Expos, Hall C) [90 vendors]
(second Sunday of month except May)
(8 A.M. to 1 P.M.)

BOURG-EN-BRESSE (covered market) [35 vendors]
(second Sunday of month)
(7 A.M. to 6 P.M.)

CHÂTENAY-EN-BRESSE (R.N. 73, Les Vignes Renard)
[30 vendors]

CREPIEUX-LA-PAPE (pl. Canellas) [15 vendors]
(second Sunday of month from September to June)
(7 A.M. to noon)

DIJON (Quartier des Antiquaires) [20 to 25 vendors]
(second Sunday of month)
(9:30 A.M. to 6 P.M.)

*DIJON (Forum, rue Général Délaborde) [30 to 60 vendors]
(last Sunday of month except July)
(9 A.M. to 6 P.M.) ($)

ÉCHIROLLES (Parking du Cinéma Pathé) [125 to 130 vendors]
(6 A.M. to 1 P.M.)

GIVRY (near Le Creusot) (pl. de la Poste) [50 to 70 vendors]
(second Sunday of month)
(7 A.M. to 6 P.M.)

*GRENOBLE (Parking du cen. com. Atac, rue Stalingrad)
[80 vendors]
(6 A.M. to 1 P.M.)

*GRENOBLE (Parking du cen. com. Intermarché) [100 vendors]
(6 A.M. to 1 P.M.)

OULLINS (rue D. Crancre, Quartier de la Saulaie) [80 vendors]
(7 A.M. to 6 P.M.)

ROGNY-LES-SEPT-ÉCLUSES (Ferme du Bourg) [10 vendors]
(first Sunday of month)
(10 A.M. to 7 P.M.)

SERRIÈRES-EN-CHAUTAGNE (center) [30 to 35 vendors, projected]
(9 A.M. to 6 P.M.)

VESOUL (pl. P. Renet) [60 vendors]
(third Sunday of month)
(8 A.M. to 1 P.M.)

VILLENEUVE-SUR-YONNE (near Sens) (boul. E. Peynot)
[30 vendors] (third Sunday of month from May to August)
(7 A.M. to 7 P.M.)

*VILLEURBANNE (near Lyon) (1 rte. du Canal) [400 vendors]
(6 A.M. to 1 P.M.)

Regional Overview

GETTING ORIENTED: ABOUT THE REGION

This chapter combines the flea markets of four regions—Burgundy, Franche-Comté, Alsace, and the Alps—all located in eastern France. For these purposes, Burgundy (in which I have included Lyon) is roughly the area from Nevers on the west to just past Dijon on the east, and from Sens on the north to Lyon on the south. Alsace is the narrow north-south strip bordered by Germany and Switzerland, between the Vosges mountains and the Rhine River valley. Franche-Comté is the area sandwiched in between Burgundy and Alsace, with the Swiss border and a rough line from north of Dole to north of Belfort forming its other two boundaries. Finally, the Alps is the area from just west and south of Grenoble, to Lac Léman (or Lake Geneva) in the north, and bordered on the east by Italy and Switzerland.

A primary reason for including these regions in the same chapter is their relative proximity. For example, the distance from Lyon to Annecy is only 140 kilometers, Belfort to Dijon is 183, Grenoble to Lyon is 106, and Strasbourg to Belfort is 143 kilometers. Also, tourists often combine two or more of these regions in a single trip. From the point of view of flea market schedules, an interesting itinerary (with markets close together, in terms of both time and distance) becomes apparent.

And what a great corner of France in which to spend some time, where the countryside is clearly the biggest attraction. Burgundy is a haven of rolling fields dotted with small, rustic villages (albeit also with a number of impressive and prosperous-looking towns, such as Beaune, Dijon, and Mâcon). Renowned for its wine, this is also a great gastronomic region of France. The powerful dukes of Burgundy reigned here with great fervor until the late 15th century, making this a center of intellectual and artistic activity. Burgundy's history is, however, far more ancient than that, with the Celts predating the Romans here. Today this region feels like a bit of an oasis in the late 20th century; although quite close to Paris—about an hour and a half from Dijon, by TGV, the high-speed train—Burgundy has managed to retain much of its traditional and rural character.

Franche-Comté, to the east, was at one time also part of the holdings of the dukes of Burgundy. This is a rural area, as well, much of it occupied by the Jura mountains, with their forests and plateaus; cross-country skiing and hiking are favorite pastimes here. Its big towns are Besançon, the capital—with a population of around 114,000—and Belfort, at just under half that size. The old county of Franche-Comté only really became part of France in the latter half of the 17th century.

The Alps is composed of the former provinces of the Savoie, in the north, and Dauphiné, in the south. Dauphiné joined with French in the middle of the 14th century, while the Savoie had a more turbulent history, and was part of the powerful duchy of Savoie. When the duchy's capital moved to Turin in the 16th century, Savoie became Italian as well, instead of French. Only in the latter part of the 19th century was the Savoie returned to France; in a plebiscite held in 1860, the vote was over 550 to one in favor of France.

This is a region of extraordinary physical beauty—while not always in view, the mountains are an ever-present reality in the lifestyle and culture of this part of the world. The rugged and bracing physical environment is reflected in many other domains, including the cuisine of this region, which is hearty and rich—fondue, raclette (melted cheese served with boiled potatoes, pickled cucumbers, and onions), *tartiflette* (made with potatoes, cheese, and ham), and gratin Savoyard, for example. The principal centers here are Grenoble, with a population of around 150,000, and Chambéry and Annecy, each with just over 50,000 people.

Like the other regions included in this chapter, Alsace is primarily composed of small towns and villages (although its capital, Strasbourg—with a population of over a quarter million—is distinctly urban and cosmopolitan). Its hillsides covered in vines, and its impossibly picturesque villages (with their tidy half-timbered buildings almost invariably decorated with overflowing flower boxes), make this one of the most quaint regions in the country. Officially becoming part of France in the mid-17th century, Alsace was annexed by Germany twice—from the Franco-Prussian War to the end of World War I, and during World War II. The Alsatian language, a kind of German dialect, remains alive here, where there is a strong sense of regional identity.

This is one of my favorite parts of France for wandering around the countryside visiting all the picturesque little gingerbread villages along the way, sampling wines and Muenster cheese, and checking out ceramics shops. Alsace is criticized by some as too pristine, and even kitschy, but I love it anyway. While this region is clearly very popular with European tourists, North Americans seem somewhat slower to discover its charms.

MARKET RHYTHMS: WHEN THEY'RE HELD/WHEN TO GO

While many of the markets in this area are year-round (Belfort is an important exception), it is nonetheless a good idea, if possible, to come to this corner of France other than during the winter. In February, for example, it is quite a bit colder here than farther south—the average daily maximum temperature in Burgundy then is 5.9°C. (42.6°F.), in Franche-Comté it is 4.8°C. (40.6°F.), in Alsace it is 5.3°C. (41.5°F.) and in the Alps region it is 3.7°C. (38.7°F.). By contrast, in both Provence and the Côte d'Azur it is 11.9°C. (53.4°F.).

Although the winters are fairly cold, the spring and fall (after March and until November) are quite nice, and the summers have the real advantage of being comfortable—neither too humid nor too hot—with July/August average daily maximum temperatures of between 24° and 27°C. (75.2° and 80.6°F.).

The flea markets here are held almost exclusively on weekends, with Saturday as popular a day as Sunday. Also, many of the flea markets are monthly only, which means that you should plan your trip carefully before you come so that your itinerary coincides with the markets you want to see. As for the time of day to come, while many of the markets here are all day, a few notable exceptions include Belfort and Villeurbanne (on the outskirts of Lyon), both significant markets.

MARKET FLAVORS: HOW THEY LOOK/HOW THEY FEEL

While none of the regions included in this chapter is noted for the plenitude of its flea markets, taken together they offer an impressive selection to the visitor. They also include some of the largest, most interesting, and most beautiful markets in France. Annecy's market is wonderful in all respects—

setting, size, variety, and range of collectibles—and clearly one of the best in the country. And while less breathtaking than Annecy's, the market in Belfort is slightly larger, and also of great interest to collectors of all descriptions. The Villeurbanne market is one of the biggest in France, and a haven for both bargain hunters and rustic-ware collectors. And the hodgepodge of markets clustered in and around Grenoble, taken together, offer interesting browsing, particularly for those looking for everyday items or a bargain.

It is, however, difficult to generalize about the markets in this region of France. Some—such as Annecy, Belfort, Dijon, and Grenoble's Quartier Hoche market—are quite high-end, while others are much more basic and modest, and as down-home as any in France. The ambience is partly a reflection of the markets' range, with the more high-end ones (such as Annecy and Belfort) offering a very pleasant and cogenial environment for market-side café-sitting and people-watching. Many of these markets take place in the center of town, benefiting from the architectural, and sometimes the natural, beauty of their surroundings. While Annecy's market is the beneficiary of both, in spades, others owe more to the aesthetic results of human efforts (the Strasbourg and Belfort markets, for example).

THE COLLECTIBLES: WHAT YOU'LL FIND/WHAT TO LOOK FOR

One generalization that can be made about these markets is that they tend to feature collectibles distinctive of their region. Also, while you will see items from other parts of France, this is not a fruitful area for finding wares from other countries (except perhaps from Germany).

In the Alps, you will see traditional Savoyard ceramics in the trademark shades of rust, dark brown, straw yellow, and green. (Blue is apparently a 20th-century contribution.) These functional wares (lots of jugs, especially, and bowls), in their characteristic simple shapes, are decorated with the traditional Savoyard motifs—polka dots, lines and squiggles, and primitive images of mountain flowers and birds. Some also have a marbled appearance —as a result of a technique called *jaspé.* You will also see wooden bowls and utensils, carved in ash and beech; mountain gear, such as old skis, snowshoes, leather packs, and fishing items; collectibles relating to milk, butter, and cheese (the Reblochon, *beaufort,* and *tomme de Savoie* for which this region is renowned)—butter churns, butter molds, drainers, milk jugs, wooden pails, etc.; cow and sheep bells and harnesses; agricultural tools of all kinds; wooden shoes; rustic furniture in fir, larch, and other woods; copper pots; and pewter.

In Alsace, you will find traditional Alsatian ceramics (notably from

Soufflenheim, northeast of Strasbourg)—sometimes in primitive folk-art floral patterns or animals—in light yellow, green, an orangelike rust, and brown (with blue a more recent addition). You will also see gray stoneware jugs with dark blue blotches (from Betschdorf, north of Stasbourg), as well as ceramic baking molds (in the undulating circular form used to make the traditional kugelhopf cake, or shaped like lambs or fish, for Easter). Ceramics from Lunéville (actually located in Lorraine), decorated with a prominent Alsatian symbol—the stork—are also to be found, as well as dishware from Sarreguemines (also in Lorraine) decorated with Alsatian folk motifs. You will also see Alsatian furniture, made of walnut, massive oak, or other woods indigenous to the region, in folk shapes and motifs (especially the chairbacks). Advertising signs featuring beers of the region, and bright embroidered linens, can be spotted as well.

You will see mountain gear of different kinds in Franche-Comté, including old cross-country skis, snowshoes, and packs; decorative clocks and clock faces (Besançon has been a major clock-making center in France); rustic furniture; copperware and pewter.

And, finally, from Burgundy, you will see wine collectibles of different kinds—wine tasters, corkscrews, bottles, corking machines, etc.; mustard pots (some quite decorative) from the many mustard producers here, such as Maille and Amora; rustic items, such as tools and agricultural implements; copperware; and pewter.

BUYING: PRICE LEVELS/BARGAINING OPPORTUNITIES

Given the diversity of the regions and markets included in this chapter, it is difficult to generalize about price levels. Also, as elsewhere, prices tend to be partly a reflection of the attributes of the market itself; in other words, the price of something at a low-end market, such as the Villeurbanne market (outside Lyon) or the Grenoble Sunday markets, will likely be significantly less than at a high-end *brocante* market, such as Annecy or Belfort.

Prices for regional collectibles are generally fairly high. For example, old Savoyard or Alsatian jugs may be as expensive here, if not more so, than elsewhere in France, where the value of the object may not be fully appreciated. (Some of my best bargains in France have been made buying one region's collectibles at a market at the opposite end of the country, or in Paris.) Of course, one great advantage to being here is that you will find a much better selection of the region's wares.

Bargaining is conducted on about the same scale as elsewhere, except perhaps Provence and Languedoc-Roussillon, where haggling is especially enthusiastic. (I have wondered whether the Villeurbanne market's active bargaining has anything to do with its location close to Provence, or whether it is simply attributable to its no-frills, rough-and-ready character.)

GETTING AROUND: HOW TO TRAVEL/WHERE TO GO

As elsewhere in France, the best way to see these markets is by car. Not all are easily accessible by train, and having a car will allow you to visit many more of them in a short time. Speed of travel is a real factor here, where the markets are bunched together on Saturday and Sunday, and where some are held only in the morning. Having a car will also permit you to explore the extraordinary countryside, clearly a prime attraction of this part of France.

If a car is not a possibility, you can still get to many of the markets relatively easily by train. Also, many—the Annecy, Belfort, Strasbourg, and Grenoble markets, for example—are located a reasonably short distance from the station. If you can, check out train schedules ahead of time, to maximize your market experience.

If you are only in this area for a short time, I highly recommend that you base your plans on being in Annecy on the last Saturday of the month and in Belfort on the first Sunday of the month; other markets can then be fitted into this schedule. If you are a bargain hunter, make sure also to see Villeurbanne's Sunday-morning market. (Both the Villeurbanne and Belfort markets start early, so that, if necessary, you could even see both on the same day.) Grenoble's Quartier Hoche market, on the first Saturday of the month, is also of real interest. Bargain hunters should also try to stay until Sunday, when they could take in three markets in one morning—Grenoble's rue Stalingrad and Parking Intermarché markets, and the market in Échirolles, just south of the city. Since Strasbourg and Colmar both have markets during the week (Colmar's small market is every other week, however) you might want to save Alsace for midweek (although the Strasbourg market would be more interesting on Saturday than on Wednesday).

Market Close-Ups

The markets of six places are featured below—Annecy, Belfort, Dijon, Grenoble, Strasbourg, and Villeurbanne (on the outskirts of Lyon). They represent both widely dispersed geographic locations and the different regions of the area covered by this chapter.

ANNECY (last Saturday of the month)

No. of Vendors: 170
Price/Quality Range: ✦✦✦ – ✦✦✦✦
Scenic Value: ✦✦✦✦
Amenities Nearby: ✦✦✦ – ✦✦✦✦

Featured Items: Savoyard ceramics, Savoyard furniture, skis, snowshoes, cow-bells, farm implements, cheese-making items, coffee mills, wooden utensils, fishing gear, glassware, dolls and toys, linens, books, silver, pewter

WHEN, WHERE, HOW: Annecy's flea market takes place all day on the last Saturday of the month, from 8 A.M. to 7 P.M. The market is held in the old quarter, along the southern edge of the Canal du Thiou (near the Palais de l'Île), and on nearby streets on the north side. If you have a car, parking can be found in lots on the edges of the old quarter or, if you're lucky, on the street. If arriving by train, the market is about a ten-minute walk southeast of the station. From the exit, take the rue de la Gare south, turning left (east) on the rue Royale (the eastern extension of the avenue de Chambéry), and then right (south) on the rue de la République to the canal. You will see the market from here.

Tourist Office: 04-50-45-00-33

I CANNOT RAVE enough about the city of Annecy, and the breathtaking countryside of the Haute Savoie, which surrounds it. Though well accustomed to the sense of marvel one often experiences when first encountering a new part of France, I was truly unprepared for Annecy. The city is in a stunning setting, at the northwestern end of the magical turquoise-colored Lac d'Annecy, and is edged by mountains, particularly to the east. The old quarter is a wonderful maze of narrow, cobblestoned streets, lined with boutiques, cafés, and restaurants. One of Annecy's best features is its canal system; little branches of the Canal du Thiou run through the old town, crisscrossed at regular intervals by small stone bridges.

While it has a long history, Annecy feels youthful and energetic. On sunny days its lakeside park is filled with cyclists, joggers, walkers, and in-line skaters. Boats of all sizes and shapes bob along on the shimmering lake, and car after car streams by, loaded with hikers (skiers in winter) heading to the mountain resort towns, such as La Clusaz, nearby. You cannot help but share in the feeling of well-being and robust health that infuses this town, which has enjoyed a resurgence in the last few decades.

THE MARKET

Appropriately, Annecy also has a wonderful flea market, which takes over much of the old quarter on the last Saturday of the month. This is a large market, with about 170 vendors, whose stalls line the south side of the canal and fill the narrow streets to the north.

I have not seen anywhere in France a more appealing setting for a flea market than this, especially on a sunny day. The combination of colorful half-timbered buildings, crisp blue sky, and mountain peaks reflected in the water of the canal is pretty overwhelming, in a picture-postcard way. The ambience is similarly congenial; while this is a busy market, a feeling of easiness and well-being permeates. Alongside the canal, and on neighboring pedestrian streets, strollers take a break from browsing at outdoor cafés and restaurants, turning their chairs and faces to catch the rays of the sun.

Of equal interest are the wares to be found here. Alpine and Savoyard collectibles, in particular, abound. Perhaps most notably, you will see numerous examples of Savoyard ceramics, in the functional, simple shapes so typical of this region. Decorated with polka dots, mountain flowers, or primitive birds, or in a marbled motif, their trademark colors are straw yellow, green, dark brown, and rust. You will also see carved wooden kitchen utensils of all kinds; sturdy, rustic Savoyard furniture; old skis and leather carrying bags; snowshoes; farm tools; cheese drainers; milk pots; butter churns; butter molds; large copper pots; cow and sheep bells in all sizes; fishing gear; pewter; and wooden shoes. Many other collectibles, not particular to this region, are also to be found here, such as linens, glassware, toys, coffee mills, silver, and enamelware.

This is a high-quality flea market, and prices generally reflect that. For example, expect to pay at least 350 francs for an old Savoyard pitcher in good condition. You will not see many vendors whose wares are piled chaotically on the ground and selling for a song. However, some good buys can certainly be made. In my endless quest for more and more nail-studded *boules,* I managed to find a quite beautiful matching pair here for 200 francs (the vendor was asking 250 francs), and I think if I had tried, I could have done even better than that.

I would highly recommend that you plan your trip to this region so as to be in Annecy on the last Saturday of the month. The combination of its setting, regional focus, and size makes this flea market one of my favorites in France.

OTHER THINGS TO DO

Annecy has a number of good restaurants where you can sample the classic Alpine dishes, such as fondue, raclette, and *tartiflette.* One place I particularly like is La Taverne du Fréti at 12 rue Ste-Clair in the old quarter (04-50-51-29-52); the restaurant is warm and casual and the food hearty, flavorful, and not terribly expensive. This is a good spot for a romantic dinner over the simmering fondue pot. (I had it with my noisy children instead.)

But my favorite place by far, and one of my favorite restaurants in France because of its robust Savoie fare and rustic ambience, is L'Auberge des Dents de Lanfon (04-50-02-82-51), in Veyrier-du-Lac d'Annecy (Col de Bluffy), about a 20-minute drive along the lake southeast of Annecy. Not only is the restaurant filled with Savoyard ceramics to die for, but there are heartwarming views of the green, green surrounding countryside from the dining room windows (recalling those long-lost Heidi fantasies from childhood). A huge lunch can be had here for 80 francs (around 110 francs for dinner). The last time we came, we started with a fresh salad with lardons and cheese, followed by a massive gratin Savoyard (dripping with cheese) to accompany our main dish, and then, to finish off, a fabulous *fromage frais* with a *coulis* of berries. Needless to say, this is not low-fat fare, but you will certainly leave here sated and feeling that you have had a great, authentic culinary (not to mention life) experience.

If you are interested in Savoyard ceramics, a potter who is especially faithful to this tradition is Jean-Christophe Hermann, whose Fabrique des Poteries Savoyardes studio, shop, and museum is located in Évires, about a 35-minute drive northeast of Annecy (on the N203). Monsieur Hermann not only adheres to traditional Savoyard patterns and designs, he also continues to fire his work in a wood-burning kiln. The decoration and detailing is high quality, and the result is a classic, simple, yet harmonious look, typical of the ceramics of this region. (I have purchased several pieces of Monsieur Hermann's over the years, and they remain among my most highly prized possessions.) These ceramics can be found elsewhere, but usually at much higher prices than those charged at his studio. Another huge attraction to coming here is that you can visit Monsieur Hermann's extraordinary collection of old Savoyard pottery, housed in a large barn next door. Be sure to phone ahead to make sure the shop and museum will be open (04-50-62-01-90). Finding the studio can be a little complicated. Near Évires, follow signs to the *poterie*. The road to this quite isolated spot is fairly winding, but if you follow the signs, you'll get there.

Another studio of considerable interest is the Poterie Guyot (04-50-98-35-49), in the tiny village of Marnaz, about an hour's drive northeast of Annecy. While this place—in operation since the late 18th century—similarly generally follows traditional Savoyard shapes and decoration, it has also expanded upon them. As well, the ceramics are no longer fired in a wood-burning kiln, a gas oven having apparently replaced the old kiln about thirty years ago. Prices at this studio are also reasonable. (To get here from the Fabrique des Poteries Savoyardes, continue northeast on the N203, which becomes the N205; Marnaz is about ten kilometers west of Cluses. Avoid the rather tortuous route over the mountains from La Clusaz, which we took, much to my spouse's consternation and my regret.)

BELFORT (first Sunday morning of the month, except January and February)

No. of Vendors: 170 to 220
Price/Quality Range: ✦✦✦ – ✦✦✦✦
Scenic Value: ✦✦✦
Amenities Nearby: ✦✦✦

Featured Items: Alsatian ceramics, Alsatian baking molds, enamel advertising plaques, clocks, glassware, snowshoes, skis, militaria, copper and brass ware, porcelain, pewter, linens, figurines, art deco, furniture, toys, silver, Quimper, trunks and luggage, mustard pots, absinthe *pelles*, paintings, frames

WHEN, WHERE, HOW: Belfort's flea market is held on the first Sunday morning of the month (except January and February), from 6 A.M. to noon. The market takes place in the old quarter, in the place d'Armes (in front of the City Hall) and in surrounding streets. If arriving by car, the market is in the center of town, east of the Savoureuse River, which runs north-south. If arriving by train, head northeast along the pedestrian Faubourg de France, cross the river, go northeast on the boulevard Carnot, and continue past the place de la République, on the rue des Nouvelles, to the place d'Armes (the next *place* farther east).

Tourist Office: 03-84-55-90-90

LOCATED ON THE edge of Franche-Comté, just west of Alsace, the town of Belfort probably does not attract a huge number of tourists. Its reputation is that of an industrial center, and its commercial core (west of the Savoureuse River, which divides the city in two) is not particularly appealing. On the other hand, the old quarter of Belfort, on the east, is very pleasing, its narrow streets lined with solid, old buildings in all shades of color.

Above the old quarter is the town's large fort, near the site of Belfort's most famous attraction—a gigantic lion carved into the rock. (Its creator, Auguste Bartholdi, was also responsible for the Statue of Liberty.) The lion commemorates Belfort's great victory in resisting a siege during the Franco-Prussian War. That success prevented the city's annexation by Germany, a fate that befell nearby Alsace-Lorraine.

THE MARKET

Like Annecy's, Belfort's flea market, on the first Sunday of the month (except January and February), is one of the best in France. It is both very large, at up to 220 vendors, and high-quality, with an emphasis on both regional items and general collectibles from across the country. Also, the market's setting— in and around the place d'Armes, in Belfort's old quarter—while not spectacular, is appealing in its denseness and color. In this part of town are also located several antique and *brocante* stores, many of which are open at the same time as the flea market.

This market gets going quite early. At dawn, you will already see quite a few dealers and avid collectors scouring the stalls for early finds. In fact, some arrive before daybreak, armed with flashlights. Between 7 and 8 A.M., things are well under way, even though a few vendors may still be setting up or awaiting the assignment of their spaces. During the next hour or two, the air is charged and intense, as bargains are struck and transactions are made. You may notice many of the buyers speaking German; this is apparently a popular market among both the Germans and the Swiss, who come to do some serious buying. Some of the vendors also speak German and even accept payment in marks.

As the morning progresses, a real change in the atmosphere (and language) is noticeable. For one thing, the market becomes much more crowded. This is when you will see lots of French families and couples, out for a more casual stroll. The pace slows down as it becomes more difficult to move from stall to stall. The pace of buying also seems to become more relaxed, as people spend more time browsing, holding and turning objects in their hands, and chatting among themselves and with vendors.

This is one of the best markets in France for finding a wide variety of things, but one of its greatest features is its emphasis on regional collectibles —not just from the surrounding area, but also from both Alsace and Burgundy, its neighbors to the east and west. From Alsace, you will see the traditional and functional glazed ceramics, in green, yellow, an orangelike rust, and brown (often from Soufflenheim, near Strasbourg); gray stoneware jugs, with blue blotches, from Betschdorf (also close to Strasbourg); ceramics with Alsatian motifs from Lunéville or Sarreguemines (in Lorraine); ceramic and copper baking molds; rustic furniture; enamel advertising plaques; beer collectibles; and linens.

You will likely notice, among other things, decorative mustard pots from Burgundy (from makers like Maille and Amora), which are very sought after in France and not cheap; wine-making collectibles; and advertising items.

Suggesting a provenance closer to home, you will see mountain gear of various kinds, such as skis, snowshoes, and leather carrying bags. (Belfort is located, essentially, in between the Vosges and Jura mountains.) I also noticed a lot of decorative large clock faces, some no doubt from nearby Besançon (apparently a major center for clock-making in France).

And the list of items goes on—militaria, copper and brass ware, pewter, porcelain and ceramics from all over France, art deco, linens, trunks and luggage, toys and dolls, silver, lamps, and figurines. Some things are fairly exotic (at least to North Americans), such as absinthe *pelles* (large flattened spoons —shaped like pie servers—with holes, once used in the consumption of absinthe), and little glass flower holders, once used to decorate motorcars. While there is a fair range in prices, this is not a market for finding lower-quality items at a correspondingly low cost. Bargaining is active, but I noticed that sometimes the vendor initiated the negotiating, by offering a reduction when the prospective purchaser hesitated. For example, before my friend had said anything, a child's porcelain food bowl—initially quoted at 120 francs—was then 100 francs, and finally 80 francs, at which point the deal was concluded.

That heightened state of being so familiar to avid flea marketers—the thrill upon arriving, the mesmerized stupor while browsing, and pangs of regret when leaving—is sure to be experienced here, clinching this market's position as one of the top flea markets in France. I also recommend it to general tourists, as well as collectors. While not flashy, or obviously festive, it is irresistible in its denseness and liveliness.

I am told that during the months of January and February—when the Belfort market is not on—a separately administered market is held indoors, in the Parc des Expositions, in Andelnans, not far south of Belfort. For information (dates and times) you should contact Belfort's tourist office, or call the organization which runs the Parc des Expositions, at 03-84-21-65-65.

OTHER THINGS TO DO

After you have scoured the market, you will no doubt need a break. Sit down at one of the cafés around the place d'Armes itself or in adjoining streets. A popular spot is Brussel's Café on the corner of the *place*, where you can watch the whole scene in front of you, but other appealing-looking cafés and little restaurants are also in the vicinity. Before heading out of town, take a stroll by the massive old fort and get a closer look at the gigantic lion statue— Belfort's mascot—carved in the rock nearby.

DIJON (last Sunday of the month, except July)

No. of Vendors: 30 to 60
Price/Quality Range: ✦✦✦
Scenic Value: ✦ – ✦✦
Amenities Nearby: ✦✦

Featured Items: Furniture (armoires, tables, chairs), paintings, crystal, ceramics (Quimper, Gien, Limoges, Monaco), silver, art deco, figurines, clocks, pewter, jewelry, wine collectibles, mustard pots

WHEN, WHERE, HOW: Dijon has an indoor flea market, all day, from 9 A.M. to 6 P.M., on the last Sunday of the month, except July. The market takes place in a building called the Forum, off the rue Général-Délaborde, in the northeast corner of town. If arriving by car, the market is near the place Jean Bouhey (northeast of the place de la République). You will have no difficulty finding parking nearby.

If arriving by train, the market is about a 30-minute walk from the station. From the exit, follow the boulevard de Sévigné, which becomes, successively, the boulevard de Brosses (past the place Darcy), the boulevard de la Trémouille (past the place St-Bernard), and the boulevard Georges Clemenceau (past the place de la République). At the place Jean Bouhey, veer to the northwest, toward the group of large buildings you will see; the Forum is at the near end, off the rue Général-Délaborde. Public transit is not convenient; there is apparently no bus service until the afternoon, when you can take the #6 bus (from the corner of the avenue Maréchal Foch and the place Darcy, but ask at the tourist office, located at the *place*). There is also an entrance fee for this market.

Another smaller *brocante* market (not described here) takes place on the second Sunday of the month, from 9:30 A.M. to 6 P.M., in the Quartier des Antiquaires (the rue Auguste Comté, the rue Chaudronnerie, and the rue Verrerie). It has about 20 vendors, in addition to the antique dealers permanently located here.

Tourist Office: 03-80-44-11-44

DIJON IS A prosperous-looking bourgeois city, with a rather impressive history. While it dates as far back as Roman times, its real heyday was in the 14th and early 15th centuries. That was when, as the capital of the duchy of Burgundy, it was ruled by a succession of powerful dukes, who made it a center of the arts and built its magnificent Palais des Ducs. After Burgundy became part of France near the end of the 15th century, Dijon remained the capital of the province of Burgundy, and an important center. Its population really expanded, however, about a century ago with the advent of the train, which made Dijon a major transportation hub. It is also, of course, a prominent nucleus of the region's great wine-making industry.

It's virtually impossible to talk about Dijon without discussing mustard. Some Dijonnais, apparently, claim that we owe the word *mustard* to the dukes of Burgundy, who saw this condiment as a good way to, in effect, prolong the shelf life of meat. Dijon is certainly mustard's most famous center in France. The Grey Poupon boutique, on the rue de la Liberté, displays antique mustard pots attesting to this product's longevity and importance.

History aside, the Dijon of today is a pleasant city in which to spend some time. Its core is small and easily navigable. You can happily while away a few hours wandering through its narrow cobblestone streets and gazing at its beautiful old buildings, some with roofs decorated in the multicolored geometric designs typical of this region. The area around the large covered food market is especially promising for restaurants and cafés, while the rue de la Liberté and surrounding streets make for some good shopping and strolling.

THE MARKET

Sadly, Dijon's monthly flea market, which takes place inside a building called the Forum on the northeast edge of town, does not live up to the standard set by the city itself. The market is disappointing not only in being indoor and beyond the parameters of Dijon's historic center, but also in its lack of vigor and liveliness. The number of vendors varies significantly, from 30 on a quiet month (I am told that August is particularly slow) to around 65 at its peak. (This is also one of the few flea markets where an admission fee is charged, which may account in part for its relative unpopularity.)

Also, it is not at all easy to find the market building, even when you are right in the vicinity. My friend and I took a taxi from the train station, and we then drove around in circles until one of us spotted a lonely vendor set up outside the market site. More well-placed signs would be a good idea.

The emphasis in this market is on high-end, high-quality items. You will see beautiful furniture, crystal, and ceramics from all over France (including Quimper, Limoges, and Gien), fine glassware, figurines, clocks, paintings, jewelry, silver, and pewter. Some regional collectibles are also to be found— mustard pots, for example, and items having to do with wine and wine-making (wine tasters, corkscrews, glass wine containers, or old corking machines). Not surprisingly, given the quality and condition of the merchandise, prices are fairly high. What I did find surprising in such a formal atmosphere, however, was the willingness of the vendors to talk and share information about their wares.

If you are interested in high-quality decorative objects, or fine furniture, you might find some things of real interest here. On the other hand, if, like me, your flea market tastes are more plebian (or eclectic), this is not a market I would recommend. Its unappealing setting might also detract from your experience of this beautiful city.

OTHER THINGS TO DO

For a delicious, regionally based, and reasonably priced lunch in Dijon, I recommend Le Bistrot des Halles (03-80-38-05-05) at 10 rue Bannelier, facing Dijon's food market. The three-course lunch menu here is around 100 francs. If Alsatian food appeals, I enjoyed *choucroute* at the Taverne Maître Kanter (03-80-30-81-83) on the rue Odebort, also facing the food market. To taste *pain d'épice*, a local specialty, head for Mulot et Petitjean, with one of its stores at 16 rue de la Liberté. (I find *pain d'épice* dry and uninteresting, but others do rave about it, especially the kind made here.)

While you are in Dijon, be sure to visit the Musée de la Vie Bourguignonne, at 17 rue Ste-Anne, in the southern end of the old quarter (open daily, from 9 A.M. to 12 P.M. and 2 P.M. to 6 P.M., except Tuesday. Phone: 03-80-44-44-52). Here you will find interesting displays of everyday 19th- and early-20th-century life in this region—household items of all kinds (including kitchenware), traditional Burgundy dress, and re-creations of typical shop windows from the period (such as a millinery shop, a furrier's workshop, a pharmacy, and a general store).

If you are here on the second Sunday of the month, a smaller *brocante* market takes place then in the Quartier des Antiquaires (along the rue Auguste Comte, the rue Chaudronnerie, and the rue Verrerie). From 9:30 A.M. to 6 P.M., about 20 *brocante* vendors, offering generally high-end collectibles and furniture, join the permanently installed antique dealers.

GRENOBLE (first Saturday of the month)
                    (Sunday morning)

QUARTIER HOCHE
    No. of Vendors: 75
    Price/Quality Range: ✦✦✦
    Scenic Value: ✦✦ – ✦✦✦
    Amenities Nearby: ✦✦✦

Featured Items: Savoyard ceramics, furniture, paintings, books, rustic items, silver, linens, china, tools

RUE STALINGRAD
    No. of Vendors: 80
    Price/Quality Range: ✤
    Scenic Value: ✤
    Amenities Nearby: ✤ – ✤✤

    Featured Items: Kitchenware, hardware, tools, secondhand clothing

PARKING INTERMARCHÉ
    No. of Vendors: 100
    Price/Quality Range: ✤ – ✤✤
    Scenic Value: ✤
    Amenities Nearby: ✤

    Featured Items: Kitchenware, ceramics, books, records, secondhand clothes, and tools

WHEN, WHERE, HOW: Grenoble has three regular flea markets—the Quartier Hoche market (on the first Saturday of the month, all day from 8 A.M. to 6 P.M.), and the rue Stalingrad and Parking Intermarché markets (both on Sunday mornings, from 6 A.M. to 1 P.M.).

If you are arriving by car, the Quartier Hoche market is in the lower part of the old quarter, at the southern end of the boulevard Agutte Sembat (the extension of the boulevard Édouard Rey), in and around the place André Malraux. The rue Stalingrad is a little farther south and runs south off the boulevard M. Foch, just west of the place G. Rivet. The market is located partway down this street, in the parking lot of the Atac store. The Parking Intermarché market is across the Isère River north of the center of town, in the lot of the Intermarché store, just northwest of the place Aristide Briand (off the boulevard de l'Esplanade, by the Parking Esplanade).

If you are arriving by train, all three flea markets are within a 15-to-20-minute walk from the station. For the Quartier Hoche market, head east on the avenue Alsace-Lorraine, turning southeast (right) on the boulevard Gambetta and then east (left) on the rue Hoche, which will take you to the place André Malraux, the site of the market. For the rue Stalingrad market, follow the directions above to the boulevard Gambetta, continue on it south, past the rue Hoche, to the place Rivet. Jog a tiny distance west on the boulevard M. Foch, and you will see the rue Stalingrad running south. The Atac store is a short distance along, on the east side. For the Parking Intermarché market, from the station take the rue Casimir Brenier east to the place Hubert Dubedout, cross the Isère River, and then, just west, at the place Aristide Briand, head northwest on the boulevard de l'Esplanade, and you will see the market on your left.

Grenoble's tramway system will take you quite close to the Quartier Hoche market (get off at the stop just north of the place Pasteur and walk the short distance northwest) and the rue Stalingrad market (get off at the avenue Albert 1er de Belgique and head west, just past the place G. Rivet, and then south on the rue Stalingrad).

Tourist Office: 04-76-42-41-41

GRENOBLE IS WIDELY recognized as the most important economic center in the Alps, with its big chemical, electronics, and nuclear industries and facilities. It is also an intellectual center, its large university (whose students comprise almost one-tenth of the city's population) dating from the 14th century. While Grenoble's history is long—almost two thousand years—perhaps its greatest claim to fame is its role in the French Revolution. A giant statue in the place Notre Dame celebrates the acts of the Parlement de Grenoble in 1788, resisting the right of the king to tax without the consent of the people, one of the factors leading Louis XVI to call the Estates General in 1789, which triggered the Revolution.

The first time I visited Grenoble, I was struck by how sophisticated the city seems and how much its buildings and wide avenues resemble those of Paris. Given its mountainous setting, I was expecting Grenoble to have a rustic, alpine look. On the contrary, this is a grand, impressive city, which can be reached by TGV from Paris in around three hours.

Although its buildings project a somewhat sober and conservative image, Grenoble is vibrant and youthful. Its old quarter is pleasing, with little winding streets leading into café-filled squares—the large and spacious place Grenette, the pristine and quaint place de Gordes, and the place St-André, dominated by the splendid Palais de Justice, to name the most prominent ones.

One of the best features of Grenoble is its Jardin de Ville, on the edge of the old quarter. Its highlight is a classic recessed rose garden, with rows of roses in all shades of red, pink, orange, and yellow, flanked by rather incongruous palm trees. This appears to be a favorite spot of romantic young Grenoble couples. I remember one especially demonstrative pair being taunted by children who kept chanting, *"C'est beau, l'amour"* (I don't think that needs translating), which rang true in that setting.

QUARTIER HOCHE MARKET

The Quartier Hoche *brocante* market, held all day on the first Saturday of the month, is a quite substantial and interesting collectibles market. Its site is not, however, the most scenic of Grenoble's settings, the place André Malraux being a modern square, in front of the city's Chambre de Commerce et de l'Industrie, also of recent vintage. About 75 vendors set up here and in the immediate vicinity. Most have tables to display their wares, although a small minority—with more rustic items—simply lay their things out on the ground.

This as a moderately high-end market where the carefully selected merchandise is almost uniformly of good quality and in good condition. A wide variety of things is to be found—paintings, books, silver, glassware, linens, china, well-polished rustic items, pristine kitchen collectibles (such as coffee mills, tins, and copper pots), ceramics of different kinds (including Savoyard ceramics), and a fair amount of furniture. Prices are moderately high, but not outrageously so, and bargaining is possible. I bought a small *jaspé* pitcher from the Savoie in good condition for 120 francs, which is a fair bit less than I would have paid for a comparable one in Annecy, for example. (The initial asking price was 130 francs, and my offer of 100 francs was, quite reasonably, rejected.) I also bought a large tin decorated with images of the conquests of Napoleon, in good condition, for 40 francs (talked down from 50).

In this somewhat low-key market, vendors are approachable and willing to spend time sharing information. The people I encountered strolling along were also especially friendly; one older gentleman even accompanied me on my rounds, discussing French history with great enthusiasm (he had seen me buying the Napoleon tin). We had a wonderful time browsing through old maps of French holdings in North America while he expressed his views about the wisdom of Napoleon's sale of the Louisiana territory to Thomas Jefferson. It was one of those larger-than-life experiences one seems to have a little more frequently in this country.

I would recommend this market to collectors and also to general visitors to Grenoble. However, don't arrive either too early in the day—at 8 A.M. some vendors are still setting up—or too late, as some may pack up before the 6 P.M. official closing time.

RUE STALINGRAD MARKET

For a real contrast to the Quartier Hoche market, bargain hunters and eclectic collectors should consider the Sunday-morning junk market in the parking lot of the Atac store, on the rue Stalingrad. This is a basic, no-frills market where all sorts of low-end everyday items (only some of which can remotely be classified as collectibles) are sold at rock-bottom prices. About 80 vendors set up shop here, seemingly mostly ordinary folk and families trying to dispose of their personal belongings and junk for whatever price they can get. In keeping with the level of wares here, the setting is anything but aesthetically pleasing or appealing, although a couple of food trucks sell light snacks, such as sausages and fries, and coffee.

Little effort is made here to present the merchandise in its best light; generally, things are piled on blankets on the ground or spill out of old crates. You will see cheap plastic kitchenware mixed in with old tools, farm implements, discarded toys, and secondhand clothes. The great thing, however, is that you may also find a really interesting collectible here—regional ceramics, lovely old wooden toys, antique glassware—for just a few francs. I bought a large old porcelain bowl, in perfect condition, for only 10 francs. I also bought a set of six wooden *boules* in nicely burnished shades of green, red, and yellow (complete with a little *cochonnet*) for 30 francs, and I am sure I could have bargained the price lower if I had tried.

This is a good place for those looking for everyday kitchenware from the 1940s and 1950s, or for collectors of rustic items in general. While it is a bit of a junk market for the intrepid, I enjoyed coming here and would certainly make this a regular haunt if I lived in the area. This market would not, however, appeal to general tourists or to collectors of more high-end decorative objects. If you do come, arrive as unencumbered as possible; for example, leave your camera in the hotel.

PARKING INTERMARCHÉ MARKET

A slight step up from the rue Stalingrad market (but only a tiny one) is the Sunday-morning flea market in the parking lot of the Intermarché store, across the Isère River north of the center of Grenoble. The setting is perhaps a bit more inviting than the Atac parking lot, in that it is more spacious, and the goods are more spread out and somewhat more nicely displayed. As well, while in the same genre as the rue Stalingrad market, this is a marginally more upscale scene.

Along with the usual piles of secondhand clothes and truly junky kitchenware, you will see a few vendors selling somewhat more carefully selected ceramics, glassware, books, and records. Prices are generally low. I found a couple of little pastel-colored bowls with scalloped edges, which I collect, at five francs for the two.

This is your basic low-end junk market, and unless you are a bargain hunter or a keen collector of everyday objects or rustic items, I would not recommend making the trek here. If you are on your way out of town, one advantage of this market is that is close to the A48 autoroute, heading in the direction of Lyon and Paris.

OTHER THINGS TO DO

If, after visiting the flea markets, you are looking for a café or something light to eat, head to the place Grenette, the place de Gordes, or the place St-André.

The first has the biggest crowd scene, the second is quiet and intimate, with the most congenial-looking outdoor eating possibilities, and the third has the Café de la Table Ronde—founded in 1739—reputed to be the second-oldest café in France. To sample something sweet with walnuts (a specialty of this region), drop in at Les Écrins, at 11 rue de Bonne in the old quarter.

If you are keen and you have time, another weekly flea market is not far south of Grenoble, in Échirolles. This market (which started fairly recently) is large, with over 100 vendors, and takes place on Sunday mornings.

STRASBOURG (Wednesday and Saturday)

No. of Vendors: 25 to 40, with more on Saturday than on Wednesday
Price/Quality Range: ✦✦ – ✦✦✦
Scenic Value: ✦✦✦
Amenities Nearby: ✦✦✦ – ✦✦✦✦

Featured Items: Alsatian ceramics, baking molds, Lunéville ceramics, Alsatian dishware, linens, beer steins, silver, watches, dolls, clocks, glassware, toys

WHEN, WHERE, HOW: Strasbourg has a twice-weekly flea market—on Wednesday and Saturday—on the rue du Vieil Hôpital and the place de la Grande Boucherie in the center of town. While the market is all day, from 9 A.M. to 6 P.M., a number of vendors start to leave just after noon and others pack up midafternoon. If arriving by car, the market is in the center of the old quarter, between the place Gutenberg and the place de la Cathédrale. Try to find parking in the lots in either the place Gutenberg or the place du Château, southeast of the cathedral.

If arriving by train, the market is a short 15-minute walk from the station. From the place de la Gare, take the rue du Maire Kuss, crossing the Ill River; continue east on the rue du 22 Novembre, and turn right (south) on the rue des Francs-Bourgeois and then left on the rue des Serruriers, which runs into the place Gutenberg. On the other side of the *place*, follow the rue Mercière; the first street on your right is the rue du Vieil Hôpital. You can also take Tram A from the station to the Langstross-Grand'Rue stop and walk the short distance east from there.

Tourist Office: 03-88-52-28-28 and 03-88-32-51-49

LOCATED ON THE Rhine bordering Germany, and almost 500 kilometers from Paris, Strasbourg is one of the most prominent and urbane cities of France. A primary reason is its role in the great European project—this is where you will find the Council of Europe, the European Court of Human Rights, and the European Parliament. Strasbourg has also come by some of its cosmopolitan character the hard way. Between 1871 and the end of World War I, and from 1940 to 1944, it (along with the rest of Alsace) was annexed by Germany. Many people here speak German, as well as Alsatian, a kind of German dialect.

While a significant city of over a quarter million people, Strasbourg still exudes some of that homey feel so typical of Alsace. Its narrow streets are lined with charming half-timbered buildings, some dating from as early as the 15th century. And, though international and cosmopolitan, Strasbourg retains a strong regional identity—not surprising, since it only became part of France in the latter half of the 17th century. The city also feels very prosperous, solid, and established. First settled by the Romans about two thousand years ago, and part of the Holy Roman Empire a thousand years later, it was already a wealthy trading center in the Middle Ages.

THE MARKET

Since Strasbourg's twice-weekly flea market is not large, you might expect it to be uninteresting and high-priced, catering essentially to the tourists who frequent this historic part of town. In fact, despite its modest size, this is a fairly significant and varied market (a welcome thing in this corner of the country, which has few flea markets of any note). You will, however, see quite a few tourists here—mostly Germans, rather than English-speaking visitors —and you will also hear some vendors conversing fluently in German and quoting prices in marks.

The market takes place just a couple of streets away from Strasbourg's great cathédrale Notre-Dame, and not far from the touristy and quaint quarter called Petite France. Its site, the rue du Vieil Hôpital, is not quite as picturesque as some of the neighboring streets, but it is pleasant and quiet. Between 25 and 40 vendors (fewer on Wednesdays than on Saturdays, when the market also spills into the adjacent place de la Grande Boucherie) set up their wares. Some display their merchandise on tables, but quite a few simply pile things out on blankets on the ground.

You will notice a pronounced regional focus in the things for sale at this market—traditional Alsatian ceramics, many likely from Soufflenheim, northeast of Strasbourg (in primitive designs—often flowers—in yellow, green, rustlike orange, and brown); gray stoneware jugs with blue splotches (apparently from Betschdorf, north of Strasbourg); ceramic baking molds (either round, for the traditional kugelhopf cake, or shaped like lambs or fish, for Easter); faience from Lunéville (in Lorraine), decorated with the trademark Alsatian symbol of the stork; dishware from Sarreguemines (also in

Lorraine), decorated with traditional Alsation folk figures; linens with embroidered folk designs; beer steins; siphon bottles from Schiltigheim (just outside Strasbourg); rustic items and tools. In addition, you will find collectibles from other places, including silver, copperware, glassware, clocks, dolls, and toys, but little furniture.

When I first saw all the things piled on the ground here, I thought that there might be a wide range in prices, or that some great bargains might be found. In fact, prices here are moderate to moderately high, especially for the much sought-after regional items. In some cases, prices are not marked, requiring you to ask. Vendors are direct and straightforward, however, and after quoting a figure may bluntly ask what you are prepared to pay, if you hesitate. My friend was initially quoted 100 francs each for a small Alsatin mold and a little Lunéville bowl, but the vendor then quickly offered to take 100 francs for the pair. (I had an even better experience. An elderly gentleman decided to just give me one of his bowls, and when I asked why, he said, "Because I'm like that." Alas, this kind of offer does not come along often.)

While this is an all-day market, which theoretically continues to 6 P.M., some vendors only stay for half the day, beginning to pack up just after noon, while others start to leave by midafternoon. As a result, I strongly recommend that you arrive in the morning, to experience the market at its best. If you have the option, come on Saturday, rather than Wednesday, as it will be busier and more interesting then.

OTHER THINGS TO DO

A couple of interesting-looking cafés and restaurants are right by the market, but if you want a place noted for its good regional cuisine and reasonable prices, try Au Rocher du Sapin (03-88-32-39-65), at 6 rue du Noyer, about a ten-minute walk northwest of the market. From the outside, this restaurant, located in a nondescript modern building, looks not the least bit quaint or regional. Inside, however, you will find the place filled with locals—many of them quite elderly—consuming onion tarts and huge plates of *choucroute* or other regional dishes (washed down with Alsatian beer), followed by a regional dessert of plum tarts. The food is delicious, the service cheery, and the price right.

Another place I like, in the middle of Petite France, is Chez Tante Liesel (03-88-23-02-16) at 4 rue des Dentelles. Regional in focus and not expensive, this tiny restaurant is decorated in that cosy Alsatian style (which appeals to some more than others; I tend to fall for it). For afternoon tea, and some pastry, try Christian, at two locations—10 rue Mercière or 12 rue de l'Outre.

While you are in Strasbourg, be sure to visit the Musée Alsacien, at 23 Quai St-Nicholas (open daily, except Tuesday, from 10 A.M. to 12 P.M. and 1:30 P.M. to 6 P.M.; Sunday, 10 A.M. to 5 P.M. Phone: 03-88-35-55-36). The museum is a two-minute walk south from the flea market, just across the bridge. This is a truly splendid place. The site—a few stories of an old half-timbered building, opening onto an ivy-draped courtyard—is splendid, and the impressive collection is imaginatively presented. You will see wonderful examples of Alsatian life and culture—furniture (armoires decorated with primitive patterns; beds; wooden chairs, their backs carved in folk shapes), regional ceramics of all kinds (glazed earthenware and stoneware), forged tools, brightly tiled stoves, traditional costumes, kitchenware, toys, religious artifacts, and displays demonstrating bread-making, cheese-making, pottery, woodworking, and wine-making.

In the area around Strasbourg, several towns are well worth a visit (albeit, to some, bordering on the almost too quaint and picturesque)—for example, Kaysersberg (birthplace of Albert Schweitzer), Riquewihr, and Colmar (one of the larger towns around, which also has a small flea market on the first and third Friday of the month). For a really delicious and hearty rural lunch, try Les Alisiers (03-89-47-52-82), an auberge in the Vosges mountains near Lapoutroie, not far from Kaysersberg. When we came here one time in December, we drove up through trees blanketed in fog, only getting a glimpse of the surrounding hills when we reached the auberge itself.

Those interested in Alsatian ceramics will find lots of shops selling it throughout the region (although the quality varies). If you have time, try to visit the historic center of Alsatian folk ceramics, Soufflenheim, about 50 kilometers northeast of Strasbourg—as well as Betschdorf, where the gray stoneware pots and jugs are made.

VILLEURBANNE (LYON) (Sunday morning)

No. of Vendors: 400
Price/Quality Range: ✤ – ✤✤
Scenic Value: ✤
Amenities Nearby: ✤ – ✤✤

Featured Items: Furniture, ceramics, paintings, books, rustic items, kitchenware, garden ware, hardware, tools, linens

WHEN, WHERE, HOW: There is a giant flea market every Sunday morning from 6 A.M. to 1 P.M. in Villeurbanne, a few kilometers northeast of the center of Lyon. The market is right along the Canal de Jonage, at 1 route du Canal, and has a sign,

Canal des Puces, in front. You should have no difficulty finding parking along the side of the road.

If you are arriving by car, there are various possible routes, depending on where you have come from, so that these directions are necessarily general. If you are on the A42 or the A46 autoroute, exit at Villeurbanne/St-Jean and Villeurbanne respectively, and then, off the exit, follow the road to the southwest until you reach the Canal de Jonage, alongside of which the market is located.

From the *boulevard périphérique* circling Lyon, from the south, take the Villeurbanne exit (before the exit for Geneva). As you exit, you will go straight for a bit before arriving at a traffic circle; go in a southwesterly direction at this first circle and then northeast at the second just after, which will take you across the Canal de Jonage. At the third traffic circle in the Quartier St-Jean, veer to your left (west), passing under the A42 autoroute. Then turn left (south) toward the canal, and then right alongside the canal, which will lead you to the market.

On the *boulevard périphérique* from the north, take the exit Villeurbanne, Croix Luizet–St-Jean. You will immediately come upon two traffic circles; continue in a southeasterly direction at both, then follow the road northeast across the Canal de Jonage to the Quartier St-Jean, where you will find a third circle. Veer left (west), passing under the A42, then turn left again toward the canal, and then right alongside the canal.

As for public transit to the market, your best bet is to inquire at the Lyon tourist office. Even if you cannot get right to the market, you may be able to get close enough so that the cost of a taxi from this point will not be great. On the other hand, you might rather just take a taxi from your hotel.

Tourist Office: 04-72-77-69-69 (Lyon)

I HAVE NEVER been able (or admittedly, very inclined) to get to know Lyon. This large, sprawling city—the second largest in France in size and third largest in population—is not easy for visitors to figure out. If you are driving through, its sheer size and complexity will likely disincline you to stop, unless you have come specially to experience firsthand the proof of its enormous gastronomic reputation.

Lyon has a bit of an identity crisis; it feels neither clearly northern nor Mediterranean, positioned as it is at the crossroads between the north and the south. One thing is true, though: when you get south of here, you really do feel that you've arrived in Provence, while just north of Lyon, heading the other way, you clearly sense that Provence has been left behind. The site of a Roman colony over two thousand years ago, today Lyon is an important business and commercial center, and only two hours by train from Paris on the

TGV, the high-speed train. Positioned at the juncture of the Rhône and Saône Rivers, the core of the city is located on the peninsula—called the *Presqu'île*—formed between the two.

Lyon has also been conflicted ideologically. While it has a somewhat conservative reputation—at least with regard to certain matters—it has also had long periods under a socialist mayor. It is credited, as well, with having a major role in the development of the labor movement, as the site of some landmark labor disputes. A strike by printers in the mid-16th century was followed by a bitter conflict in the early 1830s involving silk workers, which resulted in the death or injury of a few hundred people.

It is both unfortunate and curious that the center of Lyon does not have a regular general flea market. For that you must go to Villeurbanne, a rather unattractive district to the northeast. When I asked a vendor at Villeurbanne why this was, his reply was unhesitating. The Lyonnais, he said, are a cold and conservative people who like to *"garder leurs sous"* (keep their pennies). The one advantage of this market's location is that those interested in seeing the flea market only, and in bypassing the center of Lyon, will be able to do just that.

THE MARKET

The Villeurbanne flea market is one of the great junk markets of France and fun to visit, to boot, despite its unappealing setting. It can be tricky getting here; if you don't have a car, it is downright difficult, and even with a car you may get lost a few times before you actually find it. Since I wanted to arrive early in the morning, my spouse and I did a practice run the day before. Not only did we get horribly lost and disoriented (despite being given directions beforehand), we also flirted briefly with some serious marital discord until we finally located the place. Unless you have a great sense of direction (which I clearly don't), it is easy to lose your way on the vast and intertwining autoroutes and ring roads of the region outside Lyon.

The good news is that this market is well worth the trouble you may have getting here, especially for eclectic collectors, collectors of rustic items, and bargain hunters. Its rather shabby location casts no sinister or unfriendly light on the proceedings; to the contrary, one feels quite at home in this place. I found the vendors especially loquacious and entertaining. I remember strolling about at daybreak, absorbed in taking notes for this book, when a couple of them approached me and jokingly asked what I could possibly be doing. I replied (in my obviously foreign accent) that I was a tax inspector, which they found wildly amusing and repeated to others around. In conversation with another vendor, I revealed that I was Canadian; he nodded wisely and launched into a discussion about the extraordinary infiltration of Canada by religious cults, an impression I was entirely unable to dislodge (despite my best efforts), but it was a lot of fun trying.

If you arrive at this market early, you will see vendors unloading chairs, crates, armoires, and piles of boxes from their precarious perches on top of old vans and cars. Before dawn a few purchasers are already about—some dealers, but also some obsessed collectors hoping to find a treasure. While coming really early is interesting—the place has a magical quality then—you don't actually have to get here at the crack of dawn. I've seen vendors still arriving after 7 A.M., and a few pulling up even later than that.

The market consists of a large warehouselike building housing about 100 permanent stalls (also open on Thursday and on Saturday morning), and several rows outside. Inside the building, and in a roofed-over area along the middle outside, are a couple of wonderful dimly lit, tiny café-bistros. Through the glass, you can see vendors consuming sandwiches and other dishes even before dawn. Signs outside post the meals for the day—maybe *andouillettes* or *blanquette de veau*—served beginning late morning (which is actually midday for these early risers).

You could come across just about anything here—some of my favorite finds were a painting of a *sanglier* (or wild boar) head, a huge iron gate, and an entire outbuilding roof in tin, complete with weather vane. You will see lots of rustic furniture, kitchenware of all kinds, ceramics, farm implements, tools, paintings, books, and linens. The emphasis here is on rustic items from the area around Lyon (and Burgundy) and Provence. The quality runs the gamut, as does the presentation of the wares. Some stalls have piles of junk laid out on the ground or in boxes, while other vendors, recognizing (or wishing to demonstrate) the value of what they are selling, have their things more tastefully displayed.

Though prices vary, they are generally quite reasonable. Especially good deals can be made on collectibles from outside this region. I spotted a Savoyard pitcher here, at a price much lower than would have been asked in Annecy, for example. Vendors are generally happy to bargain and expect to do so. Be warned, however, that they may quote you a price in *balles,* a slang word for "francs" (used elsewhere, as well), which I found quite unnerving the first time I heard it.

I was thrilled to discover the Villeurbanne market. Unlike some others of its genre, the chances of finding something great here among the junk are fairly high, and the price also stands a good chance of being attractive (or close to it). If you are a bargain hunter or a collector of rustic items, I recommend that you plan your travels so as to make a quick Sunday-morning stopover here. General tourists, and collectors of fine decorative items (who don't mind paying the going rate), should probably skip this market.

OTHER THINGS TO DO

If you can contemplate a serious splurge on lunch after seeing the market, make a reservation at Alain Chapel (04-78-91-82-02), about a 30-minute drive north, in the tiny village of Mionnay. This beautiful Michelin two-star restaurant offers a combination of wonderful food, refined ambience, and extraordinary service. (Dishes seem to magically appear, then are whisked away as soon as you are finished without your even noticing.) All of this does not come cheap, but if your budget can be stretched to accommodate it, go for it. Remember, it's not often that you get to come to France.

Selected Bibliography

BOOKS

Albert, L. *Guide de la Brocante et des Antiquités*. Paris: Éditions de Vecchi, 1994.

Ardagh, J. *Provence, Languedoc & Côte d'Azur*. London: Collins, 1990.

Baillie, K. *Provence and the Côte d'Azur*. London: The Rough Guides, 1992.

Baillie, K., and T. Salmon. *France*. London: The Rough Guides, 1997.

————. *Paris*. London: The Rough Guides, 1993.

Bedel, J. *Les 1000 Questions sur les Antiquités, l'Art, la Brocante*. Paris: Hachette, 1992.

Berenson, K. *Quilts of Provence*. New York: Henry Holt and Company, 1997.

Birnbaum, S., and A. M. Birnbaum, eds. *Birnbaum's France 1992*. New York: HarperCollins, 1991.

Boyer, M.-F. *The French Café*. New York: Thames and Hudson, 1994.

Clemente, M. *The Riches of France*. New York: St. Martin's Griffin, 1997.

Dannenberg, L., P. Le Vec, and P. Moulin. *Pierre Deux's Brittany*. New York: Clarkson N. Potter, 1989.

Dubin, M. *The Pyrenees*. London: The Rough Guides, 1994.

Giscard d'Estaing, L., ed. *Le Guide Emer de France, 1995–1996*. Paris: Emer Édition, 1995.

Lahaussois, C., and B. Pannequin. *Terres Vernissées: Sources et Traditions*. Paris: Éditions Massin.

Le Stum, P. *Arts Populaires de Bretagne*. Rennes: Éditions Ouest-France, 1995.

MacLachlan, C. *Bringing France Home*. New York: Clarkson Potter, 1996.

Manston, P. B. *Manston's Flea Markets, Antique Shows and Auctions of France*. Sacramento, Calif.: Travel Keys, 1987.

Michelin. *Brittany*. Clermont-Ferrand, Michelin and Co., 1997.

————. *Chateaux of the Loire.* Clermont-Ferrand, Michelin and Co., 1998.

————. *Côte d'Azur.* Clermont-Ferrand, Michelin and Co., 1998.

————. *France 1998, Hotels and Restaurants.* Clermont-Ferrand, Michelin and Co., 1998.

————. *Normandy-Seine.* Clermont-Ferrand, Michelin and Co., 1997.

————. *Paris.* Clermont-Ferrand, Michelin and Co., 1998.

————. *Provence.* Clermont-Ferrand, Michelin and Co., 1998.

Moulin, P., P. Le Vec, and L. Dannenberg. *Pierre Deux's French Country.* New York: Clarkson N. Potter, 1984.

O'Byrne, C. *Les Objets de Charme de la Maison Française.* Paris: Éditions du Chêne, 1997.

Porter, D., and D. Prince. *Frommer's 99 France.* New York: Macmillan, 1999.

Rambali, P. *Boulangerie: The Craft and Culture of Baking in France.* New York: Macmillan, 1994.

Un Grand Week-end pour Chiner. Paris: Hachette, 1998.

Verlingue, B. J., and E. Mannoni. *Les Faïences de Quimper.* Paris: Éditions Ch. Massin, 1995.

Vialle, C., and B. de Goutel. *Guide du Chineur Parisien.* Paris: Éditions Parigramme, 1998.

Vidal, V. *Le Guide des Collections.* Éditions Alternatives, 1997.

Wells, P. *The Food Lover's Guide to France.* New York: Workman Publishing, 1987.

————. *The Food Lover's Guide to Paris.* New York: Workman Publishing, 1993.

ARTICLES

Arren, J. "Les plaques émaillées alimentaires." *Brocante & Collection* 1 (February 1997): 20.

Barbet, M. "Des Cafetières sur un Muret." *La vie du collectionneur* 172 (April 4, 1997): 7.

Bedel, J. "Des Cuivres plein la cuisine!" *Antiquités Brocante* (November 1998): 104.

Berger, G. "1320 outils de jardin à Paris." *La vie du collectionneur* 168 (March 7, 1997).

————. "250 biberons d'autrefois." *La vie du collectionneur* 170 (March 21, 1997): 38.

Bordet, D. "Les biscuits LU, 1re partie: affiches, chromos, calendriers, cartes, menus." *La vie du collectionneur* 167 (February 28, 1997): 8.

————. "Les biscuits LU, 2e partie: boîtes, seaux et céramiques." *La vie du collectionneur* 188 (August 22, 1997): 14.

Cabré, M. "Bagages en voyage." *Aladin* 109 (July 1997): 44.

————. "Cafetières grands-mères." *Marie Claire Idées* 21 (June 1996): 90.

————. "Grain de folie." *Marie Claire Idées* 18 (September 1995): 70.

———. "La seconde vie des arrosoirs d'antan." *Aladin* 108 (June 1997): 44.

———. "Le charme des verres à boire." *Aladin* 115 (January 1998): 24.

———. "Les boîtes à bonbons." *Aladin* 111 (September 1997): 38.

———. "Les cuivres de cuisine, une collection savoureuse." *Aladin* 116 (February 1998): 26.

———. "Parfums et haute couture." *Aladin* 112 (October 1997): 39.

———. "Santons de Provence." *Aladin* 114 (December 1997): 36.

Cagnolati, D. "Les pressophiles européens cultive l'art de vivre." *Aladin* 112 (October 1997): 66.

Dian-Dumond, C. "Les barbotines." *Aladin* 121 (July 1998): 58.

Donsey, S. "Trésors de vannerie." *La vie du collectionneur* 215 (March 6, 1998): 22.

Franck, C. "Un moulin de comptoir dans votre cuisine!" *Antiquités Brocante* 10 (June 1998): 108.

Gosselin, M. "Les boîtes d'aiguilles de phonographes." *La vie du collectionneur* 211 (February 6, 1998): 12.

Goudet, A. "Moulé à la louche!" *Brocante & Collection* 4 (April 1997): 9.

"Le biberon à travers les âges." *Brocante & Collection* 3 (March 1997): 4.

Lerouvillois, M. "Les pots à moutarde." *La vie du collectionneur* 168 (March 7, 1997): 14.

"Les échantillons de parfums." *Brocante & Collection* 2 (March 1997): 18.

"Les tire-bouchons se mettent à table." *Aladin* 107 (May 1997): 44.

"Les yaourts sont bien dans leurs pots!" *Aladin* 106 (April 1997): 43.

"Objets de cuisine et art domestique." *Aladin* 121 (July 1998): 62.

Ploëscat, M. "Les capsules de champagne." *Brocante & Collection* 4 (April 1997): 20.

Pomeau-Peyre, C. "La vannerie utilitaire et domestique." *Antiquités Brocante* (July/August 1998): 24.

Prioton, P. "1500 flacons à parfum." *La vie du collectionneur* 170 (March 21, 1997): 8.

———. "Les outils du jardinier." *La vie du collectionneur* 170 (March 21, 1997): 10.

Riva, H. "Les fers à repasser." *Brocante & Collection* 7 (June 1997): 32.

Taralon, C. "L'osier le haut du panier." *Marie Claire Idées* 16 (March 1995): 87.

Tieblemont, A.-L. "Les verres et taste-vin . . . à consommer sans moderation!" *Aladin* 112 (October 1997): 48.

Vidal, V. "Les télécartes." *La vie du collectionneur* 191 (September 19, 1997): 10.

Vincent, J.-S. "Le jeu de boules, une vielle histoire." *Aladin* 110 (August 1997): 26.

———. "Objets de la vigne et du vin." *Aladin* 110 (August 1997): 44.

Viotti, D. "Les biberons." *La vie du collectionneur* 223 (May 1, 1998): 18.

Ybert, C. "Biberons: Du 'gutti' au 'Pirex.'" *Aladin* 105 (March 1997): 29.

Zelitch, P. "Boîtes à biscuits LU: une variante inconnue?" *La vie du collectionneur* 197 (October 31, 1997): 6.

WEB SITES

Brocante.org: www.brocante.org
Forum brocante: www.chez.com/bibliophile/forum.html
Les Puces: www.les-puces.com

Index